NEYMAR

About the author

Luca Caioli is the bestselling author of *Messi, Ronaldo* and *Suárez*. A renowned Italian sports journalist, he lives in Spain.

NEYMAR

Updated Edition

LUCA CAIOLI

ICON

This updated edition first published in the UK in 2018 by Icon Books Ltd

Previously published in the UK in 2014
by Icon Books Ltd, Omnibus Business Centre,
39–41 North Road, London N7 9DP
email: info@iconbooks.com
www.iconbooks.com

Sold in the UK, Europe and Asia
by Faber & Faber Ltd, Bloomsbury House,
74–77 Great Russell Street, London WC1B 3DA or their agents

Distributed in the UK, Europe and Asia
by Grantham Book Services,
Trent Road, Grantham NG31 7XQ

Distributed in Australia and New Zealand
by Allen & Unwin Pty Ltd, PO Box 8500,
83 Alexander Street, Crows Nest, NSW 2065

Distributed in South Africa
by Jonathan Ball, Office B4, The District,
41 Sir Lowry Road, Woodstock 7925

Distributed in India by Penguin Books India,
7th Floor, Infinity Tower – C, DLF Cyber City,
Gurgaon 122002, Haryana

Distributed in Canada by Publishers Group Canada,
76 Stafford Street, Unit 300, Toronto, Ontario M6J 2S1

Distributed in the USA
by Publishers Group West,
1700 Fourth Street, Berkeley, CA 94710

ISBN: 978-178578-428-6

Typeset in New Baskerville by Marie Doherty

Printed and bound in Great Britain
by Clays Ltd, Elcograf S.p.A.

Contents

Chapter 1
Prose and Poetry

A conversation with José Miguel Wisnik

Who are the best 'dribblers' in the world and the best goal-scorers? The Brazilians. It goes without saying that their football is football poetry: it revolves around dribbling and goals. *Catenaccio* [an extremely defensive style] and triangulation represents football prose: it is based on synthesis; a collective and organised game, i.e. reasoned execution of the football code.

Writing in a 1971 essay entitled '*Il calcio "è" un linguaggio con i suoi poeti e prosatori*' ('Football "is" a language with its poets and writers of prose'), Pier Paolo Pasolini, film director, writer and great football fan, set out the similarities between literary genres and styles of playing football, offering a significant distinction between football poetry and football prose: a dichotomy which José Miguel Wisnik, Brazilian musician, composer, essayist and professor of Brazilian literature, uses as the basis for his analysis of the game he so dearly loves. He is a huge fan of Santos.

His reasoning is set out in a book, *Veneno remédio: o futebol e o Brasil* ('Poison remedy: football and Brazil'), published a few years ago. Today he reflects on what Neymar means, or what he could mean, for the history of football in his country. This is a player whom he jokingly describes as 'the

Baudelaire of football'. Sitting comfortably in his study in São Paulo, he takes his time before the verbal floodgates open.

'Brazilian football created a tradition which is based on the *ellipse*, a style of play which consists of creating non-linear ways of occupying space and breaching the defence. I based my ideas on what Pasolini wrote about football prose and football poetry. We say that football prose is more linear, more tactically responsible, collective, defensive; it involves counterattack, triangulation, cross-overs and rational movements. The idea of football poetry is that of a football which creates new spaces out of nowhere in a non-linear way, using dribbling as the deciding factor. It can be used to penetrate the opponent's space or just to be effortlessly beautiful or effective. It can be a means to an end or a way to get to goal. Mané Garrincha, for example, took dribbling to the extreme but at the same time was very effective. In the history of Brazilian football, there were glorious moments where dribbling was just for the sake of it but at the same time effective.

'In the 1930s, when Gilberto Freyre analysed Brazil from a sociological, anthropological and historical perspective, he noted that the identity of Brazilian football was closely linked to the identity of the half-caste people. The Brazilians took the English choreographed, formulaic style and turned it into more of a dance, mixing nifty footwork and capoeira and samba dance skills. This obviously has had a huge impact on how our culture is interpreted: the idea that efficiency is only valued if it is accompanied with pleasure; in other words, the ideal situation is bringing together the concepts of work and partying. Brazilian football, in this context, is both the poison and the antidote because it is a form of cultural realisation like popular music or carnival, but it is also a problem because it promotes the idea that our culture glorifies laziness and gratuity over efficiency.'

Can we go back to the concept of football and poetry and how it takes us to Neymar?

'Sure. That was just an introduction. So, Brazilian football gave a style to English football which Freyre defines as curvilinear and Pasolini poetic. A style of play which was developed in South America in the 1960s and reached a climax in the 1970 World Cup in Mexico. At this time, Brazilian football created a repertoire of non-linear moves which can be considered as ellipses, a concept of both geometry and rhetoric. Moves which are based on curves or freezing of time. Just think about all the various types of dribbling: dummies to the left, shimmies to the right, fakes, using the moment to beat your opponent in a static situation. Also the one-two, the lob, the "falling leaf" where the ball would deftly swerve downwards just at the right time. A classic repertoire which existed in Brazilian football from 1962 to 1970. It then existed only as a trait or style but from the 1970s onwards Brazilian football adapted to the new reality in international football, i.e. physical and athletic fitness, team play, different formations and specialisation of attackers and defenders.

'In the World Cups of the 1970s, 1980s and 1990s, Brazil tried various solutions. The football poetry was still there somehow, with players like Zico, Sócrates and Falcão playing in 1982, or with Romario, who in 1994 still played *ellipse* football in a national team which had adopted a more prosaic style. Up until the arrival of Ronaldinho, a footballing genius who brought back the entire repertoire of Brazilian football. You could see Didi's "falling leaf", Pelé's lob or Garrincha's dribbling. Ronaldinho was an artist of mannerisms, almost as though he was "quoting" other players' famous moves. Ronaldinho is well aware of this and as an author quotes another writer, he "quotes" a goal of a player from the past.'

And now we get to Neymar …
'Yes, all of the above was to get to Neymar. In a time when no one believes a poetic tradition exists and that it is disappearing even in Brazil due to a tendency to play football prose, along comes Neymar. A player who represents someone who wants to keep this poetic style alive.

'Neymar has an extraordinary dribbling repertoire. Impressive, I would say: a repertoire that shocks you with its inventiveness, its freshness. It is pure *ellipse* football. If you don't believe me, watch the dribbling with his heel against Seville in one of the first games of the [2013/14] Spanish league season: something unexpected, which no one even dreamed of.

'At Santos, from when Neymar was thirteen years old, he was marked out as the future champion. He is part of a generation which has been trained and grown to be something important. Often important groundbreaking news does not live up to the hype. Neymar, however, completely lived up to the qualities that were ascribed to him. In addition to his magical ability on the ball, he has a natural charisma, extraordinary likeability and the ability to manipulate his public image, just like a pop star. He has conquered the hearts and minds of girls and the public alike and is acknowledged by other clubs' fans and by great players from the past and present. In his years at Santos he showed all his exuberance, all his ability to dribble the ball, thus confirming that the tradition continues with him.

'Yes, Neymar is a poet, a graffiti artist: his sonnets are daubed all over the city's walls. His hair, his way of putting his shirt collar up and his celebrations are all part of his poetic performance. Neymar is a sort of modern-day man of the people, full of energy and life and an absolute star of the current era. He has great vision on the pitch, he has killer passes and he has a superb ability to capitalise on opportunities. He is not just a great dribbler; his relationship with dribbling is not merely rhetorical, as with Robinho who was a poor finisher and whose one-two passes were often just for effect. Neymar has a technologically advanced style, intricate but frighteningly effective. Efficient but without losing its appeal for the spectator. It is on another level, brand new and gives a new dimension to poetic football.

'I see him being in a very interesting situation. Much has been said about him being able to adapt to the *Seleção* [Brazil's national football team]; he proved this during the Confederations Cup. La Canarinha [another nickname for the national side] has found a style of play which exploits Neymar's potential to the maximum. The great expectation is how he will fit in at Barcelona. Santos managed to keep him until 2013. Seeing that a player who was at the height of his powers was not sold to a European club or an East European club straightaway was important for Brazil's self-esteem. To be honest, at Santos he was left to his own devices and I hoped he would go to Barcelona to mature in international football.'

Can Neymar's poetry and Barcelona's prose fit together?
'Barcelona's football is not football prose. It is a complete mutation in how to play football in that it combines occupation of space and expansion of the area of play on the wings, which echoes the Dutch style of play, with South American football traits such as the *tiki-taka* heel flick. You could define it as football written in prose, extremely agile but not overly

structured. The presence of Messi and the dribbling which pierces the defence leaves one in no doubt of the determining presence of South American football. I believe that Barcelona, in its great moments, has squared the circle. To bring together prose and poetry, to bring together European football and South American football and to go beyond football's classic dichotomy. What will happen now there is Messi and Neymar? They have different styles. Messi's dribbling is not as exuberant as Neymar's: it is efficient; there is a sense of mystery about the way he moves forward with the ball – you can hardly tell how he does it. He does not move like a Brazilian. His intuition is out of this world, he has a sixth sense for when his opponent is about to present him with an opportunity or when space is opening up. Messi is the straight line to Neymar's ellipse.'

Chapter 2
Mogi das Cruzes

Chaotic traffic: scooter and motorbike horns blasting. Flyovers, skyscrapers, low-level housing, viaducts searing above traffic jams, industry, roadworks, *favelas*. São Paulo, a megalopolis with 11 million inhabitants, seems to go on forever; it seems to want to keep visitors in its clutches and not let them go. The city spreads along the three-lane Rodovia Ayrton Senna, the newest of its kind in the country, dedicated to the eponymous national hero and São Paulo racing driver who died during the Imola Grand Prix on 1 May 1994.

The bus leaves from the Rodoviario de Tiete Terminal (the largest in Latin America and the second largest in the world after New York), with passengers scurrying here and there as they go on their way. The bus is perfectly on time but struggles to get out of the city traffic jams; it scrapes past lorries and cars which dart in and out of the lanes. A toll booth, and it changes motorways. As it heads for Itaquaquecetuba, the city finally lets the bus out of its clutches into the open countryside, which is green and with a plethora of hills that look as though they were sketched out using a ruler. Kites fly high in the sky and bone-dry, dusty football pitches, dotted between the vegetation, mark the *favelas* clinging on to the hillside: red bricks that look like they have been stuck together by a kid playing with Lego, makeshift roofs, satellite dishes, large sheets to cover construction works that have never been completed. Stagnant water, burnt-out cars, kids crossing the motorway on their bikes to get back home with their shopping.

Then the sharp downhill of Serra de Itapey. At the bottom, the skyscrapers of Mogi da Cruzes, one of the Alto Tiete municipalities, an area to the east of greater São Paulo. It was here that Neymar Santos da Silva played football, and here where his son, Neymar Junior, was born: a place with 40,000 inhabitants, its population having doubled in the last fifteen years as commuters have flooded in. They live here and every morning head off to work in the capital; every evening, on the platform at Estação da Luz in São Paulo, they wait patiently to be squashed into the carriages on Line 11 of the Companhia Paulista de Trens Metropolitanos, a creaky and rickety local train which takes them home.

At least there is work in Mogi, where industrial behemoths such as General Motors, Valtra (manufacturers of tractors), Gendau Group (steel works) have plants and employ a large portion of the population. The tertiary sector boasts companies such as Tivit and Contractor, two of the largest telemarketing companies. Agriculture is booming: vegetables, mushrooms, persimmon fruit, medlar and flowers (principally orchids). Stunningly beautiful examples of the latter – in an explosion of colours, whites with shades of fuchsias, violets and lilacs such as the *Olho de Boneca* (*Dendrobium nobile*) – are on show in one of the town's tourist attractions: the *Orquidario Oriental*. 'Oriental'? Yes, you read right: the East.

At the start of the 20th century, Mogi experienced an influx of immigrants from Japan: men and women who worked in agriculture, horticulture and trade. They created a lively and flourishing community that did not lose touch with its roots: there are monuments, restaurants, cultural associations, festivals, schools, and the town has been twinned with

Toyama and Seki. It is a shame that Torii, the Japanese-style gate, symbol of the Japanese immigrants, which was situated at the entrance to the town, was taken down in the spring of 2013 for health and safety reasons. The heavy rains had severely damaged it.

Luckily, one of the other icons of Mogi has not been ruined by the bad weather. A massive shiny sculpture in stainless steel, towering thirteen metres into the sky, at first sight it looks like Don Quixote from La Mancha but it is actually an homage to Gaspar Vaz for the 450th anniversary of the founding of the city. Gaspar Vaz was the rusher who opened the way to Mogi from São Paulo and founded the town in 1560. From Avenida Engenhiro Miguel Gemma, where there is a shiny statue of the adventurer who came to the area looking for gold (or natives who he could turn into slaves), the bus reaches the Geraldo Scavone terminal in a few minutes. Exactly one hour to travel around 50 kilometres between São Paulo and the town.

Through the cobbled streets of Vila Industrial and we arrive at Estádio Municipal Francisco Ribeiro Nogueira, better known as Nogueirão. The large gate is shut but someone comes and opens it. This is the home of União Mogi das Cruzes Futebol Club, a club which celebrated its centenary on 7 September 2013. It was founded by Chiquinho Veríssimo, a white textile tradesman, and Alfredo Cardoso, a black shoesmith. The club was born on Brazil's Independence Day. The football kit is red and white or completely red, with a Tiete valley snake for its mascot (*Mogi* in the local native tongue means 'the river of the cobras').

União is one of the oldest footballing clubs in the region. Over its long history, it has seen the first touches of players like Cacau (now playing for Stuttgart), Maikon Leite (now playing for Náutico) and Felipe (now playing for Flamengo).

It has always been a club which fluctuates between amateur football (in 1947 it was champion of the regional Amador tournament) and the lower Brazilian leagues.

Its golden era was from the 1980s to the start of the 90s, when it fought for promotion to the first division of the Paulista league. However, it did not make it and the only league title it has won is the 2006 Campeonato Paulistão Second Division title. Three years later came its worst year ever: União, or *Brasinha* as it is known in the town, became 'the worst team in the world': eighteen defeats in nineteen matches and 75 goals against, a record which relegated the club to the fourth division. Today it is not doing much better, in terms of either its results or its finances – in fact the situation is so bad that the centenary celebrations were a washout. Senerito Souza, the chairman of the club, said better celebrations may be held in the future.

Meanwhile, the players train for the next league match. At 11.30am the first team play a friendly against the reserves. The sun beats down and the red-brick chimney stack on the far side of the stadium casts its shadow over the green pitch.

On the pitch, behind the metal fencing that separates the pitch from the stands (which can take up to a maximum of 10,000 spectators), sports manager Carlos Juvêncio, or 'Pintado' ('painted' – due to vitiligo which left white blotches on his beautiful black face) watches over the youngest players. When the players get to the changing rooms, I get the chance to have a chat with him.

'How was Neymar da Silva Santos O Pai, Neymar Jr's father, as a player?' I ask.

Pintado replies, 'A good forward, a number 7. He played on the wing; he was quick, skilful, good at dribbling, he always targeted his opponent. He was a cheery chap, extrovert, a nice person, easy to get on with.'

It is a view shared by his ex-teammates, such as defenders Montini and Dunder and goalkeeper Altair. Everyone agrees that Neymar was good with the ball at his feet. An old-fashioned forward who did not score many goals but was good at playmaking and crossing the ball.

Things change when I pose a question about the skills of both the father and son, about what Neymar Jr has inherited from his dad. Pintado, who played alongside 'Pai' in 1993 and 1994, wearing the number 3 shirt for União, well remembers Neymar Jr from when he was just a little boy: 'Pai brought him to training. He was the team mascot.' He recalls how both father and son had the same touch and ability to dribble; Neymar Jr was quicker though, lighter on his feet, faster, more creative. Ex-Seleção goalkeeper Valdir Peres, who played in the Spain World Cup in 1982 and was União coach in 1993 and 1995, is of the same opinion. 'Neymar Jr,' he says, 'is a better dribbler and always looks to finish off his moves and score goals.' 'He has a better technique,' adds Lino Martins, who at the end of his professional career played at União with Neymar Pai and then coached Neymar Jr in Santos's Juniors team.

Neymar da Silva Santos arrived at União Mogi in 1989. He was 24. He was born in Santos on 7 February 1965, the middle son of Berenice, a housewife, and Ilzemar, a mechanic. He has a brother, José Benicio, or 'Nicinho', and a sister, Joana D'Arc, or 'Jane'.

He grew up playing for the Santos Juniors team. When he was sixteen, he moved to Portuguesa Santista where he became a professional footballer. He then began a sort of pilgrimage from one club to another, all of them small fry: Tanabi in the São Paulo region, Iturama and Frutal in the state of Minas Gerais. There, in the south-east of Brazil, Neymar Pai contracted tuberculosis. This put him out of action for a year. He decided to quit football and to go back to work as a mechanic at his father's garage. However, he then received an offer from Jabaquara, a historic club in the metropolitan area of Baixada Santista.

His father was not enthusiastic but Neymar accepted anyway. During the week he worked as a mechanic and at weekends he played. He strung four good games together, one of which was a friendly against União Mogi. The referee for the match, Dulcídio Wanderley Boschilla, pointed him out to the managers of Mogi, who were immediately interested. At the end of the first interview, he was sent to train with the first team. At the end of the second interview with the chairman at that time, José Eduardo Cavalcanti Teixeira, or 'Ado', Neymar signed a contract, for one season, expiring in 1989. 'In those days the salaries were not very high,' Pintado recalls, 'The sponsor was UMC, the University of Mogi. We were paid more or less 350 reais a month but it was enough to live on.'

After years of flitting from one city to another, from one changing room to another, Neymar found himself at Mogi. He was amazing on the pitch and a real success in that A3 league. He played so well that he attracted attention from other clubs in the region. Officials at Rio Branco do Americana, a club in the small city of Americana in the state of São Paulo, were impressed by Neymar when he played against their team at the old stadium in Rua Casarejos and they wanted him, whatever the price.

Despite their loss to União, Rio Branco won the title. A striker was needed to strengthen their line-up. They offered Neymar a decent amount and Neymar was about to accept. It was a one-off chance of a lifetime. União's former treasurer Moacir Teixeira recalls, 'He needed money for his family. He wanted to buy a house for his folks who lived in Baixada Santista.' Neymar made his wishes completely clear to the club's managers – who had no intention of letting him go.

'He was our best striker; he was a great person who deserved everything he had worked for,' says the former treasurer. So Moacir, together with nine other União fans, formed a group to match Rio Branco's offer using their own funds. The agreement was made on 21 December 1989 with ten signatories. The group of investors bought Neymar's registration and ensured he could continue to play for Mogi. The transaction value was 100,000 cruzados novos, 10,000 per signatory, 'and with no interest, with no economic return,' comments Moacir. In today's money it would be around 55,000 reais (about €17,000).

This was a lot of money at the time! Neymar was finally able to buy a house for his mother at São Vicente and he bought himself a car: a Monza. He felt rich, but economic and financial reforms introduced as part of the Collor Plan led to him losing his savings. In the first half of 1990, he played for União; in the second half of the year, as the club was not taking part in any tournaments, he played for Coritiba, Cataduvense and Lemense. By this time, he wanted to have a family. So in 1991, at age 26, in the church of São Pedro 'O Pescador', in São Vicente, he married Nadine Gonçalves. They had met when she was sixteen and he was eighteen and a rising star at Portuguesa Santista.

Their first son was born at 2.15am on 5 February 1992, in Mogi das Cruzes. Nadine's waters broke the day before and she was taken to Santa Casa de Misericordia hospital: an impressive white and pale blue building which stands out from the city streets. The birth was natural and there were no complications – mother and son were fine. The baby weighed 3.78kg, about 8lb 5oz. The new parents found out that it was a boy only when he came into the world – an ultrasound was too expensive for them.

The first doctor to look after mother and son was Luiz Carlos Bacci (now deceased), followed by Benito Klei. It was the latter who discharged them. Being a fan of the club, he knew the baby was the son of a União player, but only when reading the birth certificate years later did he realise that he helped bring the Santos star into the world. 'At that time Neymar Jr did not have the Mohican hairstyle so it was difficult to recognise him,' jokes the director of the department of gynaecology and obstetrics at Santa Casa. The da Silva Santos family was accompanied home by União's physiotherapist, Atilio Suarti. Neymar O Pai had called him and asked him to come and pick them up.

But what was the name of the little baby? Both parents were unsure of what to call him. First Nadine wanted to call him Mateus; his father agreed. They used this name for a week but they were not convinced and, in the end, when Neymar Pai recorded his son's name at the registry, he changed his mind and gave him his own name: Neymar, adding 'Junior'. Within the family walls, he was known as 'Juninho'.

Nadine and Neymar Pai were happy with the arrival of Neymar Junior. Valdir Peres recalls, 'He turned up at the hotel where the club was staying in a euphoric state. He swore that his son would one day be the best Brazilian football player ever.' This was a statement that triggered a whole host of friendly insults and snide remarks.

The da Silva Santos family lived on the fourth floor of block C of the Safira flats, number 593 of Rua Ezelino da Cunha Glória, barrio Rodeio, a middle-class residential development three kilometres from the town centre, built by a metallurgy cooperative syndicate. The pastel-coloured buildings cling to the hillside at the foot of Serra do Itapeti, where the view opens out over Mogi. Theirs was an average-sized apartment paid for by União Mogi. Today not many remember that little boy with curly hair who lived there until he was four. 'They were a quiet, shy family who did not attract much attention,' recalls Licianor Rodrigues, one of the da Silva Santos family's neighbours.

One Sunday in June 1992, after a league match against Matonese, during which he scored the equaliser for União, and before starting training, Neymar Pai decided to go and see his family in São Vicente. He loaded up his car and headed off. Nadine was sitting at his side and Juninho, just four months old, was sleeping on the back seat. It was a rainy day and the tarmac was wet. The Rodovia Indio Tibiriça was a two-way road. It was the long descent down the Serra and it was always tricky and dangerous. Every few hundred metres a sign warned of fog and reduced speed limits: just 40 kilometres per hour in some places. Suddenly a car on the opposite side of the road tried to overtake and cut into the oncoming traffic. Neymar Pai swerved and tried to accelerate out of the way but he was in fifth gear and the impact was unavoidable. The other car hit Neymar's car head on and wedged itself into the driver's door.

Neymar Pai's left leg ended up on the right: his pelvis and pubis were dislocated. He could not move. Distraught, he spoke to his wife and told her he was dying. The pair looked behind them and Juninho was not there. They thought that he had been thrown out of the car on impact. They thought they had lost him forever. Neymar Pai prayed for God to take his life but save Juninho. Their car was teetering on a ledge, above the river. Nadine could not get out on her side as she would have fallen into the raging torrent below. One or two cars stopped to help and Juninho was found underneath the seat, covered in blood. His parents were beside themselves with fear for their son. An ambulance took them to the nearest hospital.

When Neymar Pai was reunited with his wife and son, Nadine was fine apart from a few scratches. Juninho had a large plaster on his head – the blood had come from a small cut on his head, caused by a piece of flying glass.

Neymar Pai was not so lucky: he had a dislocated pelvis – a serious injury. He had to have an emergency operation. He spent ten days in hospital and then four months at home in bed, suspended from a machine. He was unable to play for almost a year and had to undergo treatment, rehabilitation and physiotherapy with the help of Atilio Suarti and União masseur Antonio Guazzelli. This had been a serious accident, and it affected the rest of Neymar Pai's career. He was not able to regain his touch. However, he did not stop playing. This was his life, his livelihood.

On 31 May 1995 he donned the famous red União Mogi centre forward shirt for a friendly exhibition match. The match was being staged to celebrate the reopening of Nogueirão. The opposition was Santos Futebol Clube, who played in the Divisão Especial (today League A1), whereas Mogi were in Intermediaria (today League A2). At Santos there were players like Toninho Cerezo and Jamelli. Mogi were coached by Valdir Peres and boasted players such as goalkeeper Haroldo Lamounier and Ricardo.

The match put Edson Cholbi Nascimento, or Edinho – Pelé's son – and Neymar da Silva Santos, father of the future Neymar Jr, up against each other. On the one hand, a boy who had listened to the advice of his father on how to behave in life; on the other, a father who was to give to his son (as he continues to do to this day) advice on how to become a great footballer and on how to choose the right career path.

Edinho, a goalkeeper, was 25 years old and was playing a routine match. Neymar Pai was 30 and will always remember the match, because it was a match against Santos and he was asked to take the free kicks. Edinho saved his attempts with ease: Neymar bodged them all. A shame. Mogi wanted to win but against professional players it was not possible. The match ended in a draw: 1–1. One goal for Jamelli of Santos and one for Gilson da Silva of Mogi. A good result in any case. The reopening event carried on according to plan.

One year later, on 11 March 1996, the da Silva Santos family welcomed a new member: Rafaela was born.

After many happy years playing for União, Neymar decided to embark on a new adventure. He went back to his parents' house in São Vicente in barrio Nautica 3 for a time, and started to look for a new contract. This time he ended up at Operário of Várzea Grande, Mato Grosso.

The chairman of the club, Maninho de Barros, saw Neymar Pai play for Batel de Paraná. He was looking to strengthen his team. He did not know the name of the foot-baller who was playing such an excellent match, even scoring a goal. At half time, he asked Laurinho, a striker for Batel, who he was and at the end of the match he met up with Neymar Pai and offered him a transfer to Várzea Grande.

Neymar wanted to think about it, and to discuss it with his family. It was only after speaking to an executive at Operário and learning that he could move his family there that Neymar Pai accepted the offer. He was to wear the tri-colour shirt of Várzea Grande.

His opening match was the semi-final of the state tourna-ment and the hopes of the chairman were realised: Neymar scored and provided the final pass for another goal in the 4–1 win against Cacerense. In the final, Operário faced União de Rondonópolis. In the first leg, away from home,

Neymar did not play and the match ended in a draw. In the return leg on 3 August 1997, Neymar Pai played and the match ended 2–1.

For Operário it was a twelfth Mato Grosso league title. For Neymar da Silva Santos it was the only league title of his career, a career which ended in 1997 at the ripe old age of 32. He felt old: since the accident, his body had not responded as he wanted it to; the pain during matches and training began to hit home. The continuous transfers began to weigh on him and his family. The contracts were less lucrative and he had no hope of achieving anything else in his profession. He headed home to start a new life with plenty of surprises in store.

Chapter 3

São Vicente

Cups, trophies, medals of all types, shapes and sizes from various sports: the display cabinets of the Clube de Regatas Tumiaru are full of souvenirs of past titles spanning its 108-year history.

It started with the aim of 'bringing young people together via sport and in particular water sports'. The club's first premises were on the waterfront in São Vicente, right next to the historic port of Tumiaru from which it gets its name. Today the clubhouse is located at number 167 in what is known locally as 'post office square' but officially is Praça Coronel Lopes. The black and white two-storey building bears the club's coat of arms: two crossed oars, a lifebuoy and the date 1905. We are in the centre of São Vicente, the first city founded by the Portuguese in South America, on 22 January 1532.

São Vicente is a municipality of the small region of Santos and shares the island with the neighbouring city. It is known for its tourism and its trade, attracting hoards of visitors. Of note is the monument celebrating 500 years of Brazil, designed by architect Oscar Niemeyer: a white platform on the top of Ilha Porcha, which provides an incredible view of the coast. It is not to be missed.

The guided tour of Clube Tumiaru is also worthwhile – the city centre site, that is, not the site on the waterfront. There is an open-air swimming pool, training rooms, a gymnasium for *capoeira*, dance, tai chi chuan, judo and gymnastics, and the *futebol de salão* hall. The hall is enormous, with semi-circular vaults, large windows which light the hall, stands to the side, and wooden parquet floor ruined by years of matches. The hall is empty, as it is early morning. Training and lessons take place in the afternoon. Here on this pitch, at age six, Neymar Jr began to play football for a club.

A bola (the ball) has always been his love, his object of desire. His uncontainable passion for the ball is so strong that in May 2012 he stated, '*a bola* is like the most jealous woman in the world. If you do not treat her well, she will not love you and she can even hurt you. I love her to bits.'

He has shown this passion right from when he was a young boy. His mother, Nadine, remembers one time at the market when she was buying potatoes. He was only two years old at the time and 'Juninho' risked his life crossing the road to chase after a little yellow plastic ball. And just like Neymar has said a thousand times, Nadine remembers that he used to sleep with a ball. After only a few years, Neymar had collected no fewer than 54 balls in his room. It was not Neymar's room; more like the balls' room. The room was so full of balls that Neymar had to scrunch himself up in the corner of the bed. *A bola* was even in the photos of his childhood. In one photo of him, taken when he was just a young boy, he is wearing the Santos shirt and under his arm he is carrying a black and white patched ball.

Neymar Pai was amazed that when Juninho was only three years old, instead of grabbing the ball with his hands and shouting, 'It's mine', he gave it back with his feet. For him, football was important, something serious; he had what Brazilians call *jeto*; that is, aptitude, talent. In his grandparents' house in barrio Nautica 3, father, mother and kids all slept in the same room. Between the mattress, the wardrobe and the chest, there was very little space but Juninho made the most of this tiny corridor by playing football. The mattress was perfect for training as a goalkeeper: blocks, dives and saves on the line. When he was tired, he could always use his sister and cousin Jennifer as goalposts while he practised free kicks and penalties.

And yet when Neymar Jr first makes his mark, it is not with the ball at his feet. Roberto Antônio dos Santos, aka Betinho, passionately tells the story of the first time he saw Neymar Junior: 'It was the end of 1998 and I was watching a match on Itararé beach in São Vicente. Tumiaru were playing Recanto de la Villa. I was concerned for my son, I looked around to check where he had gone and a little boy, as thin as a rake, with short hair and stick-like legs, caught my eye. He was running up and down the stands which they had installed for the event. He ran effortlessly, as though he was running on the flat, as though there were no obstacles in his way. He ran without stopping for one second. His fitness, his agility and his coordination made an impression on me. It was something rare for a tiny young boy. This made a difference to me. A light came on in my head. I asked a friend, "Who is that boy?" He told me that it was son of Neymar Pai who was playing in the match for Recanto and had just missed a penalty. I looked at the father: he was well built and had good ball control. I looked at Nadine, who was attending the match: she was tall and thin. I immediately began to think about the genetics of Neymar Jr's parents: they were two fine biological specimens. This made me wonder how the little'un would play football.'

This was the discovery of the star about whom everyone is talking.

Fifty-six years old, with a laugh that regularly breaks up his discourse, Betinho is a former right-winger at amateur level. Born in São Vicente, Betinho works in Santos's youth set-up and travels all over Brazil, indeed all over the world, looking for new talent. In 1990, Betinho discovered Robson de Souza, aka Robinho, in Beira Mar, a futsal club in São Vicente. Robinho now wears number 7 for AC Milan.

In his office on the second floor of Vila Belmiro, Santos FC's stadium, Betinho does not hold back from telling me about the young Neymar Jr: 'At that time, I was coaching Clube de Regatas Tumiaru. I was putting together a team of young kids born in 1991 and 1992 to play in the São Vicente league. At the end of the match, I went to speak to his father to see if he would let me take Neymar Jr to Tumiaru for a trial. Neymar Pai accepted and the boy came with me. The first time I saw him touch a ball, my heart started beating like mad. I saw the footballing genius that he could become. I realised that lightning had struck twice in the same place. First Robinho and now another rare pearl, both in São Vicente. You find footballing talent where kids are most in need. And in São Vicente there are lots of people who come from poor regions. Families who cannot afford to live in Santos because it is too expensive. Here there is a gold mine of talent.'

It is almost impossible to get a word in edgeways with Betinho. But I want to understand how he worked out, from just a glance at Neymar Jr running up and down the stands, that he could be good at football. Betinho's answer is inspirational: 'God gave me the talent to see players who can make the difference and are one step ahead of the rest.'

It is worth noting that by the time he discovered Neymar, Betinho had already been working as a talent scout for five to six years – something which, together with divine intervention and the undoubtedly talented kids of Mogi Da Cruzes, helped him to choose.

But what were Juninho's talents at that young age? 'Football was something which came from the inside for Neymar Jr. At six years old he already had his own style. He was fast and poised, he had great imagination with the ball and could make something out of nothing. He loved dribbling, he knew how to kick the ball and was not afraid of taking players on. He was different to the others, you could have put him with 200 kids his age and he would have stood out just the same.'

Betinho gets up to explain a fundamental concept, starting with music, in particular the samba. 'When I used to put samba music on, I would see him move, gyrate, dance as he did when he had the ball at his feet.' Despite being a little bit overweight, Roberto Antônio dos Santos demonstrates a few steps to explain that without this movement of the hips and legs, you cannot become a great Brazilian footballer. He continues, 'Neymar at that time did the *ginga* movement.'

Ginga is the fundamental movement of *capoeira*, the Brazilian martial art introduced to the country by African slaves, which combines combat, dance, music and corporeal expression. Ginga is a coordinated movement of both the arms and the legs which prevents an attacker from having a fixed target, thus tricking him and making him attack so that the *capoeirista* can then counterattack. The word stands for movement of the body that can represent sensuality, malice, skill or dexterity. The etymology of the word could be the ancient French *jangler*, which derives from the Latin *joculari*, meaning 'joke, pretend and have fun'.

Leaving etymology to one side, ginga is something magical; something Brazilians have in their blood from birth: a gift, an innate talent for movement, for dance, for football, for shimmying, for dummying opponents on the football field. It is the spirit and identity of Brazilian football. And this quality is one that Juninho had in spades at only six years old, according to his talent scout.

Betinho continues: 'What was lacking was strength and stamina, something which is completely normal for a kid at that age. He needed to refine and improve on his skills, his technique, by playing in a team but without losing his passion for dribbling the ball.'

Betinho gave his body and soul to make sure Juninho's skills developed. He took him to play in a futsal tournament in Jabaquara, a nearby town. The team won the trophy. Neymar Jr was the leading goalscorer and the best player of the competition. Betinho also took the young Neymar with him to teams where he coached: Portuguesa, Gremetal and a second spell at Portuguesa.

With curly hair and a few milk teeth missing, and wearing the white shirt with sky blue trim and the coat of arms with the crossed oars on the chest, Neymar started to make a difference on the coloured parquet *salão* pitch. (The game of *futebol de salão*, or *futsal*, where small-sided teams play on indoor courts with a smaller than usual ball, was invented in 1933 in Montevideo by Professor Juan Carlos Ceriani Gravier, who wanted to get his students playing football in a small gymnasium.) He wore number 7, and his Clube de Regatas club membership card, no. 1419, had a serious-looking photo of the young star.

Betinho's hopes were realised. He knew that he had a pearl in his grasp. He continues, 'Neymar was different: he was a very intelligent player. He thought quickly, his mind saw things before the others did. He was always one step ahead. He knew where the ball would end up and how his opponent would react. He took on board my advice and that of the other coaches. He then metabolised the advice and put it into practice. He was the first to arrive at training and the last to leave the pitch. He loved playing with the ball. I cast my mind back to Robinho at the same age and Neymar seemed more talented. I said so to his father: "You have a son who can be one of the greatest footballers. He will be at least as good as Robinho."'

Neymar Pai, who never got to the top of his profession, believed him and had complete faith in him – though naturally he continued to monitor his son's progress.

Betinho comments, 'Both Neymar's mother and father were close to him: they always followed what he was doing. They treated him with great affection and love. Even if the finances of the family were not the best, they always did what they could for their son. They educated him to be honest, sincere – you know, a good boy.'

But what was he like when he was six years old?

'He was a happy little boy, always cheery, always smiling. He had a nice way about him. He was good at school and he liked studying. He got on well with adults and classmates alike. He was friends with everyone and a born leader. His mates trusted him because of what he did on the pitch. I am very proud of the fact that I was the first coach of a player that is now known all over the world.'

Betinho shows me photos of him with the star, including one Neymar Jr put on Instagram after a match. He also shows me a white Santos shirt with a dedication: 'To my first coach with love from your friend and athlete Neymar Junior.'

That the young man now wears the number 11 shirt for Barcelona is thanks to Betinho and his eagle eyes; his having seen Neymar's potential and opened the doors to the world of football. In turn, Betinho is indebted to Neymar Jr and his family for their loyalty and decency: 'In 2002 when Santos tried to coax Juninho away from the team but without me, Neymar Pai did not accept. He said, "My son needs Betinho at the moment." When Santos tried again and managed to agree a contract, Neymar Pai required that I went to Santos with Neymar Junior. I have Neymar Pai to thank for my job.' Betinho laughs when telling this story.

When asked how he sees his pupil now, Betinho answers, 'As of 2009 when he started playing for Santos's first team, Neymar has been miraculous. He has matured. He has refined his skills. In a few years, he has won individual and team titles. This is the experience he has taken with him to Barcelona.'

But will playing with Messi, Iniesta and Xavi influence his game? 'When Pelé played for the Brazilian team which won the 1970 World Cup, he played with Rivelino, Tostão and Jarzinho. Neymar is a star playing with other stars. I hope that he will soon be the best in the world. Yes, I am sure, Neymar will be better than Messi and after having given so much joy to my country, he will give joy to the entire world.'

Chapter 4

Praia Grande

He cleans his hands with a rag, straightens his hair, then looks straight ahead and, indicating the adjacent construction site, says, 'That there is the best goal Neymar has scored.' Gilberto Leal is a mechanic on the outskirts of Praia Grande. His used tyre shop is right in front of a white wall. On the large tin gate hangs a sign:

> *Dados informativos da obra. Cesionario: Instituto Projecto Neymar Junior. Local: Jardim Gloria Quadra 27 A y 27 B. Tipo de Obra: Costrução da Centro Social y Esportivo.*
>
> (Information about the works. Contractor: Neymar Junior Project Institute. Location: The Garden Gloria Quadra 27 A and 27 B. Type of Work: Sports and Social Centre.)

An employee with a white helmet and blue overalls opens the doors of the workshop to visitors who want to find out a bit more. It is lunchtime: builders and workmen are eating under a makeshift canopy. Two HGVs loaded with concrete pillars and a crane dominate the area which was once a football field, that of Gremio. It is here that the Neymar Institute will be opened in 2014, spread over 8,400 square metres running along the length of the Avenida Ministro Marcos Freire. It is a sports complex with a football pitch, swimming pool, gym, multi-sports hall, auditorium and refectory. The stated aim is to 'contribute to socially disadvantaged families' socio-educational development through sport'. During the first phase it will have capacity for 300 kids aged between seven and fourteen, from poor backgrounds with a per capita income of R$140. In phase two, it is expected that the institute will help 10,000 people of various ages. Gilberto comments, 'It is a good idea. Let's hope that it brings many good things to this area. Jardim Gloria is not a *favela* but almost. Life here is not easy, especially for young kids.'

This verdict is confirmed by two social workers: juvenile delinquency, street crime and lack of prospects are the problems facing the area of Praia Grande, a town with 29,000 inhabitants, twenty minutes' drive from Santos. It is a real problem zone.

On 18 January 2013, the plan for the Institute was presented at the Palacio Das Artes in the town. Neymar Pai and Neymar Jr were on the stage, together with the local councillor who was hosting. 'Juninho' stated that he was very happy with the project: '[We are happy] to be building a space for kids and for the inhabitants of Jardim Gloria. We do not want to discover a new star but rather help families realise a dream and help young kids develop and make plans for their lives. I hope the Institute can serve as an example.'

Neymar Jr is happy to be setting up this place, a place that he would have liked to have experienced when he was kid but no such place existed. He is happy to give back to the people of the area what he and his family got from them. He is happy to do something for the place where he grew up and where he spent most of his childhood. He commented, 'I played on the streets here with my friends: I had great fun in the endless marbles matches; here I played with my kite.'

Neymar Jr moved here from São Vicente with his family when he was seven years old and he lived here until he was fourteen. They lived at number 374 Rua B, Jardim Gloria:

a low-level house, painted in pastel green, at the end of the street, with a corrugated iron roof and a large patio. Neymar Pai built it on a 12m x 30m plot of land. He bought the land using what was left of the savings earned during his footballing career. Two of his friends, Toninho and Jura, helped him. One sourced the materials to build the house and the other helped with labour, all because Neymar Pai agreed to play on Saturdays and Sundays in their teams in Várzea Grande and Baixada Santista.

Today, number 374 Rua B is home to one of Neymar's cousins. As you wander through the run-down area, you realise that Juninho's childhood could not have been easy. 'I am not a daddy's boy. I grew up in a *favela*. My family was humble. We had serious financial problems,' commented the Brazilian icon years later.

After finishing his professional career, in 1998 Neymar Pai took part in an open trial for a job at the CET – the Companhia de Engenharia de Tráfego (traffic engineering company) – in Santos. He was selected and got the job.

Being an assistant builder is not what he wanted, or what he knew how to do: Neymar Pai trained as a mechanic. But for the moment it would have to do. CET was building new canopies for Santos bus shelters. Neymar Pai dug, mixed cement, placed pillars and mended pavements. Four months later he started doing vehicle maintenance and he ended up looking after the Military Police motorbikes. Thanks to Senai training courses, he would become head of department.

He would leave the company in 2009 to manage Juninho's career. But that was in the future: for now, the CET minimum wage was not enough. To make ends meet Neymar Pai sold water purifiers and on weekends he did removals in his trusty old Volkswagen Kombi van (a model famous in the 1960s and 1970s). Nadine looked after the house and the kids but also worked as a cook in a welcome centre for children in need.

Juninho split his time between school and football. He attended the Escola Municipal José Julio Martín Baptista and when the bell rang he would shoot off like a bolt of lightning to football training, where he gave 110 per cent. He played at home, dribbling around chairs and tables and anything that got in his way. He used the door of his bedroom as a goalmouth and tackled the sofa, which knocked him to the ground – penalty. He played against walls, he took the ball on the volley, he headed and chested it and kept it in the air with his thigh, using his left side wherever he could. With a child's size football he scored goal after goal between the legs of the armchair. He imagined various matches: league games, semi-finals and finals.

Sometimes things got damaged. His mother's poor vases took a bashing. Nadine told him off, but not too much. Her father, Arnaldo, whom Juninho never met, had played football. She was understanding and did not prevent her son from having fun with the ball.

The young Neymar did not stop playing football for a moment: he played at home, at school, on the beach with his father when he had a spare moment, and on the street with his friends – a tarmac pitch where the goals were made from any available object and the touchlines were the pavements. The street was on a slope, and every three goals the teams would swap sides to make it fair.

Gustavo Almeida remembers that 'it was difficult to stop Juninho both up and downhill' and he recalls the time when Betinho came to find his pupil to take him to training: 'He parked his car nearby to come and see the match but he forgot to put the handbrake on. The car slowly began rolling downhill and started to gather speed. Luckily we were able to run and catch the car and stop it. It would have been a disaster.'

In Jardim Gloria, many remember Juninho as a shy boy who did not speak much. He loved to collect toy cars; he played on the street, knocking the ball against his neighbours' gates. He trained at the Gremio Praia Grande pitch (where the new Institute is now being built) or in the pitch his father had set up in the backyard to his house. It was grass and it was amazing.

One day Juninho called his friends for a match. There were twenty of them. They started playing at midday and did not stop until six o'clock when it was dark. It was only then that they noticed that the grass pitch had turned into a sandpit. There was not even a single blade of grass. Neymar Pai was bound to be angry: all that hard work ruined in one match. One of Juninho's friends had an idea: he should go to sleep, or pretend to sleep. Neymar Pai would not wake his Juninho. And so, for almost two weeks, Neymar Jr became sleeping beauty: by the time his father came home, Juninho was already in bed.

There are lots of stories of those who knew the most famous neighbour in the neighbourhood. But there are also those who are not old enough to have seen him play in Jardim Gloria but know where he went to school, where he lived or where he played: just like two kids I see cycling home after school, they are proud of someone who has made it, who has become the number one footballer. They also dream about leaving their town one day, just like Juninho ...

But let's get back to Neymar Jr's career. Betinho was the one who guided him. After Tumiaru, Betinho went to coach Associação Atlética Portuguesa for a while, as a springboard to get to Escolinha at Gremetal: Gremio Recreativo y Esportivo Sindacato Metalurgicos de Santos.

It is an association, founded in 1972, whose members, in 1995, decided to start a sports project for kids as a reaction to the increasing use of drugs among the younger population in Santos. Today Escolinha de futsal has 200 kids aged between four and fifteen. A large concrete structure with white and blue stripes in Rua Paraná in Santos is the clubhouse. The club crest stands proudly over the entrance.

Inside, kids are training. White shirts against tanned skins on a light blue pitch. In the corridor there is a large green screen which reads 'Silverware of the club. Athletes who have been through Gremetal and now play football in Brazil and abroad'. There are lots of club membership cards with photos and names. From Adriano Bispo Dos Santos (Gremio) to Anderson Carvalho (Santos); from Renatinho (Hangzhou Greentown, China) to Rodolfo (Vasco Da Gama). And, obviously, Neymar. There are four photos of the star, together with his teammates when he played here, and then later with Gremetal's youth squad when he was already famous.

Elton Luiz, manager at Esportes Futsal, explains: 'He came to us in 2001. Betinho took him, together with a group of fifteen kids. He was in a league of his own both on and off the pitch. He just loved playing with the ball. Training was three times a week but he showed no sign of it bothering him. At the club we always try to get all the kids involved and playing. We make them play in all positions, even in goal, and we work hard on the basics. They need to know how to kick with the right and the left foot, have good ball control and work well with their teammates. Let's not forget the relationship with the family. We work closely with parents because our job, at the end of the day, has a social aspect to it. In Neymar's case, his father was very doting. He talked with the coaches to give them some tips, being an ex-footballer himself. We get the kids ready for competitions and internal tournaments and regional championships. When Neymar was here, we won cup after cup.'

He breaks off mid-sentence and asks someone else in the room to go and find the photos of the victories. Here is Neymar, together with his teammates, wearing the yellow shirt with the green collar, crouching, football in hand, and with a smiling Betinho standing behind. Here he is again, with a white shirt and a 'Cascão' haircut, i.e. the one like a sort of toupé which Ronaldo Luís Nazário da Lima sported in the 2002 World Cup in Japan and South Korea. Ronaldo was his idol at that time and Neymar wanted to be at least as good as him. Standing in the photo is coach Alcides Magri Junior.

Alcides is training the under-11s. At the end of the match, he has a few minutes to chat to me about one of his ex-athletes: 'He was nine at the time. He was a smart kid, lively, always happy. I remember his smile and the fact that he was great friends with his teammates. He was a great player and had great skills. When he was on the pitch he changed. Nothing challenged him. He was able to turn a match around on his own. But he did not want to be treated differently to the others. He liked being in the group. When you have a talent like Neymar, often you get jealousy, conflict or envy amongst the players but not with Neymar; there were no problems whatsoever. He was a nice kid, a team player. His teammates admired him. No, Ney was not a show-off on the pitch.'

We talk about his development at Gremetal: 'Betinho worked with him for one or two months and then he came to me at the under-11s team and then the under-13s. This change was due to the fact that Neymar was so good that we moved him up a level almost immediately. He started playing with kids older than him, one or two years older. I remember that when he finished training he went to the technical office and Edy told him, "Hey kid, go and eat in the canteen with the rest of the players", but he did not want to and continued practising on his own. The first title? The Copa Uniligas. The final was against Santos and we won 3–1. Two cutting crosses from Neymar and two goals from Leo Dentinho, then a magnificent ball from Dentinho allowed Neymar to score the final goal. Those two players understood each other perfectly, they complemented each other perfectly. Dentinho with number 10 set up the play and Neymar, number 14, finished off. Or vice versa. They were a fantastic pairing. When they were on the pitch, we never lost. Unfortunately Leo has not had a successful career like Neymar.'

I ask him what a coach can teach to a little footballing genius like Neymar? Magri answers, 'My role was to give him freedom, not block his talent and try to improve his technical abilities. I didn't need to teach him how to dribble …'

And what has futsal given Neymar? 'In futsal space is limited; the player has to think and move quickly. There is no time to stand still with the ball at your feet. You have to dart here and there, pass the ball, shoot. It is a much quicker game than eleven-a-side. The player has to have quick reflexes, be ball smart and have a particular style. Just look at the short and concise dribbling which Neymar employs. In futsal you have to work the ball more, to be more agile and have incredible ball control. This develops into freestyle, which Neymar is such a master of. Let's not forget that 80 to 90 per cent of Brazilian players playing at the highest level, those that get to play for the national team, the *Seleção*, have played futsal. It is an experience which improves the creativity of the player. It means he is more confident when switching to eleven-a-side.'

While we have been chatting, Elton Luiz has pulled out more photos. One by one he points out the players in the teams and the coaches such as Carlos, Eduardo and Amorini André who at Gremetal followed Neymar's development in awe. He points to Neymar celebrating a title. This time his hair is normal but on his forehead he is wearing a white band with writing on it. It is hard to make out but Magri steps in: 'Yes. When he was eleven or twelve years old, he loved playing with a sweatband on his head. His mother had made it for him so that God could protect him, even though his father told him to take it off because his teammates called him 'the masked man'. The writing says 'Jesus is faithful' or '100 per cent Jesus'.

Chapter 5

100 per cent Jesus

A conversation with
Newton Glória Lobato Filho

The church service is over. The priest, Newton Glória Lobato Filho, says farewell to the congregation. He inquires about the health of a relative, shakes hands, hugs a young boy and has a moment's prayer with others. Sunday Mass, in the *Igreja Batista Peniel,* a huge sky blue warehouse in Avenida Martín 781 in São Vicente, was intense and emotional. A real show, lasting about three hours. On the stage, behind the Plexiglas lectern with Jesus written on the column, Newton Glória used every oratory device: from ranting and raving to witty remarks, from a falsetto voice to baritone, from shouting at the top of his voice to a hushed whisper. First he asked the congregation to take part in the 37th anniversary celebrations of the Ministerio Peniel as set out in the pamphlets provided. After the reading of I Samuel 24, 25 from the Bible he started his sermon: a speech with a sentence repeated over and over again: 'God will come and visit you tonight. Prepare your soul for this visit.' The standing congregation answered him with raised palms in an emotional trance. The lights beamed down on the stage below, illuminating a simple white cross, two massive screens to the side, and a large blue, red and yellow banner:

Ministerio Peniel Face a Face com Deus 37 anos restaurando vidas ('Peniel Ministry Face to Face with God, 37 years of restoring lives')

Three TV cameras filmed the sermon, the whole piece to be sold on DVD. There was lots of music, with electric guitars, keyboards and drums. The song was '*Abraça-me*' ('Hold Me'), a religious gospel by André Valadão. The song was sung by the congregation, with the chorus – 'Hold me, heal me, anoint me, touch me' – repeated again and again. With its catchy tune it gets stuck in your head and you cannot forget it.

The members of the congregation approached the stage and the 2,000-strong crowd took the Holy Communion: wine from plastic cups and a bit of toast for the bread. Now the service was almost over but first there was the presentation to the worshippers of a newborn baby and a new couple.

Before letting the congregation go, yellow envelopes were held aloft on the stage and in the wings. These were for the collection of an 'offering to God' with each member of the congregation giving what they can afford. The envelopes are also used to collect the 'tithe'. According to Leviticus 27, 30–32 in the Bible, the tithe is the offering to the temple of the tenth part of the earth's produce and of the flock. Today the tenth part refers to a tenth of a worshipper's earnings.

When the enormous warehouse is almost empty at 9.30pm, Newton opens a stage door and goes to his office. On the wall behind the desk is a framed page of a newspaper: it shows Neymar sporting his Santos shirt. Accompanied by his son, who helps him at the ministry, the minister talks about *Ministerio Peniel* and its famous follower in a calm voice. He explains that in Baixada Santista and the coastal region there are 58 churches and more than 12,000 followers. The majority of them (almost 70 per cent) are young men and women, white and coloured in equal measure. They are schoolgoers, university students or in work. 'But some of them are from difficult backgrounds. They grew up without a family. They have had drug problems and been involved in criminal activity. In our church they find support, a new family, an identity, community and the word of God, which can ease their pain. There are lots of them who come here as young kids, as did Juninho. Some get married here, some have their kids baptised here and now they are devoted followers of the church,' comments the Minister.

Let's talk about Neymar Jr.
'He came to our church when he was eight years old. He lived in Praia Grande. The first time he came with his father, and then with his mother, sister and his friends. He was baptised in our church when he was fifteen years old, on the first Sunday of December, 2007, on Gonzaguinha beach in São Vicente. [This ceremony attracts around 10,000 followers every year and they remain immersed in the sea during the christening.]'

Why did he wear that headband when he was a kid?
'It is a sign of faith, a way of paying tribute to his Creator.'

What about the '100 per cent Jesus' band Neymar wore in 2012 during the celebrations for the tricampeonato Paulista.
'I was with him then. It is something we must thank Him for.'

What is Juninho like from a spiritual and human perspective?
'He is a very nice person. Very human. He always says hello and hugs the other followers. He always makes time for the handicapped kids. He speaks to them, signs autographs and lets them take pictures with him. From a spiritual perspective you should note that, despite his commitments and other problems he may have had, he always came to Thursday Mass when he played for Santos. He sat on the last row and listened to the sermon and the praises made to the Lord. This shows his faith in God and his spirituality.'

Did he ever speak in front of the congregation like some did this evening?
'No. He never did that. One time I said to him, "How come you are on television and you sing, dance or go on stage at a concert but here you are too shy to speak in front of the others on stage?" But he still did not want to do it.'

How did religion help him?
'I believe that all stages in his life are linked to his faith. Throughout all the challenges he faced, I prayed with him and the community prayed for him. Each step he took, each category he moved into, when he signed his first professional contract, when he played his first match with Santos and his first time with the Brazilian squad, we prayed for him. The prayers and the word of God have been a spiritual guide in his life and they have helped him get to where he is today. He could have lost his way as a result of the fame and fortune he has had but it has not happened. The values of the church and his family have been passed down to him and ingrained in him.'

What values did your church give to him?
'Giving glory to God, loving and respecting your family, your friends and your neighbour. These are the values we try to instil in our followers.'

But how do you combine faith in Christ with nights out in nightclubs and relationships outside of marriage?
'It is difficult but this is not only true of Neymar. It is the same with other young followers of our faith who are neither as famous nor as rich as he is. It is an age thing: there are no inhibitions. I pray for people not to have sex before marriage but you need to understand and be tolerant. We need to open our arms and our hearts to the congregation. We cannot shut the door on anyone.'

What did you think when Neymar Jr was nineteen years old and discovered that he was a father?
'I spoke to his father, his mother and to him. I told him that he had to love his child, to help him, because it was his son and a creature of God. In a moment as difficult as this for a young man, his family values passed down to him from his mother and father were of fundamental importance. When David Lucca was born, we presented him to the world here in the church before the congregation, just like we did this evening. His family and his friends were all there.'

Does Neymar pay the 'tithe'?
'He is generous. He began to pay it when he was a young kid. He contributed to the life of the church with 20 or 40 reais. His father and mother paid the tithe for him. He still helps the church every month but he does not pay the tithe.'

Is it true what certain Spanish newspapers wrote a few years ago, that in his contract with Real Madrid or with Barcelona, Neymar Jr wanted to include a clause which covered the costs of plane tickets for you to go back and forth from Brazil, so that he could have his spiritual guide always by his side?
The minister laughs heartily. Wiping away the tears from his eyes, he quips, 'I did not know that.'

How do you see Neymar in this new adventure of life and football?
'It is something natural. It was meant to be. Sooner or later the time had to come when he had to leave Brazil and go to Europe to develop. Neymar can now face this challenge calmly and confidently: he is more mature, he has more experience of the game of life. I remember when he was fifteen, during Mass one time I opened the Bible and I saw the prophetic words of God. God gave me the voice; I asked Juninho to stand up and listen to God's message. I spoke as God's instrument and I told him he would become one of the best players in the world.'

And has the prophecy come true?
'I believe so, yes. I believe the word of God represents the truth.'

Chapter 6
Liceu São Paulo

'When he was a promising talent we believed in him. It was a great privilege to have been able to help and develop one of the greatest footballers in the world. Good luck Neymar Jr.' The poster is fixed with tape to the side of the reception cubby hole at Neymar's old school. Neymar Jr is wearing a red and white top and has a football at his feet. The football pitch is an open book. The advert is simple but effective and works a treat to attract new students to the Liceu São Paulo: a red and white building with five floors, which stands out on the Avenida Ana Costa, a large street leading to Santos's beaches. The school caters for primary, secondary and further education students. It is a private school with a long history. It was opened in the 1920s and is well known throughout the city.

Maria Antonia Julião Faracco, coordinator of the school and head of years six and seven (eleven and twelve year olds) welcomes me to the school. Maria has a little pin on her top with the colours of Santos FC. She is a fan of Alvinegro Praiano and is sincerely saddened by the fact that Neymar Jr has gone to Barcelona, even though she understands his reason for doing so. She shows me down the corridor and calls the lift to take me to the classrooms, the library, the auditorium, the biology lab and, on the final floor, the gym illuminated by light which pours in from large windows – these provide a wonderful view of the city. She comments,

'It is here that Neymar played and it is here that, thanks to Copa TV Tribuna de futsal escolar, he started to become known all over Baixada Santista.' The promotion of the Liceu continues.

But let's talk about Neymar da Silva Santos Junior the student.

'He was an average student; he liked history, and physical education, obviously. He struggled with maths,' says Antonia.

'Numbers and figures were not his thing,' confirms Doña Vilma Julia Rinaldi, his maths teacher, 'but he was not a lazy or disorganised student. He studied hard.'

Maria Antonia continues, 'He was polite, respectful with the teachers and sociable with his classmates. He never missed lessons and never gave us any trouble. The thing we noted was that he was mad about football. You saw it immediately. He was always ready to play a match with his classmates. At break time, students were not allowed to play football but he always found a way around it. He would go to the headmaster and beg him to lend him a football so he could take some shots or practise keep-ups. Here in the gym, he and his friends pulled down the volleyball net so they could use the gym as a football pitch. The girls wanted to play volleyball but the boys pretended they were hard of hearing.'

I ask how a boy from a humble, modest family in Jardim Gloria in Praia Grande was able to come to such an expensive private school: surely he could not afford the school fees?

'He won a scholarship,' explains the coordinator of the school.

It is a long story which began on the football pitches of Associação Atlética Portuguesa, known to everyone in Santos as 'Briosa', a company founded in 1917 by a group of Portuguese immigrants. Most of them were builders, working on the building sites all over the city. They did not want to be seen as inferior to Italians, Spanish and Syrians who were setting up their own sports clubs. After having seen an España Futebol Clube football match, they met in a barber's shop to discuss setting up their own club. Portuguesa Santista's sports facilities are only a few hundred metres from Avenida Ana Costa where the school is. Theirs is a massive complex which includes an Olympic swimming pool, a kids' pool, a futsal pitch, party hall and even a *churrasqueria* (steak house). At the centre of the complex is the Ulrico Mursa stadium. Manuel, the association's secretary, reminds us that it is 'the first one in the whole of Latin America to have a roof of reinforced concrete'. The first team, which plays in the second division of the Paulista League is training against a junior team.

In the stands, Edu Marangon is watching with interest the moves of a new kid who has just started and has great potential. Marangon is of Italian origin (his family is from Treviso) and still speaks the language of Dante. He grew up with Portuguesa Santista, played for Torino for two seasons (1987/88 and 1988/89) and then moved to Porto, then Flamengo, then Santos, then Palmeiras, then Yokohama Flugels and finally to Bragantino. He played ten times for the *Seleção*.

Today he is director of sports at Portuguesa Santista. When speaking about Neymar, he says, 'He is different to everyone else. Not only is he a great footballer but he has the intelligence to read the game, coupled with superb physical fitness. For a time, he single-handedly transformed Santos into the *Cirque du Soleil* (the show that children and adults alike want to see at all costs). He is the new Messi.' It is, however, a shame that he has given birth to 'Neymarisation'. Marangon continues: 'Look at all young footballers. They have his haircut, they wear their clothes in the same way, they listen to their music through headsets in the same way, they copy him. If you just stand in front of the door [he points at the entrance to Portuguesa], you will see ten fathers and twenty mothers with a twelve-year-old or thirteen-year-old boy with CV in hand. They all swear that their son is the new Neymar and that they have stopped working to follow their prodigal son's career more closely. But a Neymar is born once every 50 years.' Marangon remembers clearly the boy with the Briosa shirt on this very pitch, playing eleven-a-side.

It was Betinho who brought him to Portuguesa with a group of his boys. It is here that he played his first official tournament on a large pitch. Betinho recalls, 'He played on the left side and immediately showed us what he was made of. He looked for the ball and picked it up in front of the defence. He started dribbling from way back and ran circles around his opponents and then released the ball for one of his teammates or just carried on straight to goal.'

Betinho remembers a goal that Neymar scored in the final of a tournament at Cascavel, Paraná. He reminisces, 'He created from nothing a one-two pass, in the style of Robinho, and then struck the ball which slotted into the top corner of the opponent's goal. A masterpiece. Everyone was amazed!'

The match that many still remember is the junior league match between Portuguesa and São Paulo. Neymar was eleven at the time and his teammates were all twelve. One of his friends, Dudu, with whom he played at Tumiaru and then again at Liceu and had a great relationship with both on and off the pitch, played as the number 11. Dudu started dribbling with the ball and was brought down in the area. Penalty. Number 10, Neymar, took the spot-kick. One-nil to Briosa. It was Dudu again who crossed the ball from the left for Gustavo to score the second goal. São Paulo reacted and Fabio headed in to make it 2–1. But Neymar was on fire. He dribbled the ball and went it alone. Neymar shot but the opponent's goalkeeper parried; Neymar got the ball back and passed it to Leo Baptistão, lying in wait, who slotted in for 3–1. Neymar then finished off the game straight from the centre spot. The goalkeeper read what he was doing but the ball slipped through his hands.

Four-one the final score, with 'Juninho' scoring twice. It was their third victory in the league and took them to the top of the table. At the end of the match, the coach, Betinho, effused praise for Dudu and Neymar in a post-match TV interview: 'He is a revelation for Baixada Santista youth football.' Sporting his '100 per cent Jesus' red headband, Neymar said that the rest of the team played well and, with a cheeky smile, took a swipe at São Paulo: 'We won a lot more easily than we were expecting.' Neymar stood out from the rest to such an extent that São Paulo made an offer. They wanted him in the Tricolour shirt. But no agreement was reached.

Reginaldo Ferreira de Oliveira, aka Fino, coach at Portuguesa and Liceu futsal coordinator, recalls, 'That was a proper team, that one. There was Neymar, Dudu, Gustavo and Leo Baptistão. Juninho loved playing football and always wanted to be the best. The best on the street, the best in the district, the best in the city, then the state, then the country and now the best in the world. He always wants more, every single day, and you could see this in him right from when he was a little boy. Just look at how quickly he adapted from futsal to eleven-a-side. So quickly that within six months Santos had made an offer for him.'

Fino is now a physical education teacher and coach at Escola de futebol Meninos da Vila Ct Neymar in Ourinhos.

'The only one which bears Neymar's name,' he says. 'It was his father who wanted me to train in the school his son founded, perhaps because of what I did for Neymar.'

Among Fino's many accomplishments was that of helping Neymar and his sister, Rafaela, get into the Liceu São Paulo. One day, speaking with Ermenegildo Pinheiro da Costa Miranda, aka Tio Gil, the then head at the Liceu, Fino explained that the futsal team was good but at Portuguesa there were certain players who could make it better. In particular, there was a kid who could make the difference and become the star of the team. The trouble was that his family could not afford to pay the fees. What to do? The head did not hesitate for an instant: 'If he is that good, bring him to the school and we will find a way to help him.'

The trial at the Liceu gym was more than convincing. Fino continues: 'It was Mr Miranda who registered Juninho and his sister at the school. He granted him a scholarship which included all school materials, books, uniform and the school bus for the trip to and from Praia Grande.'

Since 2003, and continuing to the present day, the Liceu has played in the intercollege league organised by TV Tribuna, an affiliated network of Globo TV. More than 80 schools from the region take part and the matches are broadcast on TV. Having a good team and winning the cup is excellent marketing for the school. That is why Tio Gil did not think twice about offering Neymar and his sister a place. In the style of the American universities, the Liceu poached Neymar and the top players from Portuguesa.

Fino continues: 'The first year we got to the final, where we lost against Anglo Americano College. Neymar and Dudu, number 7 and number 11 respectively, were the stars of the team. They were inseparable. Their life was football. So much so that sometimes they would skip lunch to play

football. They did not care that they would then have to go
to Portuguesa for training.' Neymar was a rising star and the
papers began to publish photos and articles about the young
kid from Praia Grande. 'Neymar could be next national
hero' ran the headline in *A Tribuna*, one of Santos's dailies.
The accompanying piece read: 'Neymar is cheeky both on
and off the pitch. On the field he strings together pass after
pass, he takes responsibility for the ball, he scores and creates
goals for his teammates. Off the pitch, he says he is already
used to interviews but during the league celebrations he did
not manage to dribble past the cameras of his fans and the
kisses of his college girlfriends. In the hustle and bustle he
almost lost his medal from around his neck.'

The network interviewed him, the kids asked for his autograph and girls shouted out his name. At thirteen he was
already famous. This made some schools envious and they
accused the school of having taken in Neymar just for football, without enrolling him in lessons. Ermenegildo Miranda
went in person to the directorate in Encino to show the
register and the enrolment papers to prove the other school
heads wrong. Everyone wanted a Neymar in their team.

In 2005 Juninho faced the only upset of his entire school
career. He was working with Mateus Pavão Fuschini, the PE
teacher at the time. Neymar had little or no spare time and
often missed school training sessions. His school teammates
were not happy about this, grumbling, complaining and
accusing Mateus of favouritism. How could he not train and
still be entitled to play? Mateus called Neymar and told him
to come to the school training. Neymar came, scored goal
after goal and ran rings around his opponents. And that was
that. No one had anything to say after that, especially seeing
as the school team was on top form with Neymar playing.

The school went on to win the TV Tribuna Cup. A photo

of the time shows Neymar, in his white headband and matching shirt, lifting the trophy (in the shape of a boot kicking a ball) amid a sea of people. 'We won other tournaments,' reflects Fino, 'but the televised Tribune Cup was perhaps the most important.'

Neymar left Portuguesa to join the youth teams at Santos. In turn, he also left the Liceu to study at the Lupe Picasso Institute next to Vila Belmiro, Santos's stadium. Maria Antonia comments, 'And what a coincidence that this year [2013] the two schools where Neymar studied won the Copa Tribuna de Futsal. Lupe Picasso won the women's cup and the Liceu won the men's cup, eight years after that famous victory.'

Chapter 7
Santos

The harbour, coffee houses, beaches and football. This and much more is Santos: a coastal city with around 500,000 inhabitants in the state of São Paulo, 68 kilometres from the capital. Endless convoys of HGVs loaded with containers and goods wind down the Serra do mar along the Rodovia dos Imigrantes to queue one behind the other at the entrance to the thirteen square kilometres of port, the largest in Latin America. A quarter of everything that comes in and out of Brazil passes through this port – goods and passengers. The transatlantic cruise ships of the largest companies offload hundreds of tourists here for a few hours. A quick visit to the city and then off again. Ships, petrol tankers and cargo ships which embark and disembark to and from the open sea or moor along the coast, their lights flickering on the horizon of the night sky in Baixada Santista.

Copper domes, coloured glass depicting the mythology of the country, marble mosaics, granite columns, groups of sculptures, a clock tower 40 metres high: the Bolsa Oficial de Café in Rua XV de Novembro no. 95 is a monument to the coffee heritage of the city, a testament to the golden era when Santos was the main market for the world coffee trade – so much so that certain countries only bought coffee if it had been certified here. The Bolsa opened on 7 September 1922 and for almost 50 years the shouts and cries of the traders bargaining for the seeds from the *Coffea* trees could be heard. Nowadays it is a museum – a city tourist attraction – a bookshop, and a crowded coffee house where different aromas can be experienced.

It is a meeting point in the historic centre which, with its paved streets, lampposts and pastel-coloured buildings built at the end of the nineteenth and beginning of the twentieth century, shows the trappings of the coffee economy. Here, on 16 February 1867, the first train of the São Paulo Railway arrived, connecting the production areas with the port: the point of departure for Europe and point of entry for immigrants, Italians and Japanese, who came to replace the African slaves in the plantations. Today the port is still a source of wealth, alongside fishing, trade and tourism. Santos has a flourishing economy, which in the next few years could be propelled by natural gas and crude oil. In 2008, the Carioca reserve was discovered in the Santos Basin. It is believed to contain 33 billion barrels of crude oil. It is the third largest reserve in the world. It would enable Brazil to not only be an agricultural economy, exporting coffee, sugar, soya and ethanol, but to become a petrol powerhouse.

That is for the future. For now, let us look at the present-day Santos. It is a city which comes in at fifth place in the quality of life rankings for Brazilian municipalities according to the UN Development Index, which considers education, GDP per capita and life expectancy. A city which, like the rest of the country, shows the brutal contrast between the rich and the poor, between the gleaming coastal buildings and Vila Gilda, the largest *favela* of stilt-houses in all of Brazil; between the slightly run-down historic centre where the street lights are switched off at night and the beaches on the other side of the tunnel, which are brimming with life and activity.

The beaches: seven kilometres of fine white sandy

beaches crowned by skyscrapers. Glass and concrete, dream penthouses, rooftop pools. Pinnacles, one next to the other, each more stunning than the next. A neat line which every so often is broken by neoclassical hotels from the 1920s – the first hotels to host travellers who wanted to benefit from bathing in the sea.

Shopping centres, restaurants, bars, cycle paths, tourists, OAPs jogging, young men and women going back and forth laden with surfboards, boules players and beach volleyball players. It is a constant to and fro of people in Praia Gonzaga.

On Saturday evenings, the beach becomes one big football pitch. One match after another as far as the eye can see. Lines drawn in the sand and matches played barefoot. All ages play: pot-bellied elderlies sweat and groan; fit, handsome young men; teenagers darting around and young kids pulling one trick after another. There are shouts, fouls, goals, penalties and throw-ins with balls that skim dangerously close to the massive waves of the Atlantic. There are coloured shirts of all the great Brazilian and European clubs, bare chests and makeshift kit. Five-a-side, eleven-a-side, foot volley, 'futebol society' (seven-a-side): not a single football-related game is missing in this procession of sport.

Soon it is evening and the beach slowly returns to its natural state. With goalposts and crossbars slung over shoulders, nets stuffed into bags, the footballers leave and are replaced by the laughter which burbles out of the beach bars, and by the tramps who methodically pick up bottles and cans.

Football returns to the clubs, the suburban pitches, the futsal halls, the youth clubs. It returns to the fans and to the three city football clubs: Portuguesa Santista, Jabaquara, and Santos, the club that changed forever the way football is played, according to its famous supporters' group, the Torcida Jovem.

'One hundred years of football art' is the slogan the club created for its centenary in 2012. These words can be found at the entrance to the Urbano Caldeira stadium, better known as Vila Belmiro, after the area. It is a small sports complex, opened in 1916, with capacity for 16,798 spectators. During bad times, no more than 4,000 turn up.

Everything is close to hand. You can almost touch the pitch and the players. At the heart of the stadium lie the changing rooms. A plaque marks the entrance: *Vestiario Edson Arantes do Nacimiento Pelé* ('Edson Arantes do Nacimiento Pelé Changing Rooms'). Inside is a large photograph of the great number 10: an homage to 'O Rei'.

Pelé is not the only champion whose successes are on display. In the changing rooms, each locker bears the photo of a current player and the name of one of the *Alvinegro* icons.

The history is set out over the 380 square metres of the Memorial das Conquistas on the ground floor of Vila Belmiro. Photos, footballs, autographs, football boots, newspapers, plaques, shirts and trophies representing 100 years of football.

It was on 14 April 1912 when the largest, most luxurious transatlantic liner in the world, RMS *Titanic*, collided with an iceberg and sank in a few hours. Of the 2,223 passengers, 1,518 lost their lives. In Santos, that same Sunday, 39 young men, aged between fifteen and 24, some students, others workers, all members of the well-off upper middle classes, met in the grand hall of the Club Concordia. Santista sportsmen Francisco Raymundo Marques, Mário Ferraz de Campos and Argemiro de Souza Júnio had called a meeting to found an 'important football club'. The meeting went on for a long time. It was difficult to agree on a name that hit the mark, that pleased everyone. Someone suggested Africa Futebol Clube, others Concordia, others insisted on

Associação Esportiva Brasil; and then finally, at 10.23pm, the simplest idea of all was agreed as the name of the club: Santos Football Club (in the English style, naturally).

The next day the *Diario de Santos*, edited by Tito Brasil, splashed the news all over the front page with the headline 'Sports', wishing 'a long and prosperous life to the new sports club'.

On 15 September 1912 the new team played at the pitch in Avenida Ana Costa, no. 22, where today the Igreja Coração de Maria stands. This was the first official match. The opposition were Santos Athletic Club. The final score was 3–2 to the new team. The next year Santos were invited to play in the Liga Paulista de Futebol, the first official competition. The first match was against Germânia, on 1 June 1913. One goal for and eight against – a thrashing by all accounts. If this was a sign of things to come, it was not looking good.

In fact, 22 years passed before Santos achieved their first title, winning the Paulista league in 1935. Professional football in Brazil had been around for two years by that time. It was that same year, during a match at Vila Belmiro against São Paulo da Floresta (the team which became the current São Paulo) on 12 March, that the Santos fans claimed for themselves the nickname which they had been given by other fans. Every time Santos played at São Paulo, the home fans teased the Santos fans by shouting 'rotten fish, fishmongers'. When they played São Paulo da Floresta that day, they had had enough, and retorted, 'We *are* fishmongers and we are proud of it'.

Peixe ('fish') became the nickname for Santos and a killer whale became the club mascot. But the killer whale had no bite, as, after the first trophy, a long barren period ensued. It was a dark time for the club, which writer and commentator José Roberto Torero defined as 'our middle ages'. He was not wrong: another twenty years passed before Santos won the league again. By then it was 1955 and a team made up of Manga, Hélvio, Feijó, Ramiro, Formiga, Urubatão, Tite, Negri, Álvaro, Del Vecchio and Pepe beat Taubaté 2–1 in the final.

Then in June 1956, a fifteen-year-old boy arrived at Vila Belmiro, accompanied by former *Seleção* footballer Valdemar de Brito. Born in Três Corações in the state of Minas Gerais, the boy was called Edson Arantes do Nacimiento. Yes, Pelé; who, together with Gilmar, Dalmo, Mauro, Calvet, Zito, Mengalvio, Lima, Dorval, Coutinho, Pagão and Pepe, made Santos into a team famous all over the world and Brazilian football the benchmark for footballing excellence.

The end of the 1950s and the 1960s were the golden years for the club: nine league titles, five Brazil Cups, two Coppe Libertadores and two Intercontinental Cups. Santos was also the basis for the Brazil team which won the 1958, 1962 and 1970 World Cups.

The explosion of football in this period was in line with what was going on in the world. It was in harmony with rock 'n' roll, The Beatles, the bossa nova (a style of samba mixed with jazz and classical music which influenced the world). Brasilia was founded in this period: a city with futuristic architecture, a symbol of the Brazil to come, capable of originality due to its *mestizo* ('mixed blood') origins – hopes which were abruptly dashed not long after with the military coup d'état of 31 March 1964 and the years of dictatorship which followed.

Futebol, the art of football, the Santos style, developed in the years of change and hope, continues to amaze nonetheless. Pelé is the undebated icon, the pride of the nation, the player who scored 129 goals in 1959. The game played by *Alvinegro Praiano* was football art, a show in its purest form, an expression of the joy and pleasure of football. It was something everyone wanted to see up close. And so Santos became a sort of Harlem Globetrotters, touring in 59 countries and even stopping a war in January 1969 when, during a tour in Africa, they managed to get the factions to lay down arms in the Congo; similarly, their visit to Nigeria later that same year resulted in a temporary truce in the Biafran war.

On 19 November 1969, in a Silver Cup match (the precursor to Brazil's national league competition, the *Brasilerão*) against Vasco da Gama in front of 65,157 spectators at the Maracanã in Rio, the 'Black Pearl' scored a penalty. It was his 1,000th goal. 'The entire world applauds the greatest footballer of all time,' the radio commentator said.

Five years later, the saddest day occurred. On 2 October 1974, Santos played against Ponte Preta at Vila Belmiro. In the 22nd minute, Pelé took the ball in his hands, kneeled down at the centre of the pitch and raised his hands to the sky and faced each side of the stadium. Teammates and opponents waved at him. He got up, took off his black-and-white-striped shirt, ran a lap of honour around the pitch and left in tears for the changing rooms while the whole stadium sobbed. After nineteen years, O Rei had left Santos.

'Brazil is Pelé's widow,' reflected the TV reporters. It was a hard event for the country, and Peixe, to swallow. So many years of marvellous football ended in that moment. A period of grief ensued. The story of Santos continued, but their rebirth would take four years. Only in 1978 did they once again find success again in the Paulistão, with the team of Juary, Pita, Ailton, Lira, Nilton Batata and João Paulo: the young and exuberant *Meninos da Vila* ('young kids of Vila Belmiro').

*   *   *

Emerson Leão, the coach who arrived at Santos in 2002, gave the kids of the club's youth teams a chance, just like Lula (Luis Antonio Perez) had done in the 1950s and 1960s. History repeated itself. Santos was reborn with the second generation of *Meninos*: Diego and Robinho, who took Santos to their seventh Brazilian championship in 2002 with lively and showy football. And eight years later came the third generation of *Meninos*, led by Neymar.

In honour of Pelé, the Memorial das Conquistas at Vila Belmiro dedicates an entire cabinet to memories and emotions. The only other player who is honoured in this way is Neymar. The two champions, side by side. A shiny tin statue with Mohican hair for Neymar, a copper-wire statue with the Brazil number 10 shirt for Pelé.

Chapter 8

Peixe

Though he died in June 2015, José Ely de Miranda, aka Zito, remains an icon of Santos Futebol Club. The same can be said of Antônio Lima dos Santos, aka Lima – although he is still very much alive. Zito, nicknamed 'O Gerente', arrived at the club in 1952. He had a small moustache like Clark Gable, and wore number 5 on his shirt. He was captain of a dream team which won everything there was to win in the 1950s and 1960s. And we must not forget that he won the World Cup with the Brazilian national team in 1958 and 1962. They say he was the only player able to give orders and shout at 'O Rei', the king, Pelé.

Lima played with Santos for ten years from 1961 to 1971, appearing in 696 matches, scoring 65 goals and winning every title. They called him 'O Curinga' ('the joker in the pack') because he played in every position on the pitch except in goal. He was the 'lung' of that famous team which amazed the world.

Zito and Lima were two key figures in Neymar's life. The first introduced Neymar to Santos; the second was his coach on the eleven-a-side pitch.

Speaking in 2014, Zito remembered well the first time he saw 'Juninho' and decided that the boy had to play for Santos. It was the end of 2003. At that time Zito was the coordinator for the junior teams for Santos. A Santos fan, Alemão, who was obsessed with Peixe, called him to tell him that he should go and see a certain Neymar, a young boy who was playing in a futsal tournament. Alemão added, 'He is only a kid but he plays very well. I am sure you will like him.'

Alemão is a notable character. He has thirteen Santos crests tattooed on his arms and one on his forehead. He manages a bar in front of Vila Belmiro and is a leading figure in the official supporters' club. When he saw Neymar, he saw his potential. But he wasn't the only one: lots of people had tipped off Santos about Neymar, the boy from Mogi da Cruzes. Another of these was José Luiz Pinho, a metallurgy trade unionist, who had watched the boy closely when he played on the parquet at Gremetal.

Regardless of who spotted him, Zito decided to go and see this player. He spoke to a friend and went to the Portuguesa Santista ground.

Zito said, 'I have to admit that Neymar filled me with joy. He was only eleven years old but he did the same things then as he does today. With the ball at his feet, he was incredible, sensational. He was miles above the rest. A real superstar. I went back to Vila Belmiro and I spoke to the chairman, Marcelo Teixeira. I told him that we had to get Neymar straight away before someone else snatched him up. I insisted that Neymar signed a contract which tied him to Santos for a long time. When you see a player you like that much, you know you can't be wrong. I was sure he would bring great happiness to Santos's fans.'

And so a few months later, on 10 May 2004, Neymar da Silva Santos Jr signed his first contract with Santos, for a five-year term and a salary of 450 reais per month. It was his first salary, even if he had already earned bits and bobs here and there and received a few presents for his family when he was playing for the futsal teams.

When Neymar started his Santos career, the club had no eleven-a-side team at under-13 level; so he started in five-a-side. (The efforts of Zito and the chairman led to the creation of such teams thereafter, in order to train talents like Neymar. In 2006, the Centro de Treinamento Meninos da Vila was opened, set up specifically for the junior teams of the club.) It was Lima who brought him to eleven-a-side. He recounts: 'I had heard that he was a good player but, unfortunately for me, he was playing futsal. I went to see him train and decided to get him to join my team made up of fifteen year olds, whereas he was only twelve. I spoke to Zito: "Look, if it's ok with you, I'll take Neymar in my team." His reply was clear: "Are you mad! He is not strong enough yet to play eleven-a-side." I insisted, however, and explained that I did not want him to play in the league: I just wanted him to train with the group at a different level. Zito agreed: "OK, you're the boss, do what you feel is right." And that was that. Neymar came to play for me.'

Behind his desk in his office in Vila Belmiro, the deep-voiced, stocky Lima remembers the details of those first years on the pitch: 'He played centre forward. I reflected on this and I told him that with his physique he was not able to move well in the area against defenders who were bigger and stronger than him. It was the only thing I had to tell him in three years. I suggested that we mix things up a bit and that he move to midfield, so that he could receive the ball, be in front of the defence and attack and use his speed. That way no one could stop him. I told him, "You can zig-zag your way through the field and finish off the move or assist your team-mate who is in a good position." Neymar was having none of it. At the beginning, with tears in his eyes, he said to me, "No. Profe. You want to take me out of the area; you don't want me to score." But I explained to him that it was quite the contrary and that I wanted to place him in area where he could dominate the ball. That way he would not have to take the ball from behind him, turn round or deal with taller and bulkier players.'

Players like the famous *gatos del futebol* ('football cats'): kids who were way too old for the category. Bruisers who went in hard to intimidate smaller and more fragile opponents like Neymar.

It was Neymar's build that worried Zito. 'He was not wrong,' reflects Lima. 'Look at how he is now. You can imagine what he was like six or seven years ago. He was pretty thin, but, thanks to the work of the club, bit by bit he gained seven to eight kilos of muscle mass and a top-rate physique.

'At barely fourteen, Neymar was playing in the fifteen year olds' league. He played futsal and eleven-a-side. In the morning he trained on the pitch and in the evening on the track – maybe a bit too much, and I told Zito and Neymar Pai as much. I wanted him to choose and in the end he did.

'Neymar was a quiet, polite and obedient child. It was easy to work with him. He never complained about any of the exercises: basics, finishing, physical. Training was not a burden for him. I remember that when it was time to leave the pitch and go to the changing rooms for a shower, you always had to wait for him. 'Profe. Just five more shots. Let me take this free kick,' he used to say.

'He was so determined, which is so important at that age. When I explained to him what I wanted from him from a training session, you could be sure that Neymar would always achieve what you were trying to achieve. Just like the time when for the entire week we tried and retried a set piece to exploit his speed. We got to the match against San Bernardo. I settled myself on the bench and spoke to the reserves. I had my back to the pitch. I heard shouting and I was not sure what was going on. Then one of the reserves said, "Profe. Neymar has just scored using exactly the set piece we practised all week." It was incredible.

'The only thing he did not like doing was kicking or shooting with his left foot, because he was right-footed. When I insisted, he complained. He did not want to hear about shooting with his left. "Why always me, why do I always have to do it, Profe?" he said. Today he is ambidextrous. I text him every now and then to take the mickey, just like I did after the goal in the final of the Confederation Cup. The message read something like "Not bad for someone who did not want to shoot with their left".'

Lima goes quiet for a minute and then says, 'I am certain that he will not take long to become the number one in the world' – words of honour indeed coming from a champion who has seen hundreds of players and who has himself played with the best of them all, Pelé.

Now we have heard the views of the coach, what about those of Neymar himself? What did Juninho dream about becoming when he started at Santos?

In 2004, Antonio Venancio, a Brazilian researcher, received a request from someone in England to interview some of the most promising players at Peixe, those who could become the next Robinho. The interview was to serve as the basis for a documentary on Robinho, who at that time was expected to be the next Pelé – starting with the 2006 World Cup in Germany. In the event, Brazil did not perform at the tournament, going out in the quarter-finals against France, and Robinho did not meet the expectations placed upon him. Consequently the English documentary was not made, but Venancio had already carried out his interviews, and he kept the recordings. One of the interviews was with a twelve-year-old Neymar Jr.

A close-up shot of a photo on a wall. In the photo, Juninho, with his usual red headband and Santos shirt. At his side is Robinho. The interview begins. With his short hair, bare chest and large eyes staring nervously into the camera, Neymar is clearly embarrassed but still confident. He explains that they took the photo the year before, in 2003, when Robinho wanted to get to see him because 'some say I look like him'. Venancio asks Neymar what advice the champion gave him. 'He told me to continue to work hard and study and that one day I would go far.'

'What do you want to do if you make it as a professional footballer and earn lots of money?' the youngster is asked.

'Help my family,' is Neymar's immediate response.

They go past the trophies, the framed newspaper cuttings and the golden boots for best futsal player of 2002 hanging on the wall, an award that Robinho also once won. Neymar mostly answers with 'yes' or 'no' but he wants to let us know that the trophies and cups he has won were because he was a goalscorer; that he did not get angry when the coach took him off the pitch; and that in his brief career he had only been sent off once, for pushing another player. The interviewer changes tack and asks about music. Neymar is not a big fan of music.

Venancio asks why and Neymar admits that he does listen to samba and pagode and that his favourite bands are Revelação and Sorriso Maroto. He knows the words to some songs but he is not prepared to sing.

He is asked what team he supports. 'Palmeiras,' replies Neymar with no hesitation. 'Why? Because I lived through the time when Palmeiras was always the top team, the period when Evair and Rivaldo were there [1993 to 1999, when the São Paulo club won the Paulista League, the Brasilerão and the Coppe Libertadores].'

It is not the best response for someone coming from Peixe, but each to their own: Neymar is young. And if there is something that is clear, it is that Neymar has a future career in football. Neymar nods. He would like to become a professional footballer at Santos.

Later on, in another interview, he admits he would like to go to Real Madrid or Barcelona. He dreams of following in the footsteps of Pelé and Robinho. His ambition is there for all to see.

Chapter 9

Madrid

Madrid Football Federation
05/06 season. Youth league
Player registration card application

Sporting name: Neymar
Name: Neymar
First surname: Da Silva
Second surname: Santos Junior
Address: Castillo de Alarcon, 49
City: Villafranca del Castillo
Province: Madrid
Birth place: Mogi das Cruzes
Date of birth: 5.02.92
Country: Brazil
Nationality: Brazilian
Club: Real Madrid CF
Located in: Madrid
Date: 29.03.2006

A yellow card with a photo of a smiling Neymar Jr: this is the Madrid Football Federation application form of the boy from Mogi das Cruzes to play for Real Madrid. The form was authorised on 30 March 2006. This document, taken from the Federation's archives and published on the front page of *As*, a Madrid sports daily newspaper, is confirmation that Neymar Jr, at barely fourteen years of age, could have been playing for Madrid. It could have been akin to the story of Leo Messi, who moved to Barcelona at thirteen from Newell's in Rosario to then develop at the Catalans' La Masia school. But for Neymar things were to be a bit different.

In March 2006, Neymar Jr took off from São Paulo airport for Madrid. He was accompanied on his first flight by his father and Wagner Ribeiro, his agent, the man who in 2005 sealed Robinho's transfer from Santos to Real Madrid after long and drawn-out negotiations. Ribeiro was introduced to Neymar Pai by Betinho. He was convinced of the talent of Neymar Jr right from the outset and gave the family a monthly income to help them out: he was willing to take a gamble on Neymar Jr, right from when the star was only twelve. Together with Juan Finger, the talent scout famous worldwide for having helped the likes of Maradona, Gullit, Sócrates, Dunga, Klinsmann and Kaká, and also for his run-ins with the Brazilian justice system, Ribeiro managed Neymar's entire early career. He was in the bad books of the Santos management for the Robinho deal but thanks to his contacts with Real Madrid, forged the summer before, he was able to get Neymar a trial with the Spanish giants.

Neymar stayed there three weeks. He was put up in the Colegio Internacional SEK-El Castillo in Villafranca del Castillo, a complex located about twenty kilometres from the capital. It is here where the up and coming Madrid talents live and study. The club made cars available for him so that he and his father could get around and get to know Real Madrid's many sports complexes.

The medicals went well and his first trial impressed the Madrid coaching team. Jesús Gutierrez, who trained the *Infantil A* (youth 'A' team), where the kids were fourteen, was struck by Neymar's quality from the first moment: 'He had tremendous quality. He was a lot better than the other players at that stage.' And these were not your average footballers: there was Dani Carvajal, now playing for the Real first team, Pablo Sarabia, now at Getafe, Alex Fernández, now at Espanyol, Fran Sol, now at Real Oviedo. Neymar was a clear star. Gutierrez continues, 'Everyone agreed. All the members of the management team agreed to sign him, and even our players. Normally when a new player arrives in a group that has already been formed, there is jealousy and politics. The first thing the players say is, "This kid is not as good as they say he is." This time they said, "Coach, this kid is incredible, he is awesome."'

Neymar played well and in the training matches he scored a lot of goals: as many as 27 by some accounts. It looked as though he had fitted easily into the group and was happy to be in Madrid. He would later say of Real in an ESPN interview: 'It seemed like a dream and yet Real was a reality.' Neymar was clearly emotional. He had met his idols: Ronaldo 'O Fenómeno', Zinedine Zidane, Julio Baptista and Robinho.

On Sunday 26 March 2005, he was invited to Santiago Bernabéu to watch a *Liga* match: Real Madrid *vs.* Deportivo La Coruña. Sitting in the VIP box beneath the chairman of Real Madrid, he saw the Whites win 4–0 courtesy of goals from Hector, Ronaldo, Sergio Ramos and Julio Baptista. At the end of the match Júlio Gomes, Spanish correspondent for TV Bandeirantes, interviewed him. 'Did you enjoy that?' he asked. Neymar, smiling, replied, 'Seeing Zidane and Robinho play … how could that not appeal to me?' He also said that he liked the city and wanted to stay there.

Wagner Ribeiro then stepped in: 'Neymar came here to get to know the reality of Madrid so his father could move to Europe and Neymar could become a great footballer in

Spain, England or Italy; it is just a matter of time. He is a real talent.' How did Neymar respond to this? 'I don't know anything, it is those two [Ribeiro and his father] who know everything. I just play football.'

After a few days, Real Madrid had reached their decision. The contract was drawn up and agreed by the parties. It had a term of five years. Among the various conditions were a guaranteed job for Neymar's father, appearance bonuses for Neymar and his and his sister's schooling paid for. Just Neymar's mother's signature was missing. Nadine had a plane ticket for Spain but preferred to stay home with Rafaela. Madrid wanted to sign Neymar up in time for the last few matches of the season. Some say that the new recruit was meant to play in a tournament in which the *Infantil A* were taking part a few days later, in Barcelona. But Neymar was not part of the group. He returned to Brazil.

Why?

Because the deal with Real Madrid was not signed. The reasons why do not always match up. Neymar Pai said it was *saudade*, Portuguese for 'nostalgia'. He said that 'Juninho' was getting sadder each day that went by; he had lost his natural happiness; he missed his family, his friends, his city, Santos and even the rice and *feijoada*.

Basically, Neymar Pai claimed that they went back because Neymar Jr followed his heart, even though it is not easy to say no to a new life and a large sum of money. Many criticised his choice: they said he was mad to refuse an offer from one of the most prestigious clubs in Europe; commentators said he had missed the chance of a lifetime. But Neymar Pai was convinced he was acting in the best interests of his son. Money can't buy happiness, as they say. Happiness for the da Silva family was in Santos.

Madrid did not report the matter in exactly the same

way. Allegedly the terms were virtually agreed when Wagner Ribeiro asked for a further €60,000 to close the deal. The sports management of the club agreed. The amount was not over the top. It was achievable. Ramon Martinez, technical secretary for the club, approved the deal and requested that it be completed as soon as possible. But a few of the club officials did not agree. One of them said, 'We are not paying a penny more for a fourteen-year-old kid from Brazil with his whole family in tow.' The identity of the naysayer was not revealed.

It is worth noting that at this time (March 2006) Real Madrid was going through a difficult time in terms of the running of the club. Florentino Perez, the chairman, who had initiated the 'Galacticos' era for the club, had resigned on 27 February that year. He was disappointed with the players that he said he had spoilt rotten and was leaving so that the dynamics and the results of the club could change. In his place came Fernando Martín, a building tycoon, who would act as interim chairman until the elections in June 2006. Martín, though, would leave his office as chairman before the expiry of the mandate. On 26 April 2006, barely two months after having accepted the position, he would hand over to Luis Gómez-Montejano, who was to manage the election process. In short, there was a great deal of uncertainty behind the scenes at the club at this time. And the unclear signals coming from the club's management meant that the deal with Neymar was not achieved, for the sake of the modest sum of €60,000.

Marcelo Teixeira, the then chairman of Santos, does not agree with this version of events: 'Once we heard about the deal with Real Madrid, we moved quickly and called Neymar's parents straight away. We offered Neymar a five-year contract, a pay increase and that we would provide for his family. The father and son wanted to stay in Brazil and, even before Neymar had his successes with Peixe, we had mapped out a career and professional terms and conditions.'

But that was not all. According to Teixeira, Santos contacted the lawyer Marcus Motta, who informed FIFA and the relevant authorities of Real's approach to Neymar Jr – which was not strictly by the book as Neymar was underage. In short, the ex-chairman claims it was his club that won the battle with Real and not that Real Madrid backed out over the extra €60,000.

This may be true, except for one missing detail. According to Neymar Pai, he and Wagner Ribeiro spoke to Zito and Wanderlei Luxemburgo, the then coach at Santos (and ex-coach at Real Madrid). O Pai and Ribeiro called Luxemburgo and asked him to convince the Santos chairman to back young Neymar. At any event, on Juninho's return from Madrid, the meeting held at the University of Santa Cecilia in Santos between his father, his agent and Santos's chairman was successful.

Neymar Jr and his father, at Jardim Gloria in Praia Grande, signed the contract in Zito's presence. One million reais (€400,000) and a salary of 10,000 reais per month meant that Neymar Jr remained at Santos. With so much money, his family could afford to buy a flat opposite Vila Belmiro, and they left Praia Grande.

This is the official version, although how the deal was reached is not clear.

And the story was not over. Indeed it would run and run; so much so that, on 30 August 2007, *UOL Esporte* wrote an article that the young Neymar (by then fifteen) was about to sign a contract with Real Madrid that would have locked him in until 2011. Emilio Butragueño, sports director at Madrid, was convinced that the deal would be signed within a week.

Santos would not be due any compensation for the transfer, as they only had a letter of intent signed by Neymar in which the parties agreed to sign a professional contract when Neymar reached sixteen. Wagner Ribeiro said that the final decision was down to the father and son, and that Madrid had a long-term project for Neymar like the ones that made Messi a success at Barcelona and Cesc Fàbregas at Arsenal.

On 13 September 2007, the matter was resolved: the contract for exploitation of Neymar's image, which he had signed with Santos, was extended; the essential terms of Neymar's professional contract were laid down and the break clause for $25 million was inserted.

Neymar Pai commented to ESPN Brasil, 'We are all happy to have reached an agreement. The important thing is that Juninho can relax and play without external pressures.'

Chapter 10

A Copinha

It had just struck five in the afternoon in São Paulo. It was 10 January 2008 and in the Nicolau Alayon stadium, better known as Comendador Sousa, to the west of the megalopolis, a youth football match of the Copa São Paulo was being played.

'La Copinha' is the most important youth tournament in Brazil. It was created to commemorate the anniversary of the founding of the city. The first tournament was held in 1969 and since then many talents have emerged from it: Roberto Falcão, Toninho Cerezo, Raí, Walter Casagrande, Kaká and Robinho.

The 2008 edition, which started on 5 January and ended on 25 January, featured 88 teams split into 22 groups. All of the country's states were represented, even if the majority of the teams (38) were from the state of São Paulo. Nowadays the tournament is reserved for under-17s but in 2008 it was up to the age of twenty.

Neymar Jr was aged fifteen years and eleven months. He was 1.66m (5ft 5in) tall and weighed about 50kg (7st 12lb). On 10 January, he played Santos's second match. They called him up at the last minute to give him some experience, playing against players who were three to four years older than him and clearly taller and more experienced.

The match was broadcast live on Sport TV. Jota Junior, a TV commentator, explained that the greatest hope for the Santos fans was on the bench: a kid whom everyone wanted to see burst on to the pitch as soon as possible. Thirty minutes into the second half, the linesman raised cards to indicate two substitutions: number 10 on one team and number 21 on the other. Neymar jigged up and down on the spot, waiting for Paulo Henrique, the future Ganso, to leave the pitch.

Peixe were winning 3–0 against Barra do Garças, a team from Mato Grosso: a comfortable scoreline, which enabled the coach to take a risk and try out 'Juninho'. A quick handshake and pat on the shoulder from the eighteen-year-old Ganso, the undisputed centre midfielder, and Neymar, number 21, was into the action, taking up a position just behind the centre forwards.

Jota Junior spelt out the age and place of birth of the young Neymar. Another commentator wondered if he was the youngest player of the tournament. Two minutes went by and Neymar was already in action. Square on to the area, he showed some nifty footwork and played an inch-perfect pass to Thiago Luiz, who was unmarked in the area near the penalty spot. The goalie parried the shot but the linesman had already flagged for offside. Number 21 looked at the referee with an inquisitive expression.

Into the 82nd minute: Carleto, on the right, played the ball to Serginho. He played a quick pass to Neymar in the area, who flicked it back. Two paces from the goal, a blue and yellow defender made the clearance.

The 86th minute: Juninho, on the edge of the area, hit a lobbed pass over the defenders to find Vinicius, but the offside flag was up. 'A sensational pass, deft footwork with the ball glued to his foot. There was no way that was offside – a complete injustice,' opined the TV commentator. One minute later, an assist from Juninho and another goal for

Santos. A long pass by the opposing team's goalkeeper; the Santos defence pushed out; Neymar, in his own half, headed the ball on to be picked up by Alemão, who cut into the area and struck the ball goalwards. The Barra do Garças keeper could not hold it. 4–0. Neymar ran over and hugged him and jumped on his back.

It was not over. The players from Mato Grosso scored a consolation goal and feebly celebrated. The reaction was immediate. Neymar on the left darted into the area, skimmed past a player and made an assist: a curving cross to Thiago Luiz, who just slotted it in. 5–1 the final score.

In fifteen minutes the rising star of *Alvinegro* had amazed the crowd and confirmed the hype that had been building about him. He was interviewed at the side of the pitch. They asked him what it was like to play for the first time in the *Copa*; how did he feel knowing that the match was broadcast live, and playing at such an important venue. 'When the match is on TV you get goose bumps,' he replied, 'but when I touched the ball, all my fears disappeared in a flash. Thanks be to God that we played a brilliant match. We are working towards becoming champions.' One commentator continued by saying that the only thing missing was that Neymar did not score. Juninho laughed and said, 'Let's see next time.'

That goal – a penalty – did indeed come on his second appearance, against Nacional of São Paulo. It was a shame that Santos's run ended in the quarter-finals, exiting to Internacional of Porto Alegre on penalties.

Márcio Fernández was the coach of that under-20s team. Nowadays he is coach at Shanghai Shenhua, a Chinese team which bought Nicolas Anelka in 2011 and Didier Drogba in 2012. He remembers that they used to say he was mad for playing a fifteen year old with a group of eighteen year olds: 'At first, it created a few issues at the club. Then, once people saw him play those amazing matches, they told me off for not having played him sooner. It is true that he skipped a category by coming to play for us but I wanted him to cut his losses and play in a tournament that is important for the development of young players. I put him up against bigger and more experienced players to see how he would react. He clearly showed he was up to the challenge.'

Lino Martins, who was Neymar's coach from age sixteen to seventeen, agrees. He is a friend of Neymar Pai and had known Neymar Jr from when he was a boy playing at Tumiaru and Gremetal. In a hotel bar in Santos, he tells me how he took him from Lima 'at a critical age, an age when you can see whether a kid is going to make it, if he will become a professional.'

'Neymar was different from the others,' says Lino. 'He was still developing, but he had impressive technical skills. He was faster than most players I had seen before. He played a good season in the Paulista league and a good Brasilerão. He scored loads of goals. He had charm and a strong personality. His head was well and truly on his shoulders. It is not easy at that age. If you are good with a ball at that age, you think you are a star, the best in the world, everyone like that goes through it but some lose their way. Neymar did not. I believe that O Pai channelled him very well. As an ex-footballer he knew what the risks and issues of the trade were. He knew that it is not just the footballing ability that counts but also being humble, disciplined, well behaved and with a positive spirit on the pitch. And above all, the hard work day after day.'

After one year, Lino handed his charge over to another coach. Neymar was now in the *Júniores* team, in preparation for the first team.

At the beginning of 2009, he again played in the *Copinha* in São Paulo, but this time from the start. He wore number 7 on his shirt. In the group stages, he scored Santos's third goal against Cene. A foul on the edge of the area gave Santos a free kick and Neymar took it. The position was not the best. Whether he wanted to or not, he had to take it with his left foot. It was not his favoured foot but the ball swerved beautifully through the air and past the wall and smashed into the inside of the right goalpost. Goal!

Santos got through the group stages on maximum points. In the last 32, they met Guarani. The *pequiño* ('little one'), as the TV commentator called him, was the first to score: a header, connecting with a corner taken from the left. Then he headed off to the stands and made up a celebration samba move. And that was not all: the number 7 also finished off the match in style. Chasing a long ball, he ran half the length of the pitch and dummied the keeper for 4–0.

Peixe were through to the last sixteen, where they were to face Cruzeiro. But a 2–1 win for the Belo Horizonte team saw Neymar and his teammates depart the tournament.

Straight after the match, the team started talking about moving Neymar to the first team. Márcio Fernández had been coach since the summer of 2008. He had often let Neymar train with the older players at the CT Rei Pelé. The coach liked to work with three teams on the pitch; a system called *treino alemão* ('German training'). The junior players were required to possess speed and ball control. Neymar had passed the new arrivals test with flying colours. Kléber Pereira, a 33-year-old centre forward who had the most experience in the group, came over and gave him what for – these were the tactics used by the older players to scare the novices and make them understand that professional football is not plain sailing. But the number 7 from the Under 20s team was not intimidated. He fitted in quickly and did one of his usual tricks. A few days before a match against Palmeiras, he convinced his teammates, the group who played in yellow bibs at training, to turn up to the training ground with a plaster over their mouths: a gag, to convey the message that they would no longer dare to say anything against the 'referee' in the friendly matches, namely Serginho Chulapa, a Santos idol of the 1980s.

And yet, even though Neymar fitted in very quickly and was part of the group, even though he trained hard, and notwithstanding that he was expected to play for the first team, Márcio Fernández preferred to go slowly. He was convinced that Neymar was a great player but also believed that he needed experience and a bulkier physique. At seventeen, he did not want the young man overloaded with responsibility. He stated, 'I put him in the reserve first team so that he could get experience and see what professional life was like. There was still time before moving to the first team. The fans must be patient.'

Soon he would call him up to the first team, but he did not want to set a date. On 12 February 2009, Neymar travelled with the team, which was playing against Marilia in a Paulista league match, but he did not play. Santos were beaten 1–0 and Márcio Fernández was forced to resign. 'I thought he was going to play in that match. I did not play him and I regret that,' commented Fernández a few weeks later; by which time Neymar had started to play for the first team.

Chapter 11

Pacaembu

There had never been anything like it in the history of Santos Football Club. Or at least no one can remember a player who received as many standing ovations even before he got on the pitch, the euphoric fans chanting for the seventeen-year-old to be sent on.

It was Saturday 7 March 2009 at Pacaembu, São Paulo's municipal stadium. Santos were playing in the Paulista league against Oeste from Itápolis. The 22,000 paying supporters were mostly Peixe fans.

The match started at 6.30pm and immediately the fans started chanting for Neymar to be sent into battle. Vágner Mancini, the coach who had taken over the team on 14 February following Márcio Fernández's resignation, resisted until thirteen minutes into the second half. He whispered a final few instructions and, two minutes later, sent him on. Neymar strode on to the pitch wearing the black and white shirt, with number 18 on his back. He substituted Mauricio Molina, a Colombian midfielder. A huge roar boomed around the stadium. The moment Neymar Jr, and the fans, had been waiting for had finally arrived.

On the right of the area, Neymar dribbled around one player and then released a missile which hit the cross-bar and the post, narrowly missing the goal. This was his first involvement. It could scarcely have been a better start for the boy from Mogi das Cruzes. At the end of the match (which finished 2–1 to Santos), the number 18 jogged off the pitch to a round of applause. He headed off to play football with his friends. He had made his first appearance and helped the team, who had been unable to break the deadlock in the first half, to win. He did not let anyone down. It was a debut that Vágner Mancini remembers fondly.

Today Mancini is 48 years old. The coach, of Italian descent, now works for Esporte Clube Vitoria. From Salvador de Baia he recalls his time at Santos, when he strung together a series of good results and gave the number 18 his chance to shine:

'When I arrived at Peixe, Neymar was already in the first reserve team but he had not had chance to play. At that time, Santos had players with a lot of experience, but the results were not there. In order for the club to progress, it needed to renew itself.

'The young Neymar had showed me what he was capable of doing in the training sessions. However, lots of people said he wasn't ready and that he should wait another year before moving to the next level. Everyone treated him as a prized jewel, a diamond which needed carefully looking after; something which needed to be cared for and which could not be ruined or broken. I went against the grain a bit: I did not agree with the general opinion of the club because, put simply, I thought he was ready to play.

'I gave him his debut at Pacaembu. All the Santos fans eagerly awaited the arrival of Neymar on the pitch because he had shown such promise right from the under-17s to the under-20s. The expectation which he had created was truly incredible. Everyone wanted to see him on the pitch; they hoped he was the heir to Robinho and Diego.

'I cannot take much credit. I did not launch his career – he did. I gave him an opportunity and Neymar immediately showed he was something special right from the off. His arrival was very convincing. He quickly gained a permanent place in the first team due to his speed and skill levels. The fans instantly fell in love with him. Not just for his delightful football. Neymar was charismatic and likable. He was someone who you immediately connected with. Behind the athlete and the talented footballer, you saw the human element: humble, straightforward and kind – things which are very important for a star. A quality which he has not lost to this day.'

What does a coach say to a young lad who is about to make his career debut?

'I asked him if he was ready to go on. For a seventeen year old, his reply was more than convincing. He said he was absolutely ready for this moment, which he had been building up to for a long time, and that he did not feel the pressure. My instructions were simple, those of anyone who has to deal with kids. I told him to believe in himself and not to be afraid to dribble, go for goal and play like he knew how. And he did it. He did not get scared or intimidated by the stage he was playing on.'

Nor has Mancini forgotten Neymar's great joy when he scored his first goal, eight days after his debut. It was Sunday evening, 15 March 2009. Neymar had played his first home match on 11 March at Vila Belmiro against Paulista. In the second half he replaced Domingos, the central defender, and he had given it his all: dribbling here and there, one-two passes, lobs, cutting passes, the lot. He had made it really hard for the other team's defence. He even scored but it was ruled out for offside. He smiled at the TV cameras to show how close he had come but it was not to be.

He made up for it four days later at Pacaembu. Five first-team players were not match-fit and so Mancini played

Neymar against Mogi Mirim, Rivaldo's old team. Neymar wore the number 7 shirt and in the seventeenth minute he got his first chance. He skipped around a defender and shot. Marcelo Cruz, the Mogi goalkeeper, blocked it. In the 35th minute, Paulo Henrique launched the ball upfield and dashed forward but the ball rebounded off defender Julio Cesar. The stalemate was only broken in the second half. Paulo Henrique scored in the eleventh minute and Ron in the 23rd. Santos were ahead 2–0. They kept the pressure on and five minutes later, in the 28th minute, Neymar scored his first goal.

The move started way back. Molina pushed past the half-way line and passed to Germano, who saw an opening on the left and passed to Triguinho, who in turn darted into the area and crossed it into the centre. Neymar burst forward from nowhere and with a diving header scored his first goal.

It was 6.37pm and Santos were 3–0 up. Neymar raised his index finger aloft and jumped in the air, punching the sky. He imitated the gesture of his greatest idol: Pelé. Neymar commented at the end of the match, 'I wanted to celebrate that way because I had promised my father I would do so.'

It was dedicated to Ilzemar, his grandfather, a huge fan of Pelé. It was Ilzemar who had shown him so many videos of O Rei's goals, who had accompanied him to the park and, while Neymar's cousins played with their dolls, kicked the ball around with 'Juninho'. Ilzemar, the father of Neymar Pai, died in 2008 without being able to see his grandson play for Santos. Now here was a tribute to the memory of his grandfather and a way to please his father.

After jumping to the sky, the young kid from Mogi went to hug Paulo Henrique, his friend and teammate from the Under-20s. All of this while the commentator for Sport TV, Milton Leite, announced, 'The kid from Santos shines!

This is an historic goal right here! This is an historic date for Brazilian football!'

Mancini brought the number 7 off and the fans roared. Neymar came back on at the end of the match to hug one of his opponents: the striker, Giovanni, who had been the idol of the Santos fans at the beginning of the 1990s before going on to play for Barcelona between 1996 and 1999. Neymar talked to the TV journalists and said that he was hoping to be playing the following Sunday in the match against Corinthians, for whom one of his idols played: Ronaldo Luís Nazário da Lima – 'O Fenómeno'.

In the stands, the fans were ecstatic. Many had come to see Neymar and the kid did not disappoint. 'He must play', 'He must start the match', 'He is the best player we've seen since Robinho and Diego', 'He has shown his maturity and his talent' were among the opinions from the crowd. The TV commentators also chimed in. Glenda Kozlowski, former athlete turned presenter and journalist, was the most enthusiastic. She predicted, 'Neymar could be the future Pelé.'

The young star continued to score goals. At Vila Belmiro against Rio Branco in the Brazil Cup he scored his second. This time he had agreed the choreography of the celebrations with his teammates. For his third goal, he invented a new dance, with Madson and Rodrigo Souto getting in on the act. This was a scorcher of a goal, scored on 11 April 2009 against Palmeiras in the first leg of the Paulista League semi-final, to give Santos a 2–1 lead to take into the second leg. Neymar received the ball on the edge of the box. He brought it under control and skipped and danced around his opponents and then let rip with his right foot. The ball shot through a defender's legs and slotted into the corner. Peixe won the second leg with the same result and reached the final. But against Ronaldo's Corinthians, there was no chance. At Vila Belmiro, O Fenómeno, who had come back from Europe (PSV Eindhoven, Barcelona, Internazionale, Real Madrid and Milan), scored two fantastic goals in a 3–1 first-leg victory for his team. This meant that on 3 May at Pacaembu, Corinthians needed only a draw to win their 26th Paulista League title.

After fifteen years in Europe, Ronaldo took home his second Brazilian league title. (His first was in 1994 when he won the Mineiro League with Cruzeiro.) Ronaldo was awarded best player, while Neymar Jr won the award for revelation of the year. Mancini remarked, 'He deserved it. In those two months, in those few matches, he showed great maturity, so much so that at the start of the *Brasileirão* [the national league championship, which takes place in the second half of the season] he was one of the most important players in the team.'

It was a shame that the national league campaign was to mark the end of Mancini's time at Santos. On 13 July 2009, after a terrible defeat (6–2) by Vitória at Salvador de Bahia, he was sacked by chairman Marcelo Teixeira. In his place came Vanderlei Luxemburgo, who had coached Santos on several previous occasions: 1997–98, 2004, and 2006–07. With Peixe he had won one Paulista league, one Brasileiro league and one Rio–São Paulo tournament.

On 20 July, the day when he was officially presented to the club, he said that his aim was to take Santos to where it should be, among the elite of Brazilian football. He would, he said, move Santos up from fourteenth in the table. Vanderlei's first match in the dugout was against Atlético Paranaense. Neymar came on in the second half and immediately changed the rhythm of the game. He scored the winning goal with a screamer, to save the new coach from a poor start.

On 8 August, after a draw at Vila Belmiro against Avai of Florianópolis, the manager reflected on the great joy he had had working with the youth teams. When asked why Neymar was not in the starting line-up (in the first five matches under his rule, Neymar had started only once, against Flamengo), Vanderlei remarked, 'This year, everyone has been telling me that Neymar is one of the best. At some point, he will be a top-level footballer, but I am convinced that he was introduced to the first team too early. He should have played at the lower levels for longer so he could have matured. You need to be patient with him, you need to prepare him for this commitment. He is a *filé de borboleta* ['stick insect']. He is little and cannot withstand the physical contact of a match. He looks like Robinho when he started. He needs to build up his muscle mass. I do not want to burn him out.'

This meant that under Luxemburgo's reign, Neymar was almost always on the bench. He had to go on a hypercalorific diet with meals every three hours in order to gain strength and build 3kg of muscle mass. He needed to do this, according to the technical staff, so that he could play at the top level. It was a difficult time for the seventeen year old who, only a few months earlier, had signed a dream five-year contract with Santos (expiring in 2014): 80,000 reais a month and a break clause of 90 million reais.

Club officials were worried. They were concerned that after 31 matches and eight goals, the star would not develop further, either from a physical or a footballing perspective.

Neymar did not like being the 'stick insect'. He thought Vanderlei was having a joke but he wanted to get rid of this nickname as soon as possible.

Chapter 12

Baroque and minimalism

*A conversation with Eduardo Gonçalves
de Andrade, aka Tostão*

'Last Sunday was a special day. I saw seventeen-year-old
Neymar's first match, where he played from the start, for
Santos. I was so excited, like when I saw Zico, Ronaldo,
Ronaldinho and Romário play for the first time.'

The author of these four lines was Tostão. Three days had
passed since 'Juninho's' first goal against Mogi Mirim, and
one of the greatest critics of Brazilian football, writing for
Folha de S. Paulo (a Brazilian newspaper) had no doubts when
stating, 'We are in the presence of a future star, not just an
excellent footballer.'

He stated that Neymar's touch was 'beautiful, efficient
and natural', i.e. that of a player in a different league. He
continued by saying that Neymar should have more faith
in his abilities, be more ambitious and want to be number
one. He advised him to become a warrior, someone who did
not hide, who got stronger in the face of adversity and who
sweated blood and tears.

Eduardo Gonçalves de Andrade, better known as Tostão,
class of 1947, was one of the greats in the history of Brazilian
football: the white king who, together with Pelé, Carlos
Alberto, Jarzinho and Rivelino won the Mexico 1970 World

Cup, beating the Italy of Gigi Riva, Roberto Boninsegna, Sandro Mazzola and Gianni Rivera 4–1 in the final at the Azteca Stadium. He was a doctor and university professor but after the 1994 World Cup he returned to football as a commentator. Today he is considered one of the most important analysts of the game and its heroes.

From Belo Horizonte where he lives, he talks to me about the opinion he gave about Neymar:

'Yes. It is true. When I saw him play the first few matches with Santos, he made me feel the same way as I had when watching the great Brazilian players at the start of their careers. I was not wrong. That first impression has come true over the years.'

And what is your opinion today?
'I believe that Neymar is a fantastic footballer. I am convinced that, over the next few years, he will certainly be one of the candidates for best footballer in the world.'

What technical abilities do you appreciate in Neymar's play?
'He has almost all the qualities of a great footballer: he dribbles very well and with speed; he changes direction with great agility; he can lead with his left or right foot; he is a good striker of the ball; he is very fast, creative, intelligent and has pinpoint accuracy in finishing both in and outside the box; he is a *goleador* [a top goalscorer]; he can score with his left or his right foot, his head, from a free kick; he takes corners well and can bend them into the box. Perhaps the best quality he has, which makes the difference compared to other stars, is his ability to dribble the ball with both legs and to score with both feet – something which I had only seen Pelé do.'

You said that he has 'almost every quality'. What is he missing?
'Maybe he needs to learn to not go down so easily. When Leo Messi starts dribbling and the marker goes in for the tackle, trying to block him with his body, nothing happens. Messi continues to run and dribble, to move forward towards the goal. Neymar, on the other hand, falls over, because he is still a bit weak physically but also because he likes creating a bit of theatre, histrionics, to gain the crowd's attention; you know, he fakes a foul. It is a defect of youth which he is slowly growing out of. Barcelona and European football will help him to correct this aspect of his game. Another thing Neymar needs to improve is his muscle mass. He needs to be a bit stronger without losing his agility, his speed and coordination, which are spectacular.'

What does Neymar represent for Brazil?
'Since 2011 he has been the best Brazilian footballer, without a doubt. We have great players but he is the star. He is the best that Brazilian football can offer today. At the beginning, there was a sort of reluctance, resistance against him, perhaps because of his way of playing on the pitch, but bit by bit he became the key player for Santos and the Brazilian team. Neymar brings together the *jogo bonito* ["beautiful game"], the artistic game, namely skill and creativity with productivity and efficiency. He can be one of the greatest footballers in the history of Brazilian football.'

What did he mean to Santos?
'He was fundamental in rekindling the glories of a club in crisis which had not made an impression for over 40 years. But we need to remember that at the beginning of his career, Neymar had a good team around him: Ganso, Robinho,

André … but then slowly he was left on his own. They did not sell him but they sold his teammates and he had to bear the responsibility of the entire team. His performances for Santos got worse. The moment had come that he could no longer play for Santos. It would be like Messi playing in a team in Rosario, Cristiano Ronaldo playing at Madeira and Ibrahimovic playing for a Swedish team. The gap between Neymar and the other players was too big. He was wasting his time and his talent. Fortunately, he moved to an exceptional team, Barcelona, where he could grow and develop next to players like Messi, Xavi and Iniesta. It was a test for him, an important test to understand how far he could go and to allow us to measure his brilliance. Because there are players who shine on their own but when they play with the greats their spark fades.'

You mean the Barcelona stars could have the opposite effect on Neymar?
'It is too early to tell but I am convinced that this will not be the case. I think Barcelona will have two world-class stars in Messi and Neymar. Let's not forget that before Messi, Ronaldinho was Barcelona's golden boy. Messi grew in the shadow of Ronaldinho and then he overtook him as he was a superior player and more of an all-rounder.'

Please could you try and compare Messi, Neymar and Cristiano Ronaldo?
'Messi is extraordinary: he is an incredible dribbler and finisher. Neymar has a greater repertoire but that does not mean he is better. At the moment, Messi is the best player, without a doubt. Cristiano Ronaldo's great quality is his strength. He is a player who has great stamina, a blistering

shot on him, great height when heading the ball – but he does not have the skill or magic that Neymar or Messi have.

'Neymar's style is more baroque, more effervescent than Messi's. Messi is more classic and more technical. Almost minimalist. He uses the least number of moves or touches necessary to create something extraordinary. Neymar is exceptionally theatrical in the way he plays and he is more like Maradona than Messi, but this does not mean he is not effective. Diego liked to show off but it was extremely effective. He loved a spectacle and showing how good he was with a ball. Messi is more like Pelé. Like O Rei, Messi has an incredible ability to get to the crux of a move which Neymar does not have. He would use a few moves to get to a goal-scoring opportunity. I never saw Pelé overdo it with dribbling or waste time dribbling for the sake of it. He flashed past his opponents with the sole aim of getting to the goal. Just like Messi. Pelé's game was pure. Just like a great writer who in a few words says everything there is to be said, whereas others fill pages and pages but say little or nothing.

'A Brazilian who is like an Argentinian and an Argentinian who is like a Brazilian: weird huh? But let's be clear: Neymar is not on a par with Pelé [who was the best] nor Maradona [with his endless repertoire of moves] nor Messi, at least for the time being – even if he could get there in the future.'

Chapter 13

Having fun

The music resembles a prelude to a nineteenth century operetta. Then the curtains go back and, on the black background, writing flaps about: 'De Santos FC, para Torcida Santista' (From Santos FC, for the Santos fans). At the back can be seen the pitches of CT Rei Pelé's.

Dressed in a tuxedo, Madson takes off his top hat: 'Ladies and gentlemen ...'

Wearing a black jacket, Neymar moves towards the TV camera: 'We would like to invite all the Santos fans for 17 January ...'

Dorival Junior: '... at the Pacaembu stadium.'

Madson shows the black and white striped shirt: 'Mandatory dress code: the Santos uniform.'

Neymar's turn: 'I would like to present to you the waiter for the evening, Paulo Henrique, O Ganso.'

O Ganso, dressed in evening wear, continues: 'And here we have the main dish: the match between Santos and Rio Branco.'

Neymar: 'We are counting on you being there.'

Paulo Henrique: 'Mark it in your diaries: Sunday, 7.30pm.'

Madson: 'We hope you enjoy the evening.'

He bows and the red curtain closes.

Forty-three seconds of video to invite the fans to the first Peixe match for the 2010 season: the first round of the Paulistão.

In the event it was a beautiful evening, deserving of the big build-up. There were hugs and kisses between the players after a 4–0 win: two goals for Ganso and two for Neymar.

Neymar was on form and had a new look: Mohican hair. When Neymar Pai saw two red Indians come on to the pitch (his son and André) with the same haircut, he could not believe his eyes. And to think it was he who had asked 'Juninho' to cut his hair. The boy had let it grow long and his father did not like it long, but that he would go ahead and do something like that was unbelievable.

Neymar Jr explained to a horrified Ganso, 'I wanted a change.' Ganso came straight back with 'I am not cutting my hair like that!' To tell the truth, Neymar had already had a similar haircut at the end of 2009 but it was only at the beginning of the season that he found the courage to show it off.

Cosme Salles, Neymar's hairdresser from when Juninho was fifteen, explained, 'He wanted something new so I suggested the Mohican.' Or more correctly, the Mohawk: shaved hair on the sides and a central strip of spiky long hair. It was a cut that became popular at the end of the 1970s thanks to the English punk movement: anarchy, rebellion against the state, against the establishment, and 'no future'. A 'f*** off' attitude to the world with the crest held high.

In Neymar's case, the cut was a lot softer, less aggressive and did not have political or anarchical overtones. It was a question of fashion. Nevertheless it made its mark and became Neymar's brand. Its thousands of variations (more or less gel, coloured, natural, bleached, dreads, completely shaven on the sides or large quiff at the front) were a hit. Twenty cuts over three years struck a chord and spread like wildfire. Babies, kids, fans and players both in and out of Brazil copied the look. It was an enormous success.

One of those who did not like it, along with Neymar Pai,

was João Araújo, O Didì, Pelé's barber. His barber shop is right in front of Vila Belmiro. The sign outside the shop, with a Santos crest at either end, reads 'Cabeleireiro de Pelé e de voce tambem' (Hairdresser to Pelé and to you too). The inside of the shop is a football history museum: photos, portraits, autographs, scarves and pennants which date back to 1956 when he cut O Rei's hair for the first time. He explains that 'the Mohican cut in my day was the cut of a *maloqueiro* [an offensive term used in Rio Grande do Sul to define those people living in the shacks and shanties], but I must admit that today it is possible to do a decent Mohican cut.'

Even Didì appreciates the latest fashion up to a point. Especially as Pelé has shown Neymar some photos of when Pelé was seventeen and he did his military service – he jokingly claimed that it was in fact he, Pelé, who launched the Mohican style 50 years earlier, thanks to Didì. If you look at pictures of Pelé at the 1958 World Cup in Sweden, you can see what he means.

Jokes and fashion phenomena aside, Neymar's cut appears to have brought him luck.

The new Peixe coach, Dorival Junior, who had taken over from Luxemburgo, said on 30 December 2009 (the day of his presentation) that he had a group of young players, developed by the club, who could be trusted. Neymar was one of them. And so after the nickname of 'stick insect', the star was back at the forefront again. Dorival Junior used him in an attacking trio with Paulo Henrique Ganso and André, and then integrated Robinho to create an attacking front four who would become known in Brazil as *O Quarteto Santástico* (*Santástico* being a compound of 'Santos' and *fantástico* – 'fantastic').

Robinho, Neymar's idol, had come back from Manchester City, like the prodigal son returning in the Gospel of Luke. He did not get much of a look in at Roberto Mancini's

Manchester City and was often on the bench. When he had the option to go on loan to either Benfica or Santos, he did not hesitate for a second.

On 7 February in the Baueri Arena, Robinho, the Santos star from 2002 to 2005, made his second debut in the black and white shirt. He came on twelve minutes into the second half when the score was 1–1. Neymar had scored the first goal, taking his tally to seven for the season: after a foul in the box on Auruca, Neymar had converted the penalty – five steps back, a dummy shot and Rogério Ceni, the goalkeeper for São Paulo, could do nothing but watch the ball hit the back of the net as he dived to the right. Ceni, a player with over 1,000 matches under his belt and, amazingly for a goalkeeper, 100 goals scored – an institution of Brazilian football – was dumbfounded. He gesticulated, saying it was not a *paradinha* but a *paradòn* – not a mere dummy but deception. From Madrid, via Twitter, Kaká agreed and criticised Neymar, saying that only in Brazil could you get away with a fake like that. For Ceni, the goal and the celebratory dance were humiliating, showing a lack of respect by a young player against a veteran. In the years that followed, the two often did not see eye to eye.

The match had continued and Roger had equalised for São Paulo. Then it was time for *O Rei do drible* and *de pedalada*, that is, Robinho, to come to the fore. In the 85th minute, with a flick of the heel he deflected a cross from Wesley at the near post and the ball went in. The daily São Paulo sports paper, *Lance*, reported, 'Robinho showed that he still has a lot to give to football. With an exquisite touch, he guarantees victory to Santos and top of the table in the Paulista league.'

After the 'dress rehearsal', *O Quarteto Sántastico* continued to impress. The match on 10 March 2010 saw Peixe's highest score in the history of the Brazil Cup: Santos 10 Naviraiense 0. Neymar scored the second and the seventh goal, the latter a memorable goal in the 54th minute. He received the ball from Giovanni on the edge of the box. With a series of dummies, he left the two defenders standing, a third soon followed suit and the goalkeeper had no chance. The TV commentators boomed 'Gol de Placa' – an expression alluding to Pelé's great goal on 5 March 1961 against Fluminense, for which a commemorative plaque was put up at Maracana.

This Neymar goal was of no less importance. The best goal in the *Copa do Brasil*, the best of the season claimed the TV commentators. Wait and see …

At Vila Belmiro, on 14 April 2010 – Santos's 98th birthday – Neymar scored five goals against the Guarani in the last sixteen of the cup.

2nd minute: Penalty converted with a dummy.

30th minute: Missile from his left foot on the edge of the area.

38th minute: On his own in front of goal he slotted in a pass from Arouca.

81st minute: Meeting Robinho's cross from the left, he took two touches and scored.

85th minute: Matsu stormed upfield and passed to Robinho, who flicked to Neymar: goal.

The final score: Santos 8 Guarani 1.

But it was not the avalanche of goals or beautiful play which won fans and followers over. It was the spreading of joy and the desire to have fun which oozed from the pores of the latest generation of *Meninos de la Vila*. This group of players, which harked back to the earlier generations from the 1960s, 1978 and 2002, was *brincadeira* ('fun'), as the Brazilians say.

Each goal was a party with a different jig, something fun and different. In the match against Guarani, they invented one dance after another: the baseball hat and rap, the tennis match, the motorbike, the lorry, the rolling planes, the merry-go-round, the military march, the shoeshiner and the signature dances to music from the movies. The range of dances seemed endless.

On 21 March 2010, in a league match against Ituano, even the Statue of Liberty got a look in.

Neymar was not playing as he was on a one-match ban. He was in New York with Santos B, playing a friendly against the Red Bulls. Before the match he called André and asked him to do something for him and to imitate the Statute of Liberty when they scored. André scored the equalising goal and together with Madson and Wesley he made his way to the edge of the pitch. With his hand held up high as if he were holding the torch, the three made the shape of the Statue of Liberty. When Paulo Henrique scored the second, the image was repeated, much to the amusement of Neymar, who was watching the match on TV. Neymar called his friend straightaway to thank him.

It is worth noting that, even with Neymar out and Robinho injured, the match finished a scandalous 9–1.

'When we won by [only] two or three goals, everyone said Santos was in trouble. We had fun when we played but we played responsibly. The atmosphere in the changing rooms and the stadium was awesome. It was one of the best years of my life,' commented Neymar, years later.

It was a season that brought two league titles to Santos: the first and second of Neymar's career. On 2 May 2010, Pacaembu Stadium was the venue for the away match of the final of the Paulista league. Peixe were there, having beaten their eternal rivals, São Paulo, in the semis: two brilliant victories: 3–2 at Morumbi and 3–0 at home. At Vila Belmiro, Neymar scored the first with a header. Then, from the penalty spot, another dummy. This time a little less obvious but the victim was the same: Rogério Ceni. The final was against

Santo André, another underdog team come good. The first leg at Pacaembu finished 3–2 to Peixe. Neymar was injured and was replaced by André at half-time.

In the second leg, Neymar was on top form. The match was a tough one. Santos's number 11 scored two goals. The first was a real masterpiece: Robinho flicked the ball to Neymar in the area. Neymar beat two defenders and the goalkeeper and fired the ball into the back of the net. The kid from Mogi das Cruzes scored the second as well. He was then substituted for Roberto Brun.

The scoreline now stood at 2–2. Santo André did not give up and took the lead 3–2. With Peixe suffering three red cards, it looked an uphill challenge for Santos, but somehow the eight on the pitch managed to keep the boat afloat. Paulo Henrique was called to the bench but he protested and stayed on. He even managed to invent a tactic never seen before: he moved forward on the left wing but, with no one in the centre and no other player close, he decided to leave the ball on the corner spot and wait for a player on the other team to go and get the ball. He then put the player under pressure, to waste time – when you're three men down, any move is a good move if it wastes a bit of time. The referee finally blew full-time with the score still 3–2, Santos having been behind for much of the match. It levelled the score at 5–5 across the two legs, but Santos won the title based on their superior goal difference in the earlier stages of the competition.

The crowd went wild and the fans were jumping up and down in the stands. It was party time and Neymar, with tears of joy in his eyes, received the Paulista league medal.

After the excitement of winning the great gold cup, disappointment was just around the corner. Even though the fans had shouted 'Neymar for Brazil' many times, and even though Pelé and Zico had been in favour of calling him up for the *Seleção*, Dunga, the Brazilian coach, did not buckle under the pressure: neither Neymar nor Paulo Henrique would be taking part in the 2010 World Cup in South Africa. This was a knock-back for the *Meninos de Vila* who had been on a golden run. So many people wanted to see Neymar play in the World Cup, as Pelé had when he was seventeen and amazed the world in 1958. Juninho would have to wait another four years. Brazil eventually lost in the quarter-finals to Holland. Millions of Brazil fans were in mourning.

Santos relieved the post-World Cup depression by winning the Brazil Cup. The first leg, on 28 July against Vitória at Vila Belmiro, finished 2–0 to Santos. Neymar chested the first off a cross from Pará but then spooned a penalty: the ball ended up in the goalkeeper's hands. Neymar was booed from the stands. Every time he got the ball the crowd teased him, as if to let Neymar know that sometimes his arrogance was too much to take. In the end, despite this mishap, the match finished well. In the return leg at Bahia on 4 August, despite losing 2–1, Santos took the cup. Neymar was the leading goalscorer for the tournament with eleven goals. He also scored fourteen in the Paulistão. He was the undisputed Brazilian idol.

In an interview with *Estado de São Paulo* in April 2010, Neymar told the paper that his dream car would be a yellow Porsche – with a red Ferrari in the garage (even though he had just bought a Volvo XC60 for 140,000 reais). He said he wanted to go to Disneyland because he loved the amusement parks. He collected watches, perfumes and bought designer clothes: Calvin Klein and Armani. He was enrolled on the electoral register but he had no idea who the presidential candidates were. He had not paid much attention to Lula da Silva for the time being, although he swore he would do so in the future. Basically, here was a rich and famous kid who still needed to mature. He would do so sooner than he expected.

Chapter 14

Ayrton Senna

The first offer was a tester. West Ham United offered €15 million at the end of June 2010 for the eighteen-year-old Neymar. The idea was that the Santos striker would play one or two seasons with West Ham before moving to Chelsea. The Hammers were to be the testing ground for the Blues of Roman Abramovich. A neat way to try and pay less for the end product. A similar approach worked well in 2006 with Argentinians Javier Mascherano and Carlos Tevez. Coming from Corinthians, they started at West Ham and then ended up at Liverpool and Manchester United respectively.

The offer was appealing to Neymar Pai. He was convinced that his son could adapt to English football without too much difficulty and go on to become one of the great stars of European football. Santos were not so keen to negotiate. The club, which owned 60 per cent of Neymar's registration (40 per cent was owned by Dis Group, the sports arm of Grupo Sonda, the largest supermarket chain in the state of São Paulo), knew that behind West Ham was Chelsea, and so they wanted to wait for a better offer. In the meantime, Santos reminded the bidders that there was a break clause for €35 million and that it had no intention of underselling Neymar and thus breaking up the team, which in 2010 was a dream team.

A new offer from Chelsea landed a few days later. Abramovich and his partners put €20 million on the table.

On 20 July, Santos issued a press release on its website stating that they were grateful for the interest but were not willing to start negotiations for Neymar at that price. It was horse-trading, which escalated over the following few days. The offer rose to €30 million, with a five-year contract worth €3.5 million per season to Neymar, plus match bonuses, league bonuses and various perks.

It was an offer that the da Silva Santos family could not refuse. At the beginning of August, Neymar Pai and Wagner Ribeiro flew to New York, where Brazil were playing a friendly, with Neymar due to start, to negotiate with Chelsea. Santos remained adamant that they did not want to sell to the English league champions, then managed by Carlo Ancelotti.

In an interview with *Radio Globo*, Wagner Ribeiro stated, 'Luis Álvaro de Oliveira Ribeiro, the Santos chairman, is a decent and honourable man; he has all my respect and that of Neymar's father. Objectively speaking, I think he is a dreamer. Any Brazilian club would love to have an offer like the one from Chelsea. He is the only one to have received an offer that any chairman would want but which was not accepted. It is a shame that contracts have to be honoured.'

Ribeiro had no doubt that it was time for Neymar Jr to leave Brazil. He could not see the need for the young Neymar to stay at Santos. In order to grow and develop, he needed to move. It may even have been counterproductive to stay in Brazil because, as he said, 'in Brazil there are better footballers but the league is not as good. Playing in the Champions League is totally different to any other competition in our country.' In Ribeiro's mind, it was a done deal: 'it was just down to the family now'.

But it was still Santos's move. They needed to make a winning move in a few days. Luis Álvaro de Oliveira Ribeiro called on Armiño Neto, the marketing manager for the club, who he had brought in when he was elected. Ribeiro said, 'I have €30 million on the table but I do not want to sell Neymar: I want to sell the show. We do not have the financial clout to pay the salary that Chelsea is offering. But we need to find the money to keep him here; we need to lay down a new contract, a new deal, but above all offer him and his father a career project. We need to talk about his future.'

In a room in the Hotel Porto Bay in São Paulo, a stone's throw from Avenida Paulista, Neto, the marketing manager, who left Santos in July 2013, runs through the steps of what was called 'Project Neymar'.

The idea was simple: develop the Neymar brand to find a sponsor which would enable the club to match the salary offered by the English. A complicated task because for it to work, Neymar's father, Neymar and his agent all needed to be on board. Neto was to look after the key concepts and the marketing and the chairman was to look after the financing.

On 17 August 2010, at Banco Santander's offices, the decisive meeting was held: a tense and difficult meeting which saw the participation of all the interested parties. Neto thought to himself, 'How do you tell Neymar Pai that his son is special, that he has all the characteristics of a star and could become the most loved player in Brazil? How do you convince him that it would have been a good thing to stay at Santos?'

He thought of other great sportsmen: Pelé, Roger Federer, Maradona and David Beckham. He then put his marketing hat on and thought of an image that could work.

The meeting started at 10.00am. Santos's chairman switched the lights off and pointed at the screen. The first slide of Project Neymar came up. An empty chair. Disbelief echoed around the room. Neymar Pai said, 'What's this …?

We are talking about contracts, money. What has an empty chair got to do with anything?'

The chairman explained, 'That is the chair of the great national sports hero. It has remained empty since Ayrton Senna left us. Gustavo Kuerten was about to sit there but due to an injury at only 29 years of age, he had to quit his tennis career. Ronaldo O Fenómeno left for Europe at seventeen years of age. The chair is empty. If your son rejects the offer from Chelsea and stays with Santos, it will be the first step to earning the right to sit in that chair.'

Neto remembered the speech word for word. It had a great impact and was very effective. Those attending the meeting were impressed, including Neymar Pai. It was only the first trump card from Santos. Next came the good and bad points of a career with Santos (including numbers).

At 10.40 the chairman's phone rang. Luis Álvaro de Oliveira Ribeiro gave the phone to an inquisitive-looking Neymar Pai. Who could be calling during such an important meeting? On the other end of the line was Pelé. O Rei spoke and Neymar listened. He told him it was not the time to be leaving Santos to try something new in Europe. Neymar needed to be stronger and more mature and aware of his skills so as to be able to achieve his objectives on the Old Continent. He assured Neymar Pai that if it were his son he would not make such a decision. He reminded Neymar Pai that, even though they were different times, his entire career was spent with Santos and that he won world and national titles with Peixe.

When Neymar Pai got off the phone and gave it back to Luis Álvaro, he was on another planet. His expression was one of a father who had just realised that Santos was also concerned about the well-being of his family.

Neto explained, 'The presentation ended with a short

and emotional statement saying that Neymar would indeed go to Europe but he would go after having won all he could win with Santos and he would leave as an idol for everyone. When Neymar Pai entered the room that day he was 99 per cent convinced he was going to sign with Chelsea but after the meeting he was in two minds. He asked for some time to think and to speak to his family. At 5.00pm a meeting was set up in Ribeiro's offices. As soon as I saw Neymar Pai, I knew that Neymar Jr was going to stay with Santos.'

On 19 August the final decision was made public. Neymar Jr had signed a new five-year contract with Santos with a break clause of €45 million. His salary had gone up from 170,000 to 600,000 reais a month. Other than Ronaldo, who was on 1,000,000 reais a month with Corinthian, Neymar was the highest-paid player in Brazil. And that was not all: the new contract envisaged that Neymar would receive a significant portion of the earnings from his image and a bonus if he was selected for the national team.

The chairman and Neymar Jr held a press conference to explain the details of the deal. A beaming Neymar Jr confirmed that he had taken on board the advice of many but in the end it was his decision and his decision alone. He was happy to be able to continue playing for Santos. Luis Álvaro de Oliveira Ribeiro showered him with praise: 'He is an adult in a boy's body.' He explained that the deal had been long and complex but that the end result was something that had never been done before in Brazilian football.

Neto commented: '[Brazilian] football has always sold its "raw materials" as soon as there was a chance to make money. What Santos has done goes against the grain of national culture. It was an example for other clubs.'

The contract was signed; now there was just the project to get under way. There were two limbs to it: the player and the sponsors. The club from Baixada Santista set up a task force to look after its investment. Roles were assigned: there was someone to look after his appointments and diary, someone to accompany him to away matches and matches with the national side. The eyes of Santos would never let Neymar out of their sight. Then there was the work around developing Neymar, plus the media training so that he knew how to behave in front of the cameras and the microphones. He was to have elocution lessons with Cida Coelho so that he could pronounce words properly, along with English lessons so that he could get by.

Then there was the hardest aspect of all of the project: selling the Neymar brand. Neto commented: 'It was not difficult for Neymar because he is naturally charismatic. Something which you cannot buy at the supermarket. He is a natural media icon. How can we sell him? Analysing the body and soul, we can offer different qualities to different investors. Body: his hair, his extravagance, his tattoos, his constant use of social media: Instagram, Facebook, Twitter. Neymar is a child of his time, connected with technology, music and fashion. Soul: he is a synonym for bravery, happiness and speed.

'I remember when I spoke about the possible sponsorship by Red Bull. They said to me, "Neto, we only sponsor teams, not individuals. The only individual player we sponsored was Edgar Davids because of his predatory look. Neymar does not have that sort of image. We are a better fit for extreme sports athletes." OK, I switched on my iPad and looked up Santos–Guarani in the 2010 Brazil Cup on Youtube. Neymar scored five goals. I showed them one at a time. In the end the Red Bull manager said, "This is not a football player, this is an extreme sports athlete."

'Red Bull was the third personal sponsor after Nike and

Panasonic. The others followed after that. In 2011, every five or ten days or so, there was someone who wanted a piece of the action, who wanted to sponsor Neymar. It was not long before there were thirteen sponsors.'

And yet, despite the Neymar project having worked so well, in June 2013 Neymar packed his bags for Barcelona.

Neto explained, 'Santos showed Brazil and Brazilian football that it was possible for one of the best players in the world to stay in Brazil for a while. It was an important lesson to a system which is used to selling off players. There is no doubt that Santos profited from it. Much more than if they had sold Neymar in 2010. Santos were rewarded both on and off the pitch. They won six titles; membership grew from 20,000 to 66,000; their turnover grew from 70 million reais in 2009 to 198 million in 2012. The Santos brand sky-rocketed and TV rights, sales from licensed products and earnings from shirt sponsorship all increased: from 6 million to 40 million reais. The club is in the top 50 clubs in the world according to the latest research. It is not all Neymar's doing but his presence has certainly helped raise the profile of the club.'

Why let him go then?

'Because when a player has made up their mind, there is little you can do,' comes the reply. 'All you can do is wish them well and that's it. In addition, while our club can bear the costs of a player like Neymar, the market, the footballing environment and the structure of our football cannot. We need a more professional league and club to be able to compete with the Spanish *Liga* or the English Premier League, but this is Brazil and today this is not the case. We can't even compete with Ukraine teams. It's a shame.'

Chapter 15
Monster

'I am deeply disappointed today. I have spent my entire life in football but I have hardly ever seen someone as rude [from a sporting perspective] as this boy, Neymar. I have always worked with young players and I have never seen anything like it. What he did was unacceptable. Even the Santos players did not agree with his behaviour. It is time someone educated him or we will create a monster. It is true we are creating a monster in Brazilian football in the name of *futebol arte*. I believe in the art but not this. He is all-powerful both on and off the pitch. You journalists, the referees, the club, all of us need to educate him for the good of football because at the moment he is not a man, nor a great player: he is a product of all of this. What I saw today was bad, very bad.'

So spoke René Simões, coach for Atlético Goianiense, being controversial on local TV and radio and in front of the press microphones at Vila Belmiro on the evening of 15 September 2010. What could have happened that was so bad to cause Simões to repeat the word 'monster' at least five times in two minutes while referring to Neymar Jr? What had he done that was so bad? Let's start at the beginning.

It was the 22nd round of matches in the *Brasilerão* and Santos were playing Atlético Goianiense, a Goiânia team, from the state of Goiás, at Vila Belmiro. It should have been an easy match for Peixe, who incidentally had not won any of their last three matches.

But things got complicated. Peixe were two goals down at half-time. Neymar decided to take things into his own hands and got on with turning the tables. A few minutes into the second half and the score was 3–2 to Santos. Then Neymar was fouled on the edge of the area. He gestured clearly that he was going to take the free-kick, and placed the ball, but Marcel ran up and took the kick.

With five minutes to go to the end of the match, the same thing happened again. This time the Santos number 11 was in the box. Penalty. Neymar picked up the ball and walked to the spot. Change of plan: Léo, the number 3, ran over to Neymar and told him that the coach had decided that Marcel should take the kick.

This was where the problems started. Neymar dropped the ball on the floor and started shrugging his shoulders and waving his arms about and walked over to the bench. He gave the coach, Dorival Junior, a piece of his mind – better not to repeat his exact words.

Léo went over to Neymar, hugged him and tried to calm him down. Even Marquinos, who was on the touchline, tried to placate him but Neymar slipped past him and went to the centre of the pitch with a bottle of water in his hand. He had a go at Roberto Brun and Edu Dracena, the team captain, who tried to calm him down. Marcel converted the penalty and it was 4–2 to Santos. Neymar did not care; he continued to behave like a spoilt child having a strop.

After the penalty, he went into ball-hogging mode. He was on a one-man mission. The team did not exist anymore. The coach, from the sidelines, was at his wits' end and kept shouting instructions, but to no avail. The Santos fans were on the coach's side. They chanted the manager's name rather than that of their idol, Neymar. Outside the stadium, the fans chanted, 'Santos is more important than Neymar.'

At the end of the match, the number 11 ran straight off the pitch and into the changing rooms. He dismissed the waiting journalists without saying a word. A downbeat Dorival acted as spokesperson: 'It is a difficult, serious and grave situation which I would prefer to resolve internally with Neymar, his father and the club management. I do not feel comfortable talking about it. I know René has said something about what has happened. I think I would have done the same in his shoes.'

The journalists wanted blood, they wanted to know what was happening with Neymar.

'I don't know. I am doing everything I can to help him but once the situation is taken out of my hands, it will be difficult. Thank God that in all the seventeen years of my career, I have not had a problem with discipline. With Neymar, it's different. It is a new situation. We are all learning something new, including Neymar,' said Dorival.

Dorival explained why he let Marcel take the penalty: Neymar had had three misses out of six attempts, and even in training he was not getting a good percentage of conversions.

Neymar's rebellion did not go down well with his teammates either. Marcel was succinct and to the point: 'A player must accept the decisions of his coach. The hierarchy on a football field must be honoured, just like in a company.'

The next day, Neymar, the monster, was the topic of all the TV chat shows, the critics' newspaper columns and the fans' reactions. The newspapers trotted out the previous 'bad' behaviour of the number 11: the controversial lob of Corinthians defender Chicão, the lob of Avaí defender Marcinho Guerreiro, etc. – provocations which set off the other team's players.

Antonio Lopes, the coach for the *Catarinense* team,

accused Neymar of effectively saying, 'I am a millionaire and I can do what I want.'

The latest entry on this rap sheet had come on the Sunday prior to the Atlético Goianiense match: Neymar argued with João Marcos of Ceará and nasty words were exchanged. If it were not for their teammates, punches would have been thrown.

The Brazilian press had a field day: 'It is becoming a habit for Neymar to leave the pitch at the centre of some controversy or other.'

They called him a rebel, they said he had got too big for his boots. They said he had no respect for anyone anymore. Basically he was a proper 'bad boy'. Even his sponsors started to take a step back. Three companies that were going to sign with Neymar called the club's marketing team and said that he had gone mad and that they were no longer interested. Bad news followed bad news.

An insider leaked the exchanges with the captain and then with Dorival's assistant in the changing rooms at Vila Belmiro. Neymar, who had not showed up to the press meeting the previous evening, tweeted to calm the waters: 'The argument I had on the pitch is from someone who wants to win … it is for the good of the group as a whole … Dorival Junior is a person whom I admire and respect a great deal. He has my complete backing. Everything is fine. Thank God we are back to our winning ways. Let's carry on, *profe*.'

It was not enough for the commentators or the fans. Some of the fans even put up an offensive banner in front of the 'monster's' house.

Neymar was asked to apologise in front of the group and the public and the next day he obliged: 'I apologise to Dorival, Edu and my teammates and to the chairman and fans of Santos. I apologise to all those who love Neymar and the kids who look up to me. I ask for forgiveness because what happened last night was not the Neymar people want to see. Neymar is happiness, football with a smile across his face.'

This was the show for the journalists. In private, Neymar prayed to God for forgiveness.

Years later he still remembers that day, 15 September 2010. It was one of the worst days of his life. He remembers that, after the match, he got home and found his father and mother crying. Nadine, who had watched the match from the stands, told him, 'I did not recognise you on that pitch. That was not my son today. That was not the Juninho I brought up.' Her words cut through Neymar, much more than the torrent of abuse which ensued over the following days. Neymar recalls those horrible, interminable nights when he cried like he'd never cried before. The Santos chairman confirmed this: 'I found him the next day at eight in the morning. He was red-eyed and with a puffed face. He was sincerely sorry for what he had done.

'I explained to him that he would get much more out of the sport and be more successful if his image was one of happiness both on and off the pitch. Being a "bad boy" does not pay in the long run.'

Neymar thanked him. He said that if it had not been for his family, his supporters and the club, he might have thrown the towel in that day.

He made up with Dorival Junior, allegedly, right after the match when the coach called him into his office. Dorival decided to punish Neymar and use the incident to set an example. An act of this nature, whether it be from a kid in the youth teams or from Neymar, could not be tolerated. The coach had to have a firm hand. He decided to fine Neymar 50,000 reais and suspend him from the team.

Dorival explained, 'I believe it is in his [Neymar's] interests, albeit not for the club, that we work without such an important player as Neymar. It is with a heavy heart that I punish him but I hope that this can help the boy grow.' Dorival added that his decision was fully supported by the club and that he had full authority.

On Sunday 19 September, Santos played Guarani at the Brinco de Ouro in Campinas. Neymar was not playing, having been suspended. He watched on as a fan and saw his team achieve a dull 0–0.

What now? Would Neymar play against Corinthians at Vila Belmiro, an important match in the *Brasilerão*? After training the day before the match, the press conference was held. The first question to the coach was 'Will Neymar play?'

Dorival was succinct and decisive: 'No, Neymar will not play.'

This reply marked the end of the honeymoon period between Santos and Dorival Junior. Luis Álvaro de Oliveira Ribeiro, the chairman, on hearing the news, went ballistic. He had agreed with the coach that Neymar would only be banned for one match. At least, that is the version of events he gives. He picked up the phone and called the vice-chairman and the board's coordinator to discuss the situation. The decision was taken: Dorival was out. He was called to the CT Rei Pelé that evening and at one in the morning the news was given that Dorival had been sacked.

'*Perdeu Dorival*' ('Dorival loses'); '*Neymar riu por último*' (Neymar has last laugh); '*Neymar derrumba Dorival*' ('Neymar overthrows Dorival'); '*Neymar "vence" queda de braço: Dorival fora!*' ('Neymar "wins" arm wrestle: Dorival out!') were the newspaper headlines.

As is the norm in these cases, club officials talked of a reciprocal decision in light of a relationship which was no longer working. Everyone else believed that Dorival lost the arm wrestle over Neymar. The club had to decide between a coach who had won two titles and an eighteen-year-old kid worth 80 million reais. The decision was easy. Better to have an icon, the fans' favourite, the prodigal player.

What were the consequences of this? In the São Paulo *Folha*, 'PVC', Paulo Vinicius Coelho, summed up in his column as follows: 'Neymar is now the king of the castle at Vila Belmiro, which is exactly what an eighteen-year-old kid should not be allowed to think.'

Chapter 16

Doha

Brazil–Argentina: Messi vs. Neymar Jr. For the first time they were face to face. In Doha, Qatar, at the Khalifa International Stadium.

Truth be told, the duel people had been waiting for was that between the current number 10s, Messi and Ronaldinho – the former Barcelona teammates. Neymar was still a novice who needed more experience. His name was not splashed all over the stadium posters: it was only his second match for the Brazilian national team.

His debut for the senior side was on 10 August 2010. Brazil against the USA in New Meadowlands, New Jersey. After the debacle in South Africa, Dunga resigned and the Brazilian Football Confederation decided to appoint Mano Menezes. The new man came from Corinthians, where he had won three titles in three years (first the *Campeonato Brasileiro Série B* and then, following the promotion of the team to the top division, the Paulistão and Brazil Cup in 2009). Things were looking good for Brazil, especially with the 2014 World Cup, on home soil, coming up.

Against the USA, the line-up contained the names everyone was expecting to see: Neymar and Paulo Henrique – the players Dunga had decided not to take to the South Africa World Cup. One was playing in the number 11 shirt, the same as he did for Santos, the other in the number 10.

At the end of the match, the two friends were as happy as

Larry. Ganso commented, 'I did not expect my first match to be as good as this but Mano gave us complete freedom; he told us to play as we knew how to. We were able to show off our *futebol alegre* ["joyful football"] which we have been playing throughout the year with Santos.

'Wearing the number 10 for Brazil is a huge responsibility but, thank God, we managed to play a good match and show my talent.'

And Neymar? The boy wonder did not expect to score on his debut, and certainly not with his head, but that is what happened. In the 28th minute, Robinho passed to André Santos, who was pushing forward on the left. He crossed into the box and Neymar beat the defender to the ball and headed past the US goalkeeper Tim Howard. The number 11 fell to his knees and raised his arms to the sky, and then kissed the Brazilian crest on his shirt before being mobbed by his teammates, Ganso and Alexander Pato. Pato added a second for Brazil in the 47th minute to give a final score of 2–0.

Neymar commented, 'My goal was to make sure we could relax. Everything went well after that.' Neymar's pre-match nerves were well gone. He added, 'It will be a lot easier now.'

It was easy indeed for Mano Menezes, who after the match received a standing ovation. The press effused praise for the return of *futebol alegre*: speed, dribbling, *pedaladas* (stepovers) ... after the defensive Brazil of Dunga, the poetry and attacking football were back.

The following matches were not so easy for Neymar. In the friendlies against Iran and Ukraine, he was not selected. This was not due to his performance against the USA but because of the controversy surrounding the Dorival Junior affair. Another punishment to enable the boy to grow and sort himself out.

He made his return to the team in Doha on 17 November 2010 in a match against Argentina.

Before the match, emotions were high, especially as Ronaldhino was making his return to the national team after several months. Microphone in hand, Brazil shirt on, Neymar could hardly get a word out: he was choked with emotion as he stood next to his idol: 'I am one of his fans. I love his football, his career, him as a person, everything he has done for the Brazilian team. I remember his dribbling, his lobs, the goal he scored against England in the South Korea World Cup.'

He shook hands with 'Ronnie' and passed him the microphone. The Milan player confessed in a low voice, 'I have followed his career from the beginning, as well as the new generation of players at Santos. It is pure *futebol alegre*, it is football art.

'I feel privileged to be able to play again for Brazil and to be part of this group. We hope to be able to bring great joy to the Brazilian people.'

At the Khalifa International Stadium, Leo Messi was the one bringing happiness. 'La Pulga' finally got to beat his eternal rivals at the fifth time of asking. The previous contests had seen Argentina lose three and draw one. Even at the Beijing Olympics in 2008, when Argentina *had* beaten Brazil (on the way to the gold medal), Messi had not managed to score in the match.

This time he managed to. In second-half stoppage time, Douglas in midfield made a mistake. Argentina gained possession and went on the counterattack. Messi stormed up the field. He covered half the pitch and left Lucas behind. He weaved around David Luiz and Thiago Silva and then slotted it in past Victor, the Brazilian goalkeeper, who could do nothing but watch it go in.

Messi had won the duel with his former Barça teammate, who was substituted in the second half. Ronaldinho's performance was admirable – perfect long passes, free kicks and an attempt on goal with his heel – but it was not to be.

Neymar, on the other hand, was not on the same form as in his first match. He was not key to the match; indeed he was almost playing a secondary role. On the left wing, he was the Brazilian player highest up the pitch. But he did not penetrate. He fell down too often and was substituted before the end. A leading commentator, Juca Kfouri, said Neymar was in need of more experience and maturity.

At the end of the day, Neymar had only been involved with the Brazil set-up for two years.

In 2008, Lucho Nizzo was putting together a team of players to take part in the Under-17 World Cup in Nigeria the following year. Neymar had made a good impression playing for Santos in 'La Copinha', so it was only right that the coach of the youth teams should try him out in the under-16s.

The first commitment was the Mediterranean International Cup, a youth tournament played in Spain, on the Costa Brava, since 2001. It is one of the most prestigious football exhibition tournaments in the world, where many young kids have showcased their talents on their way to becoming professionals: the likes of Cesc Fàbregas, Gerard Piqué, Juan Mata, Marcelo, Jordi Alba and Lucas Leiva.

In 2003, a certain Leo Messi turned up. Nizzo remembers it well because that was the first year the Brazilians took part in the tournament. Josep Colomer, manager of the youth teams at Barcelona, spoke well of him. The fifteen year old amazed the crowds with his skills and goals. Five years later, it was Neymar and Philippe Coutinho who were to set sparks flying.

In the 2008 edition, 144 teams (split into various

categories: *alevin, infantil, cadete* and *juvenil*) from nineteen
countries took part in the tournament. On 19 March, the
opening ceremony took place at Palamós: the teams paraded
around the pitch, huge papier mâché mascots, fireworks,
sardanas (a Catalonian dance), cheerleaders from Barcelona
and, to finish, a match between *los juveniles* from the local
team and Brazil. Finishing 1–0 to Brazil, it was a taster of
what was to come.

Philippe Coutinho and Neymar, number 8 and number 10 respectively, were the main players for Brazil.
Strangers until Nizzo selected them for the squad, they hit
it off immediately, both on and off the pitch. Coutinho, a
kid from Rio de Janeiro who played in the Vasco da Gama
youth team (and now plays for Liverpool following stints
at Inter and Espanyol), was the midfield playmaker, while
Neymar, according to the coach at the time, was 'a hanging
attacker, who cuts upfield in search of goal every time he
gets the ball'.

Within a few days of meeting each other, they got on like
a house on fire. The one-twos, the exchanges between them,
were a constant feature of the matches. How many passes,
tricks, etc. did they make over the course of the tournament?
When Neymar was asked, he simply laughed.

Brazil got through the qualifiers without any hiccups and
got to the semi-finals in Calonge. On the day of the match,
a huge storm turned the pitch into a quagmire. The ball
got stuck and bogged down; it was almost impossible to get
the ball out of the puddles and control it with any technique or Brazilian flair. The opponents, Konoplet, a Russian
team, were a physically stronger team and took control of
the game. They scored first. In the second half, the weather
improved slightly. Darkness fell and it started to get cold.
Turning the game around was not going to be easy. Coutinho

managed to strike the ball and the Russian goalkeeper could not keep it out. One-all. Neymar got injured a few minutes later and left the pitch.

It went down to penalties. Luis Guillerme, the goalkeeper for Brazil, managed to hold on to one of the Russians' strikes. The players in the green and gold went wild. They were in the final. But with Neymar having had to be carried off the pitch, his participation looked doubtful.

The sun was shining at the Palamós Municipal Stadium on Sunday 23 March 2008. The final was to take place later that day: Brazil versus Lokomotiv Moscow. Neymar was fit.

The match was not easy but the two *wunderkinder* knew what to do. Coutinho played a ball through to Neymar, who was brought down just outside the area. Number 11 for Brazil, Wellington Alves da Silva (at the time with Fluminense, now with Real Murcia on loan from Arsenal) lined up the free kick. The Lokomotiv goalkeeper did not get anywhere near. He had held the fort up to this point but there was nothing he could do this time.

It was the winning goal. Brazil celebrated. Neymar celebrated. Pictures show him with fuzzy hair and a smile plastered across his face, his gold medal around his neck. Next to him are Coutinho, flying the *Ordem e Progreso* flag, and the manager, along with the cup. Neymar thanked God that it had all gone according to plan; but who knew what the future would hold.

The future for Brazil was the 2009 Under-17 World Cup in Nigeria. On 24 October 2009, in the Teslim Balogun Stadium in Lagos, Brazil's opening match was against Japan. Neymar, wearing number 11, put his team ahead in the 67th minute. The goal featured all of the three stars who had shone in the Costa Brava tournament: Neymar, Coutinho and Wellington. Nizzo wanted these three in his team come what may.

Wellington picked up the ball in defence and then passed to Coutinho in midfield. He turned, moved forward and launched the ball to his friend, Neymar, who was waiting. Neymar ran to the ball and in front of Japan's goal he did something incredible. He flicked the ball with the end of his right foot past the goalkeeper and then shimmied the other way and slotted the ball in the net. It was almost a carbon-copy of Pelé's near miss against Ladislao Mazurkiewicz's Poland in the 1970 World Cup. Neymar's goal, though, went in.

However, it was his only goal of the tournament. After a 3–2 win against Japan, Brazil lost two matches: to Mexico and Switzerland. Brazil finished third in Group B and headed home.

Ten months later, Neymar played his first match for the Brazil first team.

In time, there would be successes to make up for the disappointment of the Under-17 World Cup. Not least in 2011.

Chapter 17

2011

There are very few occasions in life where you get the chance to experience so many emotions, so much joy, so much happiness, in only twelve months. It is rare to receive, in such a short time frame, so many important life lessons which you will carry with you for the rest of your life – for better or for worse.

It is even rarer when you are only nineteen.

In 2011, Neymar was lucky enough to experience this. This was a year in which everything happened for Neymar. He became a father, won four historic titles, entered international football, achieved millionaire contracts, became a footballing icon on a par with a popstar and was party to a debacle which sent shock waves through Brazilian football. All of this at the speed of light: a whirlwind of events which increased exponentially compared to what had happened the year before.

Let's start at the beginning.

17 January 2011, Jorge Basadre Stadium, Tacna

To get the year off to a good start, Neymar Jr scored all four of Brazil's goals against Paraguay in the first match of the Under-20 South American Championship. The Buenos Aires sports daily *Olé* went with the headline 'Neymaradona'. Ney Franco, the technical coach, had called up both Neymar and Philippe Coutinho for the tournament. Coutinho was ruled out, however, due to injury. Franco also chose the cream of Brazil's young players: Lucas Moura, Fernando, Oscar and Casemiro.

The tournament would be the ticket to the 2012 London Olympics. It looked good for Neymar at the start as he predicted 'I have to play my football' – and kept the promise right from the outset.

First he scored a penalty after a foul on Casemiro (now playing for Real Madrid), and celebrated with his *la dança do créu'* ('Mc Créu's dance') with music from Mc Créu. Then, in the 33rd minute, Lucas put the ball in the area, Neymar showed some nifty footwork and made it 2–0. The third came via a header. The fourth was a beauty: Rafael Galhardo on the left delivered a killer pass, Neymar cut into the box and, as the keeper came out, he lobbed it over him.

Brazil 4 Paraguay 2 was the final score. Next it was Colombia. Again Brazil took the points, winning 3–1, with Neymar wrapping things up with the last goal.

A draw against Bolivia and victory against Ecuador meant that Brazil finished top of their group. Six teams went through to the final heats. Brazil's next match was against Chile: it finished 5–1 to Brazil, with Neymar getting two. He was now up to seven for the tournament. His eighth and ninth were to come at Arequipa in the south of Peru – the birthplace of Mario Vargas Llosa. Everyone in this city knew the author who, in 2010, won the Nobel Prize.

Everyone wanted to see the new Pelé, Neymar, who arrived in Peru relatively unknown but instantly became a massive star. Seeing how much interest the match and Neymar had whipped up, the *Comembol* decided to change the time of the match with Brazil, switching it to prime time.

On 12 February 2011, Brazil played Uruguay. Uruguay had a one-point advantage over Brazil when they got to the last match of the tournament, as Brazil had lost to Argentina. Uruguay were the favourites to qualify in first position and earn a place at the Olympics. It was not to be: Uruguay got trounced 6–0. Three goals from Lucas Moura, one from Danilo and two from Neymar. Brazil won the tournament for the third time in succession, their eleventh title since the inaugural competition in 1954, and thus earned their place in the 2012 Olympic Games. Neymar was the leading goalscorer with nine goals and was voted the best player in the tournament.

Ney Franco confessed in an interview with *El País*, 'At the beginning some people thought Neymar was the rebellious type with his casual style, styled hair and relaxed attitude. In reality, he is someone who has a huge personality and he really showed it in that tournament. He was the centre of attention, he was a great footballer, but he was able to play for the team and be part of the group.'

The Brazilian critics stated, 'At just nineteen, Neymar is already used to stunning the crowds and creating a show with the team. He demolished Uruguay's defence, he was crucial in the Paraguay, Colombia and Chile matches. He leaves the tournament with an extremely promising career ahead of him, more than anyone could have expected.'

So much praise, and yet Neymar, while celebrating with his medal and the Brazilian flag in hand, commented, 'There are no stars here. We have created a fantastic family in two months and this is the result of work which started on 13 December [the day the pre-tournament training camp started]. Now our dream is to play at the Olympics and bring home the gold medal.'

24 February 2011, Forte dos Andradas, Guarujá

'Even without doing military service, Neymar's talent and skills can do a lot for our country. He can help promote our country in the world more than it already has been.'

These were the words of General Santos in front of the TV cameras during Neymar's visit to Forte dos Andradas.

Neymar turned up to the 1st Brigade of the anti-aircraft artillery camp sporting sunglasses, T-shirt and white shoes, the famous Mohican, now with little dreadlocks, a huge watch and a gold necklace. The cadets patted him on the shoulder, shook his hand, gave him a hug, asked for an autograph or a photo and offered him a brigade shirt and beret. Neymar was visiting the fort to get his compulsory military service exemption. While he was there he was treated to a film of Pelé, who, unlike Neymar, did do military service. (In 1959 at Fort Itaipu in Praia Grande, Pelé was there and ended up playing football for the military.)

Eventually Neymar obtained the signed document exempting him from the marching, training and the dorms … all with the kind blessing of the commander of the fort. The commander admitted that football could achieve more than arms – in the case of Neymar, anyway.

27 March 2011, Emirates Stadium, London

It was his third match with the national team and, fittingly, the Brazilian football prodigy scored three goals. The match was against Scotland, the venue Arsenal's Emirates Stadium, London. Neymar took part in his favourite pastime: scoring goals. With great ease he racked them up. The first came from a ball from André Santos on the left, which he brought down and then launched a missile into the far corner of the goal. The second was a one-man show. He danced and skipped with the ball into Scotland's area and the defender,

Adam, brought him crashing to the floor. Neymar wasted no time in converting the penalty.

The TV commentators were stunned by the technique and deadly effectiveness of Neymar's play and, while the match was under way, started to talk about his future: they concluded that his future was in the UK.

Interestingly, a large number of the fans from London booed Neymar for the entire match. At one point, while dribbling in the area, Neymar was hit by a banana: a pure act of racism. Neymar commented, 'It is always sad when these sorts of things happen. I cannot come here and see these sorts of things.' The Scottish fans denied any act of racism. They said they had had enough of Neymar's constant diving, simulating fouls – that old chestnut. But perhaps what irritated the Scots most of all was the elaborate dribbling and his style of play which destroys opponents.

15 May 2011, Vila Belmiro, Santos

'Santos ... Santos ... Goal!
Now:
Who gives the ball, it's Santos
Santos is the new champion
Glorious Alvinegro Praiano
Absolute champion this year'

As Santos's anthem, 'Leão do mar', says, the glorious Alvinegro Praiano are champions this year. The popular tune was composed by José Maugeri Neto and Maugeri Sobrinho in 1955. Now, in 2011, the music boomed around Vila Belmiro stadium. Edu Dracena, the captain, on a stage in the centre of the pitch, lifted the Paulista Cup for the second year running. It is the nineteenth trophy and the sixth 'double' (back-to-back titles) in Santos's history.

The deciding goal was scored in the second leg against Corinthians (after the first leg had finished 0–0) and it was Neymar who scored it.

Santos were 1–0 up following a 43rd-minute goal from Arouca. Neymar had already missed a chance to make it two: alone in the box, he tried to put the ball between the legs of Julio Cesar, the goalkeeper, but Cesar sensed what Neymar was doing and deflected it for a corner.

Now, in the 83rd minute, Cesar was not so lucky: Neymar struck the ball with his right foot and, although it was not the strongest of shots, it slipped through Cesar's hands and then trickled over the line despite Cesar's desperate dive to try and claw the ball back.

In the 86th minute, Morais clawed one back for Corinthians but it was too late to try for the draw. A triumphant Neymar was hoisted on the shoulders of his teammates and hugs and kisses of joy flew.

It had not been an easy Paulistão. After the dismissal of Dorival Junior, a succession of managers had failed to settle into the role: three in total. Marcelo Martelotte, Adilson Batista, then Martelotte again before Muricy Ramalho took the role on 10 April 2011. The team had been transformed: Robinho, who was one of the stars in 2010, went back to Europe; André, another friend of Neymar's, was sold to Dynamo Kiev right after Santos's 2010 Brazil Cup success; Elano was bought from Galatasary to bolster the midfield (he was no foreigner to Santos having played from 2001 to 2005) – this was a good buy but the dream pairing between Elano and Paulo Henrique was not to be as Henrique tore ligaments in his knee in a match against Gremio on 25 August 2010, meaning he could not play for another seven months. He would return in March 2011.

Neymar was engaged with the Brazil Under-20s and could

not play the first six league matches. Muricy Ramalho was unable to field his strongest line-up until the quarter-finals of the Paulistão, where Santos beat Ponte Preta with a goal from Neymar. Then it was on to São Paulo: Elano and Ganso sorted things out. The final awaited and Santos did not miss their opportunity to get another 'double', played out to the unmistakable *zumpa pà-pà – zumpa pà-pà* anthem.

22 June 2011, Pacaembu, São Paulo

Forty-eight years after Caetano's own goal and Pelé's double against the Uruguayan team Peñarol, Santos won the Libertadores against the same team.

It was 15 June at the Centenario Stadium in Montevideo and the stadium was a sea of black and yellow, the colours of the home team. When the two teams jogged onto the pitch, the light from the fireworks and flares lit up the Montevideo night sky. The roaring welcome sent shivers down the Santos players' spines. The Santos boys did not let it get to them. It was 0–0 at the final whistle. It could have been better but for Peixe it was a good result as the second leg was in Pacaembu.

For the second leg, the stadium was teeming. Santos were in a creative mood and made many chances but at first nothing came off. Shortly after half-time, though, Neymar managed to open up the game by scoring the first goal: Arouca carved out a lovely little manoeuvre from the midfield and found the number 11 free on the left; on the volley he smacked the ball past the goalkeeper into the right corner of the net. Goaaaaal!

The players were ecstatic and it was clear that the game was there for the taking. Danilo drove home the second and it looked as though it was all over. But there was still time for a comeback. In the 79th minute, while trying to clear his area, Santos defender Durval scored an own goal.

The fans could not believe it and some turned their backs on the pitch: they could not bear to watch. They only turned round when the Argentinian referee, Sergio Pezzotta, blew the final whistle.

Pure emotion took over: tears poured – and punches flew. A Santos fan invaded the pitch and attacked a player from Peñarol, who fought back. The gauntlet had been thrown down and the battle commenced. The police had to get involved to break up the two teams. It took a long time for peace and calm to be restored and the awards ceremony to take place.

Neymar knelt on the green carpet and raised his arms to the heavens. Muricy hugged Pelé and then accompanied him to the centre of the pitch. O Rei, with his red jacket on, waved to the crowds and when he was interviewed for TV channel Fox Deportes and asked about Neymar, he wore his heart on his sleeve: 'As everyone knows and as everyone can see, he is a great player with a huge talent. In the first half, he was not at his best because Peñarol defended very well. In the second half, he opened up the match and scored a brilliant goal. We will see if he can do the same when playing for Brazil. Let's hope he is not like Messi who plays brilliantly for Barcelona but not that well with Argentina.'

The journalist dared to ask the question everyone was thinking: 'Will he be better than you?' Pelé smiled and said, 'To do that he will need to score more than 1,283 goals.'

The Old King did not want to give up his crown quite yet.

A few days later Neymar was presented with his own crown. It was gold with an 'N' just like that of Napoleon. 'Reymar' was engraved on the crown and, to the side, the verdict of the São Paulo weekly magazine *Veja*, of 28 June: 'Finally we have a star who is of Pelé's calibre.'

17 July 2011, Estádio Ciudad de La Plata

It was a terrible afternoon: one of those days where the ball just did not want to go in the goal. It was cleared off the line, miraculously saved or chances were fluffed. In the ensuing shoot-out, four penalties were missed. Elano, Thiago Silva, André Santos and Fred could not do anything right. Brazil bombed out of the 2011 Copa America. It was the quarter-final and Brazil lost to Tata Martino's Paraguay, who went on to lose the final against Uruguay.

At the beginning of the tournament, which was held in Argentina, the most talked about names were Neymar and Paulo Henrique. Everyone was convinced that together they could change the outcome of a match and turn things around for Brazil. However, on Sunday 17 July, Brazil exited the Copa America without Neymar and Henrique having shown the brilliance that they regularly demonstrated for Santos – Neymar in particular.

Brazil just did not look themselves against Paraguay. In the 83rd minute Neymar was substituted for Fred. He watched the penalties from the bench, with Ganso, who came off in the first half of extra time. Mano Menezes had granted the number 11 plenty of licence to attack alongside Alexandre Pato. Neymar got his chance after only three minutes, but missed. He missed the second and third chances as well. In the second half, Pato set Neymar up beautifully but his shot was parried by Villar, the Paraguay goalkeeper.

Neymar paid dearly for his mistakes and things started to go wrong. His dribbling was not effective, he mistimed his runs and his passes went short or long into the hands of the opposition: he lost the ball nine times in total. When Brazil needed him, he was not there. Neymar's record at the end of the tournament was not great: two goals against Ecuador in the last Group B match and thirteen attempts on goal.

The critics were not amused: 'Too few goals for someone who is meant to lead the way for Brazil,' was their verdict.

27 July 2011, Vila Belmiro, Santos

A show? A spectacle? A memorable event? A historic match like in the films? An ode to football? However people chose to describe it, it was difficult to think of another match like Santos vs. Flamengo in the twelfth round of Brasilerão matches in 2011.

The 4–5 win for Flamengo reminded the older heads in the crowd of Santos's 7–6 win over Palmeiras in 1958. Two things were clear: Neymar played his best match for Santos, and Ronaldinho put in the type of performance he used to give when playing for Barcelona.

El Gaucho scored three goals, the first taking advantage of mistakes by Edu Dracena and the goalkeeper; the second from a free-kick which split the wall; and the third driven hard along the ground into the corner.

Neymar was on fire as well: from the ground, he switched the ball and set Borges up for a simple finish; he then earned a penalty, only to see Elano clip the bar with a Panenka-style kick; Neymar also scored two goals himself. The second, from a counterattack, put Santos 4–3 up with half an hour of the match left to play (prior to Ronaldinho's crucial second and third goals). Neymar's first was a work of art.

Neymar received the ball near the touchline, just inside the Flamengo half. He was marked closely by two players: Leo Moura and Williams. The players closed in on Neymar in a pincer movement. He needed to get out into the space; it looked impossible but somehow he managed it. He slipped between the two and ran forward. He saw Borges and played a one-two. Renato quickly closed in but Neymar skimmed round him and on to Ronaldo Angelim. A bit of dribbling and then the masterpiece: a flick to one side and Neymar passed around the other side of him. With a few metres to go, Neymar saw the defenders diving in and the goalkeeper coming off his line and lobbed it into the back of the net.

The goal earned Neymar the FIFA Ferenc Puskás Award for 2011.

On 9 January 2012, in the Congress building in Zurich, Neymar attended the yearly awards ceremony. Wearing a black jacket with white shirt and grey tie, and sporting styled hair with red highlights, he sat in one of the front rows. He was one of the star attractions as not only had he been nominated for the Puskás Award but he had also been shortlisted for the Ballon d'Or.

Ruud Gullit gave out the awards on the stage. The three finalists for the Puskás Award were Leo Messi, Wayne Rooney and Neymar. Messi earned his place with the goal he scored on 8 March in the Champions League against Arsenal – a fantastic flick and volley to beat the Gunners' keeper. The Red Devils' centre forward was in the running for his overhead kick in the derby against Manchester City on 12 February.

The videos of the three goals were shown and then Kate Murray, the journalist co-hosting with Gullit, introduced the person who would present the award: it was Hugo Sánchez, the greatest Mexican player of all time.

The former Real Madrid player commented, 'Scoring a beautiful goal makes you very happy but receiving this award is the best. I talk from experience.' The TV cameras zoomed in on Messi, Neymar and Rooney. 'The FIFA Puskás Award for 2011 goes to … Neymar.'

The kid from Santos removed his earphones (worn for translation purposes) and shook Rooney's hand. He got up and passed by Gerard Piqué and Andres Iniesta. Doing his

jacket up, he walked on to the stage. He said hello to Hugo
Sánchez, Gullit and Murray, then looked out at the audience.

'I am very happy to be given this award. I was up against
two of the greatest stars in football, of whom I am a great
fan. I want to thank God and all those who are here. Have
a great night.' So spoke an emotional Neymar. He took his
award and headed off to party.

24 August 2011, Hospital São Luiz, São Paulo

'Nasceeeeuu !!! Davi Lucca …' was how Neymar announced
the birth of his first son. He posted a photo online with him
holding the baby, still wearing the hospital cap and gown.

The next photos were of his father and Paulo Henrique,
friend and godfather to his child. Neymar published a note
on his official site in Portuguese, English and Spanish stating that mother and son were doing well and that he would
like to thank God 'for the little blessing in his life aka David
Lucca; 2 kilos and 810 grams of pure joy and courage.'

Neymar was over the moon and he said as much in a tweet
which topped the trending on the internet in Brazil after
only a few hours. David Lucca was the most important thing
in his life; but becoming a father at nineteen was not easy.

When Neymar heard that Carolina Dantas (then seventeen) was pregnant, he did not know what to think. He
was scared. He was not ready for such responsibility, and
Carolina was a casual partner. They had met through mutual
friends when she was sixteen. He began sending her texts
and eventually they started going out together, but it did
not last long.

When Carolina discovered she was pregnant, she first
thought of keeping it quiet and not telling Juninho, but
then she realised that one day her son would want to know
who his father was. She told him and he behaved like 'a true

gentleman' (according to Carolina when she appeared on the TV program *Domingão do Faustão*).

Neymar still had to face his and Carolina's families. He first confronted his mother, Nadine, who burst into tears. With his father, it was not as easy, especially as his father had warned him to be careful and not make stupid mistakes which could have serious consequences.

A ticking off was inevitable and O Pai duly gave Neymar Jr what for, but then the emotion, the hugs and the paternal advice of a father who wanted the best for his son gushed forth. Neymar Pai told Juninho that whatever he decided to do (i.e. whether he married Carolina or not), the little boy would always be his grandson.

Neymar's fears faded and Neymar Pai accompanied Juninho to the Dantas family home. Neymar decided to acknowledge his son and to pay a monthly payment for his upkeep.

Neymar decided to go public, although without revealing the name of the mother. Neymar stayed close to Carolina throughout the pregnancy and at 11.00am on 24 August, Neymar was in the delivery room to welcome David Lucca to the world.

The young mother (now nineteen) and medical student commented, 'Juninho is a marvellous, caring, doting father and a friend who has stood by me. When he was at Santos, he would come and see him as often as he could, he was caring and showered him with gifts. Sometimes he stayed the night to sleep with David.'

Neymar had his son baptised at the *Igreja Batista Peniel* and when the baby was but a month old, on 7 September 2011, he took him to CT Rei Pelé so that he could meet his teammates.

On 4 March 2012, David Lucca was paraded when Santos

took the pitch at Vila Belmiro prior to the match against Corinthians. He brought the team luck and Santos won 1–0. David Lucca had become a sort of mascot for Santos, as Neymar Jr had once been for União Mogi.

28 September 2011, Mangueirão Stadium, Belém

The *Superclásico das Américas* is a trophy which dates back to 1913. It was founded by the Argentinian president, Julio Roca, to develop football in Argentina and in Brazil. The first tournament was held on 27 September 1914, a few days before the death of its founder. The match was held on the Gimnasia y Esgrima in Buenos Aires and Brazil won 1–0 with a goal from Rubens Salles.

With various formulas and different outcomes each year, the trophy pitted Brazil against Argentina right up until 1976. Then it stopped, just like that.

In 2011, though, it was rekindled thanks to an agreement between the Argentinian and Brazilian federations. The biggest challenge of them all was back on. The first match was to be held in the Mario Kempes Stadium in Córdoba on 14 September, with the return leg in Belem in Mangueirão on 28 September.

In Argentina, in front of 50,000 spectators, the match ended 0–0. The blue and whites put out a 'B' team without any of their Europe-based stars, while Brazil put out a fairly strong team, albeit with up-and-coming players: Lucas and Cortes had their debut. Iconic players like Ronaldinho were also there.

Neymar played in the return leg and scored the second goal in a 2–0 win. Cortes supplied Diegou with a cutting pass and Diegou drove the ball hard into the box, along the ground. Neymar slipped in between defender and goalkeeper to score.

Mano Menezes finally got the satisfaction of beating a top international team and Neymar got another trophy to add to his already full collection.

In 2012, Neymar would double his tally for the tournament before also finding the net in the penalty shoot-out that followed the second leg – his being the deciding kick of the *Superclásico*.

9 November 2011, Vila Belmiro

At 11.30am the deal was sealed with a handshake.

At 3.00pm the deal was officially announced.

Luis Álvaro de Oliveira Ribeiro, the Santos chairman, with his sleeves rolled up, kicked off the press conference: 'Whereas Neymar shows his talent on the pitch, destroying opposition defences, his family shows its loyalty and passion for Santos off the pitch.

'I would like to thank them from the bottom of my heart. I said that the happiest day of my life was 22 June in Pacaembu, when we won in the Libertadores after 48 years, but today is an even happier day for me because a dream has become reality.

'Neymar is staying with us until the 2014 World Cup. He has signed a contract and it is a done deal. He is not going to Real, nor Barcelona. He is with Santos.'

Ribeiro's Santos had fought back, in quixotic style, against the economic power of the European clubs. How? By paying more. Neymar's salary jumped from 1.5 million reais a month to 3 million a month; with the equivalent of €14.9 million a year, he was now the eighth best paid player in the world.

Peixe went to town on the advertising rights under the contract, granting Neymar 30 per cent. The break clause was bolstered as well. And the termination date of the contract was brought forward: before it was 2015, now it was August 2014.

It was a home run for Luis Álvaro de Oliveira Ribeiro, who, on 2 December, was standing for re-election as chairman. In the press room, Ribeiro, Neymar Jr and Neymar Pai sat patiently before the announcement. Neymar Jr was wearing a baseball cap on backwards and a black T-shirt and chewing gum. He calmly explained his feelings: 'I wanted to stay here. I had always said that. I thank the two Spanish clubs for their interest. It is an honour. But I never really thought about leaving to become the best in the world. Here I have my family, my son and my friends. I could not imagine leaving to become the best in the world. I just want to play in the best championships. Santos is doing that. We won the Libertadores and we are now playing the Club World Cup.'

Case closed … for the time being.

18 December 2011. International Stadium, Yokohama

'Today we learned how to play football. Barcelona was the better team. Its players are amazing. It is the best team in the world. This is the match which we learn from.'

The final of the FIFA Club World Cup 2011 had just finished. Neymar, with his Mohican hair flattened, plaster on his nose to help him breathe and a gloomy face, answered the TV journalists' questions from the sidelines. He admitted, grudgingly that Santos had just received a masterclass in how to play football. He then had to go and receive the runners-up trophy and the trophy for third best player of the tournament. He had to say hello to Leo Messi, who was the best player of the tournament beyond a shadow of a doubt and who would collect the Club World Cup trophy.

Neymar had to settle for runner-up this time as he

watched the Argentinian put in an amazing performance. 'La Pulga' was the complete forward, and he scored two of Barcelona's four goals against Santos. The first goal was a delightful lob over Rafael, Santos's goalkeeper, and the second was a quick rifle through the defence.

While Messi constantly received passes to his feet, Neymar did not even get one playable ball. Barcelona dominated the space and left Neymar isolated, a lost soul in a sea of green. Without the ball, it was a bit difficult to play football!

In the first half, the kid from Mogi das Cruzes' only moment was when he picked up the ball on the halfway line, but he was quickly blocked by Puyol and Piqué. In the second half, he got the only chance of the match for Santos, but he mistimed the shot against Víctor Valdés coming forward. And that was that.

The only thing to add was the close-up shots of Neymar's face after every Barça goal.

The next day all the praise was for Pep Guardiola's team, who had just won their thirteenth title. *O Globo* in Rio de Janeiro laid it on thick: 'There is no other team quite like Barcelona in this world.' The *Clarín* in Buenos Aires went with 'Messi carries Barcelona to title'. *El País* preferred 'Barcelona's out-of-this-world football ends Santos's dream'.

That dream of repeating Pelé's achievement of winning the Club World Cup after 48 years (when Santos beat Milan in 1963) was shattered. The only consolation for Neymar was that Santos managed to get this far. He went home with the booby prize: Leo Messi's shirt …

Chapter 18

The gift of improvisation

A conversation with Muricy Ramalho

On entering, the security checks are strict. Before going past the double iron gates which surround the cream-coloured skyscrapers, you have to wait. There is time to take a quick glance at the road, where a group of kids are playing on a makeshift pitch on the edge of a *favela*. The rich and the poor right next to each other, one step from the ultra-modern, filiform Octávio Frias de Oliveira bridge, which stands elegantly over *rio Pinheiros* in São Paulo.

After checking on the phone, the security guard confirms, 'Mr Ramalho is in the Gourmet hall.'

The hall is accessed via the gardens. Muricy Ramalho comes and opens the door to an enormous room with settees and armchairs and an American kitchen. American coffee and glasses of water are served and the manager who won four trophies in just over two years sits down on the other side of the table. He talks about his arrival at Santos in April 2011, and about Neymar.

'Before I arrived at Santos, like everybody else who saw him, I thought he was a good player. But when I watched him close up, I realised he was much more of a player than I could have imagined.

'Why? Because I saw him every day doing things that I had never seen being done before. I, myself, did not play much football [Muricy Ramalho played from 1973 to 1985 at São Paulo and then for Puebla in Mexico] but I have coached a lot and I have seen all sorts of footballers; but what Neymar did I had never seen before.'

What was it that impressed you about him?
'It was his ability to do things that no one else could do. At the end of the day, that is what a star is all about: the unexpected play, improvisation, creativity. When you expect him to go one way, then he goes the other. This is what makes Neymar so special. The defender is convinced that he is going left and yet somehow from nowhere Neymar will flick the ball over the defender's head.

'He improvises and does not follow the established rules of football. In the beginning, I watched him closely; I wanted to see how far he could go. Well … every day he would create something new. The end result is that we haven't seen everything Neymar is capable of.'

What are his best qualities?
'His imagination; he manages to get out of situations which no one would bet on. One thing he needs to improve on is his passing, the quick one-touch passing at which Barcelona excel. His statistics were not brilliant in this area when he was at Santos. He would make mistakes in midfield. I told him that he must improve on that as it was fundamental for the team he was going to. On the edge of the box, what can I say, Neymar is in his element here.'

And his worst quality?
'His choice of music. When he goes into the changing rooms, he puts on that horrible funk, pagode, music, which I hate. It makes a right din. The music on the bus for away matches

or before entering the pitch. I must have told him a million times to turn the volume down or to switch it off. But he just does not listen. In the changing rooms, he is always dancing, talking, joking with his teammates. It does not seem like he is about to play an important match. It does not matter if it's the Libertadores final or a league match, Neymar is playing football just like he did on the beach or in the street. It is fun time. His happiness is contagious.'

And you have paid the price for this happiness on more than one occasion …
'When we became champions, the lads kept throwing water at me and Neymar was the instigator. Then there was the egg in the face for my birthday incident. The lads just kept throwing eggs, flower and water and laughed non-stop. But this is normal in a team. Neymar is very polite compared to some of the players nowadays.'

But he is still a kid?
'Yes. He is still a kid like the others. He goes to clubs, hangs out with girls and does the things kids do at that age but, compared to certain others, he is respectful and polite. He turns up to training and shakes your hand and says "hi" to everyone at all levels in the club.

'He is very friendly with people. His hair, his clothes and his practical jokes made people think he was a bit of a rebel but they were wrong; he is a kid with his feet firmly on the ground who always listens to his father, his trainers and his physio.

'He is completely focused on his job. I'll give you an example: my flat was at the training centre in Santos. Sometimes I would wake up at two or three in the morning and his car was in the car park. He had just finished a TV advert in São Paulo or Rio and instead of sleeping at home

The *filé de borboleta* ('stick insect'): seventeen-year-old Neymar Jr celebrates scoring for Santos in a Brazil Cup match in March 2009. (LatinContent/Getty Images)

(*below*) *O Quarteto Santástico*: Neymar (number 17) celebrates a goal with teammates Robinho, André and Paulo Henrique. The goals and exuberant attacking play of this quartet defined Santos's successful 2010 season. (Ernesto Rodrigues/Agencia Estado via AP Images)

Santos players celebrate Neymar's goal in the final of the 2011 Copa Libertadores against Peñarol of Uruguay. It proved a crucial strike as the match finished 2–1 to the Brazilian sid (AP Photo/Andre Penner)

Neymar, still a Santos player, comes up against Barcelona in the Club World Cup in Japan 2011. A 4–0 win for Barça underlined the gulf between Spanish and Brazilian club footbal and reinforced the notion that Neymar would one day have to move to Europe to make th most of his talent. (AP Photo/Shuji Kajiyama)

Heir to Pelé: for the friendly game against England in June 2013, Brazil coach Luiz Felipe Scolari gave Neymar the iconic number 10 shirt – an indication of the player's talismanic status for the national team. (Getty Images)

...coring the last goal in the ...hampions League final ... Berlin in 2015 to seal ...remarkable treble for ...arcelona.
...ean Catuffe/Getty Images)

(*above*) Neymar celebrates scoring the penultimate goal in Barcelona's historic victory over Paris Saint-Germain. Finishing 6–1 on the night (6–5 on aggregate), it was the bigge[st] second-leg comeback in Champions League history. (Bagu Blanco/BPI/REX/Shutterstoc[k])

(*below*) Now in the Paris Saint-Germain shirt, Neymar shoots a penalty kick to score again[st] Dijon on 17 January 2018. One of the four goals he assisted or scored, the match was a resounding success, finishing as a 8–0 win and solidifying his place in the team. (IAN LANGSDON/EPA-EFE/Shutterstock)

with his mother and father, he would come straight to the club so that he could start his day's work. He would have breakfast and then go straight to training. No one asked him to, he just did it because he is a professional.

'Another example: in March 2013, the Brazilian national team was playing in Europe: first in Switzerland, then in London. We were playing a league match in south Brazil. Neymar managed to get back the same day and played. He was the best player on the pitch. He is not like lots of other footballers who complain all the time: "Coach, it hurts here, there, etc.". He never says he is hurting.'

And yet he gets lots of knocks?
'That's true but he never gets injured. He has never had a serious injury. Why? Because he is very strong, physically. In Brazil, we play on a Sunday. Those that play on Sunday do not train on Monday. But Neymar was always there, ready to take instructions from the trainer. He was never tired, he was always fit and his medicals were the best of the team. He has an excellent aerobic stamina, which is rare for a striker, who does not need it as much as a midfielder or winger; all a striker needs is speed and acceleration. But Neymar recovers very quickly from physical effort. He can string moves together without having to stop.'

A professional who is physically strong, polite, responsible, gifted with improvisation … There must have been something other than the music which made you worry about him?
'The thing that worried me the most was his non-footballing commitments. They kept increasing and for me there were too many. Yes, he was young and, yes, he handled it well, but there comes a point where it gets too much and it tires you out. How long could he keep going like that? I spoke to him

about it a lot and also with his father, as we were worried. We were worried he would burn out and that his image was being exploited too much.'

In terms of his image, how did he become such a world phenomenon in such a short time?
'I think he became so famous so quickly because he conveys happiness, he gives you the joy of playing football that any kid has. Neymar is the image of someone who is always happy, never complaining; a boy who enjoys himself on and off the pitch, who changes his look all the time, a message which strikes a chord with the entire world.

   'We landed in Japan once to play the Club World Cup and it was unbelievable the attention he received. We played all over Brazil and the airports were always full of kids. Everyone wanted the Mohican and everyone wanted to be like him. Neymar is aware of this and knows he has a responsibility towards his fans and he knows how to dedicate himself to his people. He does not hold back when there are autographs to sign and photos to be taken.'

One moment, one match, one goal, one special memory of your time with Neymar?
'The moment that has etched itself in my heart is not on the pitch but when he became a father. We were leaving for Manizales in Colombia to play against Once Caldas in the Libertadores. I met him in the lift and he was looking sad, which I thought was strange. "What's the matter?" I asked, and he said, "No … I've done something that I shouldn't have, something bad, I've got a girl pregnant."

   'I reassured him: "Being a father is the most important thing in the world; the most beautiful thing in the world."

I was scared and concerned as I had never seen him like this before and right before an important match.

'I continued to reassure him: "There's no need to worry, no need to be sad, you should be happy." He started to lighten up and he walked out of the lift with a more serene face than when he'd got in. I went to see the baby, I met the mother. David Lucca has been to training with me. It was important to me. I am also a father to three kids. I think becoming a father has made Neymar grow up quicker.'

Let's talk about the (2013) Confederations Cup: Did Neymar's performance surprise you?

'No, not at all. A few weeks earlier, before the cup, I spoke to his father. I always spoke to his father when there was a problem. The problem was his future: should he stay with Santos, go to Barcelona or go to Madrid. He needed to make the next step in his life and this really started to weigh him down. He did not show it but I could see it, I could see he was not himself.

'The fans did not mince their words, they told him what they felt; insults flew from the stands. So much so that Neymar started to feel uncomfortable at Santos. He was also not playing particularly well for Brazil.

'The day before the official announcement, when the deal with Barcelona was done, he came to training and called me. I could see he was different. "What's the matter?" I asked. Neymar said, "Profe it's over. I signed the contract last night." He was happy. I gave him a hug and told him that I was happy for him. I knew how important it was for him. He had lifted a great weight from his shoulders. He felt relieved and I believe that it was for this reason that he played the Confederations Cup he played.'

To finish, who is Neymar in two words?

'He is a fantastic player who is different to all the others. As a coach, I see it like this: there are different, special, players and there are good players. He is in the first category. Apart from that, I believe that for a player to be different from the other players, he has to be a good person. He is that. In two or three years, he will be the best player in the world.'

Will he overtake Messi?

'It is difficult to say but he will reach Messi's level. It will happen gradually and naturally, like a handing over, as happened with Ronaldinho and Messi. Neymar is preparing himself for this role. His objectives are clear and he will achieve them. He is not the sort of player who thinks if things go well then that's fine but if they go badly then that's fine too. He wants to be the best player in the world. He does not talk about it but he thinks about it. I know this is the case. He has the personality to do it.'

Chapter 19

Remake

You know John Wayne? And his gallery of Wild West characters? Ringo Kid, Ethan Edwards, Rooster Cogburn aka 'El Grinta', Colonel York, John Bernard Books, the Shootist. All of them hard as a rock. Take Grinta, who, with his Winchester in one hand and his Colt in the other, galloping on horseback with the reins in his mouth, could take on four bandits and knock them off – even with one eye missing, a bit overweight and tipsy on whiskey.

True Grit – what a film! John Wayne won his only Oscar for that film in 1970. (And the Coen brothers remade it in 2010, with Jeff Bridges in the John Wayne role.) So what have the Old West and the Duke got to do with Neymar Jr? Well, according to João Paulo de Jesus Lopes, the best man to stop Neymar in his tracks is John Wayne. The vice-chairman of São Paulo Football Club made this humorous remark on a Paulista radio station in April 2012. A joke – but only just. The vice-chairman knew there was truth behind his words, as his team had just been brutally beaten by Santos in the Paulista semifinals for the third year running. Neymar had scored three goals in the match and no one managed to get close to him.

It was on 29 April, in a match in Morumbi. Santos were in light blue, São Paulo in white. Before the spectators had even sat down, it was 1–0 to Santos. In the third minute, Alan Kardec received the ball in the area and Paulo Miranda brought him down. Referee Paulo Cesar de Oliveira blew for a penalty. Neymar took it: a long run-up and he slammed it into the top corner. No chance for Denis. It was Neymar's 100th goal for Santos. Three years and 50 days had passed since his debut with Peixe on 7 March 2009 and Neymar Jr had already joined the elite group of Santos goalscorers.

Neymar's 100th goal in official competitions had come three months earlier, on the day of his twentieth birthday, 5 February 2012, against Palmeiras in the Presidente Prudente Stadium: a header to register his first goal of the year and the 100th of his career. Of those, 82 were with Santos, eight with the Brazil senior side, nine with the Under-20s and one with the Under-17s.

O Globo examined his track record: 70 had come from his right foot, 21 from his left foot, seven from his head, one was scored with his shoulder and one with his chest. Seventy-two goals had come from within the area, ten from outside the area, sixteen from penalties and two from free kicks.

The newspaper outlined the goalscoring progress made by Neymar: fifteen goals in his first professional season (2009), 44 in 2010 and 40 in 2011. But it was not just statistics: comparisons with other players were made.

Messi, for example, achieved his 100th goal at 22 years and three months. Ronaldo, on the other hand, achieved his century a little earlier than Neymar: 'O Fenómeno' scored his 100th goal when he was nineteen years and four days old. Pelé was only seventeen years and nine months – but he had become a professional footballer at fifteen. The milestone of 100 goals is a useful tool for journalists in Brazil to compare Messi to Neymar – albeit that it is not a fair comparison, as there is an abyss between the football played by the Argentinian and that played by the Brazilian. And Messi is a three times winner of the Ballon d'Or. But nevertheless, Neymar reached his 100th goal before Messi.

Carrying on, we come to Neymar's 101st goal with Santos, which was like a ripe pear ready to fall from the tree. It came in the 31st minute of the semi-final match against São Paulo. Rodolfo, the Tricolour number 3, failed to clear properly. The ball landed at Ganso's feet and he threaded the ball to Neymar. The number 11 skipped past Miranda and, as Denis came off his line, Neymar fired the ball into the bottom left corner.

This prompted the first remake of the series: Neymar Jr danced the corner flag dance of Jorge dos Santos Filho, aka Juary. Juary was a Santos striker who went on to play in Europe in the early 1980s, first in Italy (Avellino, Inter, Ascoli and Cremonese) then in Portugal. In 1978, at Morumbi against São Paulo, Juary scored and then celebrated with his now famous dance.

For Neymar, it was not only a call back to that famous dance, it was a tribute to Juary's 101 goals scored in four seasons with Santos (1976–79 and 1989).

In the second half, Neymar made it 3–1 and Santos fell back. Neymar went over the top with flowery dribbling and dramatic falls (Emerson Leão, the Tricolour coach, advised Neymar at the end of the match to not repeat such a show of tricks and skills when playing for Brazil), but the end result was the desired one. Peixe was in the final of the Paulistão for the fourth year running.

In the first of those years, 2009, their attempt failed as they lost to Ronaldo's Corinthians. But in 2010 and 2011 they won the title, against Santo André and *Timão* respectively. Now they had the chance to bring home the club's 20th state title and be champions for the third year in a row.

The first leg was scheduled for 6 May: an away match against Guarani in Morumbi. A goal from Ganso and two from Neymar settled it. Santos's number 11 celebrated his first goal of the match with a remake of Serginho Chulapa's celebrations. He ran along the goal line, wobbled as though running out of breath and then collapsed to the ground: Chulapa, who played for Santos as a striker in 1983–84, 1986 and 1990, had celebrated in this way when he scored the goal that won Peixe the Paulistão in 1984.

The kid from Mogi das Cruzes took his tally to 105 with the second goal against Guarani. He overtook Serginho Chulapa and João Paulo (1977–84, 1992) to become the best goalscorer in the post-Pelé era. Neymar was pleased to have reached another milestone.

O Chulapa did not mind that his record had been broken: 'I am not jealous of my record, especially as it was Neymar who broke it. He is only twenty and still needs to develop. We are expecting a lot from him. I was choked with emotion seeing him score that goal and pay tribute to me. It is nice to see that Neymar remembers the history of the club he loves and acknowledges the work we have done. I cannot wait for next Sunday. The second leg of the final.'

The *Globoesporte* reported on the second leg of the final and a day of celebration – of Santos's centenary and third Paulistão in a row, marked by three goals from Neymar:

'We used to listen to our parents and grandparents tell us the story of the future of Pelé at Santos; now we have to add the story of Neymar at Santos. It is a story which has a new chapter as of this Sunday 13 May 2012.

'Neymar's Santos won 4–2 against Guarani and claimed its third Paulista league in a row. Something no one else has been able to achieve since Pelé's Santos of 1967, 1968 and 1969.'

The black commemorative T-shirt bore the legend *Não canso de ser tri. Campeonato paulista 2010 2011 2012* ('I never tire of three. Paulista league 2010, 2011 and 2012') . Neymar was wearing it on the stage. On his head, another tribute: a white headband with the words '100 per cent Jesus' on it. He ran round the pitch, dribbled round TV cameras and photographers. He shouted 'Olé' at each slalom. In the stands, the fans started laughing.

The celebrations at Morumbi carried on. Neymar was in his pants; the only other bit of clothing he was wearing was his headband. The party had only just begun. Back at Santos, the team had a meal together in a *churrasqueria* and then on to the club. Neymar took his white Porsche to the club and was one of the first to arrive.

In the nightclub, 'Neymarzetes', there was a free bar and an exclusive guest list. The DJ cranked up the tunes and there were two bands as well, Batukada and Revelação, funk and pagode music. Neymar got on the stage and sang '*Eu sou o cara pra você*' ('I am the guy for you'), a song by his singer friend, Thiaguinho. At 5.30am the party ended.

The party for the Brasilerão awards ceremony, on 3 December 2012, in the HSBC Brazil hall in São Paulo, was more contained. The show was dominated by Fluminense, who won the national league title, and Fred, who took home three trophies. In 2011, Neymar, sporting his grey gilet, white shirt and red tie, had been voted best player in the league but this year he had to make do with the best striker award and the *Globolinha*, the award given for the best goal: this was for the number 11's goal scored against Atlético-MG on 17 October, on Neymar's 200th appearance for Santos. Neymar received a hearty round of applause when he took the stage. He accepted the trophy and said, 'It is a great season, the best of my career.' He had scored 43 goals, won a historic third consecutive Paulistão and the Recopa Sul-Americana (won in September against Universidad de Chile) with Santos, and taken a whole host of individual awards including 'best player in the Americas', a title bestowed on Neymar by the Uruguayan newspaper *El País* for the second year running.

A great year indeed but there was a gaping hole. Not in the Brasilerão, although Santos finished in eighth place, nor in the Libertadores, where Santos exited in the semi-finals against Corinthians, but in the 2012 Olympics. Brazil had never won the Olympic gold medal: it was, and remains, the only trophy Brazil have not won. Many greats have tried – Ronaldo, Rivaldo, Bebeto – but none has succeeded. Ronaldinho tried at the Beijing Olympics in 2008 but it did not work out and in the end he was consoled by Messi after Argentina thrashed Brazil 3–0 in the semi-finals.

In London it seemed like the heavens were aligning. Mano Menezes called on all the young talent for the London Olympics: Neymar, Paulo Henrique, Lucas, Oscar, Pato, Rafael da Silva; and he strengthened the team with three champions: Thiago Silva, Marcelo and Hulk. On paper, Brazil looked as though they had it in the bag.

The road to Wembley started on 26 July 2012 against Egypt in the Millennium Stadium in Cardiff. Brazil put on a fantastic show for the fans and were 3–0 up after half an hour, Neymar scoring the third with a header. In the second half, Egypt clawed two back and the atmosphere was tense right until the end.

The other two countries in Group C were Belarus and New Zealand. At Old Trafford, against Belarus, Brazil were a goal down but then Neymar provided an assist for Pato before himself converting a free kick. A third goal came via a flick of the heel from Oscar. New Zealand were next. Brazil were already through but won this game too, 3–0, without breaking sweat.

In the quarter-finals it was Honduras; Brazil won 3–2. And the semi-final against South Korea was a relative breeze: 3–0. Brazil were in the final for the first time since 1988.

Neymar had been immense throughout the five matches, with three goals and four assists. He was the second highest scorer in the team, Leandro Damião taking first place with six goals. Neymar was happy but said that his role was to do the best for Brazil, like all the other players, and help win the gold medal. He said he had not slept after the semi-final against South Korea but he had no problems with sleep now; however, he thought he might go without a night's sleep if Brazil managed to win the gold.

Neymar was to get his sleep, though. On 11 August 2012, Mexico won the final and denied Brazil the gold medal they were so desperate to win. Oribe Peralta was man of the match at Wembley Stadium. He scored in the 28th second of the match following an unbelievable mistake from Rafael and Brazil went to pieces. In the first half, they got nowhere. In the second half, they got going again and Neymar got the best chance: a good move from Oscar and the ball was about 10 metres from the goal on the left side but Neymar spooned the ball over the bar.

Peralta, the Mexican number 9, put the final nail in the coffin in the 75th minute. Unmarked in the area, he headed in for 2–0. Hulk pulled one back in the first minute of injury time but it was too late. Mexico had won the gold medal and Brazil had lost a third Olympic final, following their failures in 1984 against France and in 1988 against the Soviet Union. While the Mexicans were celebrating, Neymar cried on the Wembley turf.

The next day the Brazilian newspapers had a field day. They talked of a poor performance and a second debacle like the 2011 Copa America. Doubts were cast over the number 11's future ahead of the upcoming World Cup in Brazil. There was a lot to cry about …

Chapter 20

Thanks all for everything

There are those who think Neymar should go to Europe this year.

There are those who think it would be better for him to wait until after the World Cup.

Those who think it would be a mistake to go.

Those who think it would be a fiasco.

Those who think he needs more experience.

Those who think he is not mature enough.

Those who think he should go to Real Madrid.

Those who think Barcelona would be better.

Those who love Pep Guardiola.

Those who think the Premier League is the best.

Those who say his head is in the clouds.

Those who say he is a national treasure.

Those who say he thinks more about his hair than his football.

Those who are sick and tired of him.

Those who do not care.

Those who only care about Santos.

Those who just want him to be happy.

Those who do not know what to say.

This was not an exaggeration. In the first five months of 2013, there were hundreds of opinions on what Neymar should do. The daily debate about Paulistão football and the national team (now managed by Luiz Felipe Scolari) was superseded by talk about Neymar.

Will or he won't he? Will he stay with Santos or will he choose one of the big European clubs who have been chasing him for years? Is it absolutely necessary for him to experience Europe?

Neymar was bombarded with questions until he felt nauseous. His response was more or less the same every time.

For example, on 4 March 2013, Neymar Jr was a guest on the TV show *Programa do Jô* on the Globo Network (a US-style, David Letterman-style talk show).

Jô Soares, the presenter, a larger-than-life and highly entertaining figure, greeted Neymar with a hug and a kiss. He asked him to take off his black baseball cap to see his haircut: a peroxide tuft in the style of Marilyn Monroe, which got a few giggles from the 'Neymarzetes' (Neymar's young, female fans) in the audience.

The chat started. Not even five minutes had passed and there it was: the question of all questions. Soares launched into it: 'Everyone asks me, everyone is asking themselves, when are you going to Europe, before or after the World Cup? It looks like Barcelona has given an advance as a guarantee. Can you comment on that or are you not allowed?' Neymar smiled and said, 'I have been answering this question for years. I am happy at Santos and I want to see out my contract to the end of next year when it expires. Of course, I dream of going to Europe. It is the dream of any young boy, any footballer. But everyone has their time. Some go very young, others later. My moment has not yet come.'

Jô Soares was not deterred and kept pressing for an answer: 'But if you went to Europe which team would you like to play for?' Neymar was vague in his answer: 'There is not a team I would like to play for in particular …' Soares was not for letting up: 'Don't lie to me, boy, a bit of respect please.' Neymar laughed and tried another well-used tactic: 'When I was a little boy, I played a lot with my PlayStation and, just like lots of my friends, I put my name in the Barcelona, Real Madrid and Chelsea teams. I didn't have a favourite team as my idols played for different teams and I liked all of them.'

Jô was not satisfied and he kept banging the drum: 'Real Madrid or Barcelona?' Neymar laughed nervously but kept his nerve: 'They are two great clubs.' The anchor was not giving in that easily: 'Perhaps Bayern Munich, where Guardiola is going.' Juninho came straight back: 'Another great club and a great coach.'

Jô Soares looked him straight in the eye and asked, 'Are you a footballer or a politician?' The audience laughed raucously.

He was not a politician but he did not deviate from the script. He had learned his part and repeated it about ten days later in a TV interview with *Esporte Espetacular*.

Neymar was not budging. Without blushing, Neymar confirmed he was going out with Bruna Marquezine, a seventeen-year-old actress born in Duque de Caxias, a city in the state of Rio de Janeiro, famous for acting the role of 'Salete' in the TV soap *Mulheres Apaixonadas*. (This love story was to end on 11 February 2014 – not even a year. Bruna confirmed the end of the romance in a press conference. The reason given for the break-up was the long distance, once Neymar was in Spain. The actress deleted all her photos of Neymar from her social media pages.)

Neymar was happy to talk about it and explained that they had no intention of hiding from the paparazzi. A hint about where he was going in the future? Nothing doing. He was as quiet as a mouse.

In the bars, the stadium, on TV, the fans, critics and journalists, professional footballers and ex-pros could not stop talking about it.

Pelé argued that it was not Neymar's age that was the problem but his maturity and physical condition. In England, Italy and Germany, the game was played hard. The referees let things flow more. You needed to have experience to play in the European leagues and at that level. O Rei said that Santos needed Neymar and that therefore it would be better if he stayed, but if he wanted to go, he should go to Barcelona; it was perfect for him. And, just for good measure, he gave another piece of advice to the young Neymar: he said he should worry less about his hairstyle and more about his football.

Ronaldo, on the other hand, told him to go: 'If a Brazilian player does not weigh himself up against the European leagues, he will not be a complete player.'

Romario, the ex-Barcelona player, now a federal politician in Brasilia, could not see a reason for Neymar to go, other than a financial reason. He said the Spanish league was easier than the Brazilian league. He thought Neymar would not learn much playing in Europe.

Walter Casagrande Junior, the 50-year-old former centre forward for Corinthians, Torino and Ascoli, now a commentator for Globo Network, confessed that he had changed his mind on the matter. Sitting on the steps of the Nyon stadium in Switzerland, where Brazil were training ahead of a friendly against Italy in March 2013, Casagrande Junior explained, 'I have always thought Neymar should stay in Brazil as he had no need to go to Europe, but today I believe that he has reached the top in Brazilian football. He needs that international experience. He has to play in a more challenging league like the Spanish *Liga*, the English Premier League or the Italian *Serie A*. He needs to go now. He will be a lot better prepared for the 2014 World Cup.'

The view of one of the great Brazilian opinionists was completely the opposite: Juca Kfouri, the editor of *Folha* in São Paulo, commented, 'No. I am not one of those who believes that he should play in Europe. For me, this is the conformist position. Football in our country should create the conditions where Neymar can stay in Brazil.

'The Brazil team has won three World Cups, 1958, 1962 and 1970, with a team that was made of players that played in the Brazilian leagues. Things have changed since then. The world is global and so is football. But I believe that today with our economic boom compared to the European economic crisis, we have the chance to keep our players here. It is not just by chance that in the last few years, more than 1,100 players have come home, reversing the trend which had been in place for some time. There is more money in football. Just think, the earnings of the top 100 Brazilian clubs have surpassed US$396 million in 2003 and US$1,400 million in 2012. The Corinthians saw their income grow by 481 per cent whereas Santos has reached a record of 548 per cent. It is a crying shame that the CBF has put in place a policy which is harmful to the interests of football in our country. The CBF has focused for years on transforming the national team but has put the development of club football, like Pelé's Santos, Garrincha's Botafogo, Corinthians and Zico's Flamengo, on the back burner. When you go into a sports shop today, you find the Brazil top, but you also find the shirt for Bayern, Milan, Barcelona, Manchester United and even Boca or River but not those of our clubs. If a player like Neymar were to stay in Brazil, he could raise the level of our tournaments, our football and he could help sell it all over the world.'

The views were varied and all documented. However, the debate was not just limited to the question of Europe, and when Neymar might go. The player was also under fire. And it was not just Pelé who was giving him a ticking off. Many thought that, after three fabulous seasons, his performances were going downhill. Neymar was not shining so bright any more, either for Santos or Brazil. He was agitated; he fought with the referees, who he felt did not look out for him; he argued with opposition defenders who marked him too closely; he scored fewer goals. Why?

The assumptions and interpretations were varied. It started because Neymar turned himself into a pop star. He appeared on TV, he went out with girls who ended up on the cover of magazines, he attended parties, the lot; Neymar Jr had entered the world of showbiz. And that was not all.

The thirteen sponsors he had racked up wanted their piece of the action and required him to attend events and promos and to make TV advertisements. Neymar, at only 21, had the world at his feet. The list of clubs that were knocking on his door with offers was enough to make you dizzy, and it grew longer every day: from Barcelona to Chelsea; from Real Madrid to Manchester City. Some were prepared to go to great lengths to get the star on their team. How can someone possibly concentrate on football when all that is going on in the background?

Every time Neymar agreed to an interview, he denied that he was distracted by the questions around his future. He said you could not have ten out of ten on your school record all of the time. Sometimes you had a bad day and a bad match to boot.

A missed goal opportunity would be interpreted as a sign that Neymar was not fully focused on football or Santos, and therefore he wanted to go. A goal scored would be cited as evidence that it was too easy for him, so he needed to go, and it was better he left now.

The pressure was immense. The constant questioning and commentary around his future was enough to tire anyone. On top of that, Santos was not working out. Neymar had lost his great friend, Paulo Henrique. Ganso had left for São Paulo.

The emotion was clear for all to see when the two met as rivals for the first time on 3 February 2013 at Vila Belmiro. Neymar's reaction to the Santos fans who wolf-whistled Ganso, accused him of being a mercenary, threw coins at him and tried to attack him, was unforgettable: he defended his friend and asked the fans to keep calm.

Walter Montillo, the Argentinian Santos had bought from Cruzeiro to replace Paulo Henrique, did not achieve the level of performance that Ramalho expected.

Santos could not get into gear. Peixe were suffering, but still progressing in the Paulistão. In the quarter-finals they managed to beat Palmeiras on penalties. The same against Mogi Mirim in the semi-finals. Santos scraped through to the Paulistão final for the fifth year running.

Neymar had scored twelve goals, one less than the leading goalscorer for the tournament, Ponte Preta's William, but he did not manage to score in the quarters or the semis.

Nor the final.

The first leg at Pacaembu on 12 May ended 2–1 to Corinthians. The second leg, seven days later in Vila Belmiro, was a 1–1 draw, with Cicero and Danilo scoring. Santos's dreams were dashed. It would have been a new record for Peixe and the Paulistão. The fans were left with the bittersweet taste of an historic victory that had slipped through their hands, and the shame of seeing the Corinthians' fans celebrate in their stadium. It was not a good day for Neymar. He was nervous and argumentative. He lost the ball fourteen times (out of 40 balls received) and ended the game without having had one shot on goal.

The newspapers wrote that Neymar had spent the last week negotiating with Barcelona. Everyone believed that this would be the last final that he would play for Santos. Those in the know about Neymar's future were convinced that the agreement would be signed within the week. The countdown of matches began: 22 May against Joinville in the Brazil Cup; 26 May against Flamengo in the first round of Brasilerão matches.

The cup match at Vila Belmiro was played under a downpour and ended 0–0; Santos went through thanks to the advantage they had from the first leg. Neymar played well but did not score. It was his seventh match without a goal.

The night before the game, at the Paulista Federation party, Neymar had been voted the 'Paulistão star' for the fourth year running. When the smartly dressed Santos forward walked off the stage with the trophy in his hand, *Lance* asked the question for the umpteenth time. Neymar calmly replied that his future was here and that he was staying with Santos. He added, 'A new championship [the Brasilerão] starts and I hope we can win it.'

On Friday 24 May, Neymar visited the offices of NR Sport at Santos HQ. He talked with his father and Wagner Ribeiro before reaching Vila Belmiro. On the chairman's desk were two offers: one from Real Madrid and one from Barcelona. When he left the stadium at one in the morning, there were lots of people and TV cameras waiting for father and son. Neymar Pai spoke first: 'I will speak with my son and we will decide together. We will try and help Santos as best we can.'

Neymar, looking tired, said, 'We are going home to rest.

We will decide what is best with a clear head. I am pleased about the offers from these two great clubs.'

The next day, Juninho went to the CT Rei Pelé and, before training, he told the coach and his teammates that a decision had been reached. He was going to Barcelona. Neymar then tied a camera to his head and filmed what would be his last session with Santos.

At the end of training, Neymar wrote on the walls of the changing rooms '*Eu Vou' Mas … Eu Volto!*' (I am going but I'll be back!). A helicopter was waiting to take him to a resort on Tabatinga beach in Caraguatatuba on the São Paulo coast. He was best man at Paulo Henrique's wedding. The ex-Santos number 10 was marrying Giovanna Costi.

Neymar posed with the newlyweds for the customary photos. He was wearing a grey suit with a light blue tie. Later, Neymar got on the stage and entertained alongside singer Diego Faria. He did not shy away from dancing either and got down to '*Elas ficam Loucas*'. At the end of the party, Neymar headed to Brasilia where he would be playing his last match with Santos in the Mané Garrincha Stadium.

But first he sent a farewell letter to his fans via Twitter, Facebook and Instagram. It was ten in the evening on 25 May 2013:

'I am here with family and friends who are helping me write these words … I cannot wait until Monday … My family and friends know what my decision is. On Monday I will sign for Barcelona. I want to thank all the Santos fans for these nine incredible years. My feelings for the club and the fans will never die. They are eternal! Only a club like Santos could give me all that I have had both on and off the pitch. I am grateful to the Peixe fans who have supported me, even in hard times. Titles, goals, dribbling, celebrations and songs that the fans have created for me will be with me forever in my heart … I shall play the match in Brasilia tomorrow.

'I want one last chance to play for Santos and hear the fans shout my name … as the anthem goes, it is an honour that not everyone can have. It is a strange time for me, sad [to say goodbye] and happy [for the new challenge ahead]. God bless my choice … I will always be Santos!!'

On Sunday 26 May, at 4.00pm in the new Mané Garrincha Stadium in Brasilia (a stadium built for the 2014 World Cup), the first round of Brasilerão matches got under way and the last act of Neymar's adventure with Santos began. Nine years after arriving at Peixe, five years after his debut in the famous white shirt, and now with 229 matches played, 138 goals scored and six titles won (three Paulistão, one Brazil Cup, one Libertadores and one Recopa Sul-Americana), Neymar da Silva Santos said goodbye to the club that had seen him grow up.

The match was a sell-out: 63,501 spectators for a total gate of 6,948,710 reais – a record in the history of Brazilian football. The ratings for the live broadcast via Globo Network were higher than ever before. It was an emotional and tear-ful Sunday.

In the changing rooms before the match, Neymar, next to Rafael and Victor Andrade, formed a circle with his team-mates and, with tears rolling down his face, he said, 'I want to thank all of you for the moments we've had together, the training sessions, the victories and the titles. It is not easy for me to leave you but I am living my dream. I wanted to play today to have one last chance to play 90 minutes with you, irrespective of whether we win or lose. Thank you all for everything. I will always be your fan and I wish you all the best. I will always be your friend who will support you, wherever I may be.'

The national anthem boomed around the stadium and the emotion rose up within Neymar. More tears. It was time for the match to get under way and Neymar passed the ball for his last kick-off. The match finished 0–0 and Neymar could not manage a goal. Afterwards, at the edge of the pitch, Neymar sat with a Flamengo shirt around his shoulders, clearly choked with emotion. He thanked the fans and when he was asked what it would be like playing with Messi, he replied, 'Playing with Messi, Iniesta and Xavi is a great honour. Dani Alves, as well, he kept telling me to go to Barcelona.'

That evening, on *Domingão do Faustão*, Neymar spoke about his decision to go to the Catalan club: 'Every kid has a dream. Some dream of becoming a footballer, others a dentist or a reporter. I had one dream: I wanted to become a professional footballer. I've done it. Today, Barcelona is letting me live the dream of a young kid with the face of a man, I am a father after all. The dream of playing for a club like that is amazing.'

Chapter 21

NJR

You learn a lot walking up the four flights of stairs at the offices of NR Sports, housed in a white building with the black and yellow company logo on the façade at number 56, Avenida Ana Costa in Santos. Here, in these new offices opened in May 2013, a group of twenty manage the image, wealth, public relations and e-commerce for Neymar Junior's official products. The spiral staircase and green carpets are a nice summary of the career and brand of the prodigy. There are photos of his father wearing the União Mogi shirt, a portrait of his grandad Arnaldo (an amateur footballer), and a maxim which father and son repeat religiously before a game: 'Every weapon forged against you will fail, and you will condemn every language which judges you. This is the way of the servants of the Lord and their right. Oracle of the Lord.' Five of these words have been immortalised in one of Neymar's tattoos, together with 'Blessed' and the names of Nadine, Rafaela and David Lucca, and a cross with a crown and biblical verse (verses 24 and 27 of the letters to the Corinthians).

As you walk up the stairs, there are group photos taken with his futsal teams, trophies, boots, medals, the shirt he wore when he won the Libertadores, large photos and the covers of magazines seen by half the world: *Time* magazine ('Neymar, the Next Pelé'), *Select* ('Futebol arte'). Every step is a new phase of the player's life. At the top there are

Subbuteo players with Neymar's face, a 'Neymar Jr. Football Club' game by Gulliver and a doll reminiscent of Barbie's Ken with two Brazil kits and two pairs of boots, made by Cosmokids.

There is no doubt that Neymar sells. There are all sorts of products with his image on them, including notebooks, mobile phone covers, cups, cushions, puzzles, jeans, drinks, sportswear, football boots, model cars, scented sweets and whatever else you can think of.

Neymar is a magnet: he pulls in all the sponsors just like he attracts the Neymarzetes. There are fourteen businesses that have targeted Neymar since he started at Santos: Santander, Nike, Panasonic, Unilever, Claro, Red Bull, Lupo, Tenys Pé Baruel, AmBev, Bateris Heliar, Volkswagen, Guaraná, GSK and Mentos. These are the companies that have chosen Neymar as the man to represent their brand. It worked: in 2012, adverts starring Neymar appeared on TV 5,472 times.

And it still works: Takumi Kajisha, executive director for Panasonic Corporation, confirmed that seeing is believing: 'Our brand has become more popular thanks to Neymar. He has done wonders for us in Brazil and now, with his arrival at Barcelona, he can help us on a global scale because Barcelona is well known in Asia and Africa. Neymar, as our ambassador in these markets, can achieve even more than he already has done.'

The figures are impressive: according to *France Football*, in 2012 Neymar earned €20 million, 70 per cent of which was from sponsorship; a figure which put him at fifth best paid footballer in the world, just behind David Beckham (€36 million), Leo Messi (€35 million), Cristiano Ronaldo (€30 million) and Samuel Eto'o (€24 million). This fortune is managed by NR Sport, founded in 2006 by Neymar Pai and his wife Nadine. The group encompasses NN Administration to manage the finances, NN Store to manage e-commerce and sale of other Neymar-related products, and NN Participações to manage the star's investments.

At the helm of the group, Neymar Pai, with the help of lawyers, marketing experts and financial consultants, looks to invest the earnings of Juninho to 'provide for the future five or six generations of the da Silva Santos family'. The investments are in property, treasury bonds and shares in well-established companies. The risk profile is low because, according to Neymar Pai, 'Our objective is not to earn money on the markets.'

One thing is clear and that is that the 'NJR' brand created by the PR agency Lodocca is going great guns, just like the motto *Ousadia y Alegria* ('courage and joy') which comes from a conversation with Neymar's best friend Thiaguinho, a former member of the band Exaltasamba. These words define his way of playing: the joy of being on the ball and the courage of attacking dribbling. Neymar had these words stitched into his boots on the eve of the 2011 *Copa America*; it also became the title of a Thiaguinho album in 2012.

According to *SportsPro* magazine, *NJR: Ousadia y Alegria* represents the most lucrative and commercially valuable sports star on the planet. The magazine places Neymar in first place ahead of golfer Rory McIlroy, Lionel Messi and Usain Bolt. Neymar is an impressive media phenomenon both in terms of image and economic value. On the social networking sites, on TV, in music and even in comics he is there. He has 13 million fans on Facebook, 8 million followers on Twitter and 2.5 million on Instagram. He has not reached Cristiano Ronaldo's figures yet (more than 64 million on Facebook) or Leo Messi's (50 million on Facebook) but he is on the right track. Neymar is a hyperactive user of social media, which can't but help. He always has a photo to post, a story to tell, a face to pull. He tweets nine times a day on average, which is decidedly higher than others like him.

Let's not forget his own language: *eh toiss* – 'we are the friends'. And what about music: his goal celebration dance moves to the music of '*Ai Se Eu Te Pego*' ('Ah, when I get my hands on you') by Michel Teló or '*Eu Quero Tchu Eu Quero Tchá*' ('I want you') by João Luca & Marcelo have gone viral on the internet and have led to the worldwide success of the two songs.

Neymar has been in telenovelas such as *Amor à vida* and *Malhação*, and in TV series like *Aline* on TV Globo, guest starring as himself. He did a similar guest appearance in the kids' program *Carrossel* for SBT, where he played the coach of a group of kids visiting Vila Belmiro with their teacher.

There is a Panini comic aimed at seven to eleven year olds called *Neymar Jr*. The first issue, titled '*Um Garoto de talento*' ('A talented kid') came out on 30 May 2013. It was illustrated by Mauricio de Sousa, creator of Mônica and Cebolinha: two characters who had mesmerised entire generations in Brazil. De Sousa had already done comics of Pelé and Ronaldinho; Neymar was the obvious next step. The comic depicts him with his Mohican hair and his surfboard, going on lots of adventures on the beach and on the pitch. He is with his friends and family too.

Allan Sieber is a comic artist as well but his comic strips are not aimed at younger readers: they are sarcastic, acerbic, with a hint of black humour; they hit hard against Brazilian society. His criticisms of Brazilian society effuse from his comics and books like *Tudo Mais ou Menos Verdade – O Jornalismo Investigativo, Tendencioso e Ficcional* ('All more or less true – investigative journalism, biased and fictional').

In Rio de Janeiro, at a showing of his artwork, the bulky

bearded Sieber, originally from Porto Alegre, does not hold back when talking about Neymar's image. He is deliberately provocative and heretical. He says that Neymar's success is down to being *O Cara* ('the face, the symbol') of the 'C' class Brazilian, or rather the class that is climbing up the social ladder in Brazil thanks to the economic boom of the last few years – but above all thanks to the availability of credit on deferred payment plans. Nike goods, Beat headphones and even plastic surgery that can be paid for in 30, 40 or 50 instalments. Sieber talks of 'A generation of young people, necking a bottle of red wine, consumers who love the aesthetics of rappers, bling-bling, designer clothes, TV series, funk, pagode and *sertanejo universitário* ('backcountry university') music, who dream of becoming Neymar one day, of earning gazillions and hanging out with TV actresses. A generation which is beginning to understand the insurmountable distance between their hopes and goals and the reality of achieving them. A generation which, like the entire country, after the dream of the World Cup and Olympics in 2016, could end up like the Titanic.'

On the subject of Neymar, football and consumerism, another artist, 52-year-old Leda Catunda from São Paulo, does not agree. His works on the white walls of the Museum of Modern Art in Rio de Janeiro are a collage of logos, shirts, numbers, colours and materials from the world of football. 'Santos', a piece from 2012, the biggest at the exhibition (3.4 metres by 4 metres) merges pictures of Pelé, Neymar, the Triple title and the Libertadores. It combines the club's shield, taken from a rug, with a piece of curtain from the Peixe showers. Catunda says of Neymar, 'He belongs to a new generation which places great emphasis on how you look and your image. Just think of his hair, his tattoos, his look and his clothing. He is nevertheless always polite, religious, friendly and available with the public. Kids identify with him and his colours because in a mass-market, standardised world, people need identity, a model to follow. Sport, and football in particular, offers a democratic opportunity to identify yourself with something which, here in Brazil, has the same role as religion.' He talks about consumer society and adds, 'It is normal and integral to this generation. The order is: work, earn and consume as much as possible. And consumerism in football is emotional, pure desire which is satisfied when you buy the brand which represents a value. There is no longer "beauty" in aesthetics, there is only freedom to choose what you want to buy. Everything is sold with a logo of a team or a footballing icon like Neymar.'

Francisco Bosco, a poet, writer and doctor in literary theory at the Federal University in Rio de Janeiro, is convinced that Neymar embodies 'the essence of South American footballing talent, the gift of football, the mystery that is dribbling – qualities which had been lost for some time.' Bosco goes on: 'This is why he is the "hope of a return to that golden era of football, a renaissance in Brazilian football after the fall from grace over the last ten years".' According to Bosco, off the pitch, Neymar 'shows a charisma which neither Messi has nor Ronaldinho had. You can only compare him to David Beckham and Cristiano Ronaldo. Yes, Neymar belongs to a globalised football and is a celebrity in his own right – something which, in Brazil, began in the 1990s with Ronaldo, O Fenómeno, the first Brazilian to represent a similar transformation. Neymar is going down this path. At Barcelona he will be skyrocketed to the absolute heights of stardom.'

Chapter 22
A special day

Happiness, dream, heartfelt emotion, family, help, God, Messi, Messi again, and, once more, *Messi.*

These were the words that Neymar Jr repeated on 3 June 2013. At 6.40pm, he appeared in the middle of Camp Nou and took the microphone; at 7.45 in the 'Auditorium 1899', Neymar answered the questions of the 122 journalists with official passes. Neymar, in broken Catalan and Portuguese, explained his happiness and joy to be able to stand there at that historic club and realise his dreams. He thanked God, explained that he had chosen to come to Barcelona not for money but to help the team win and to help Messi and the others be the best in the world, and to help Messi win lots more Ballons d'Or.

Young Neymar was polite, or rather he read the script that had been drummed into him – i.e. if you wanted to come to Barcelona and Camp Nou and win the sympathy of the people, the club and the fans, it was better to tread carefully, enter quietly and pay homage to the great players at the club and the undisputed genius that is Leo Messi. Neymar had been informed that his life at Barcelona would depend on how he got along with Messi. Ronaldinho, Eto'o, Ibrahimovic and David Villa had all had to pack their bags when it came to the crunch. Better to bow your head and not overshadow the champ. Neymar was humble and sometimes overdid it. So much so that some of the Brazilian journalists lost their rag and sniped, 'Fine that you will help Messi to be the best in the world and win Ballons d'Or but have you forgotten that there is a World Cup in a year's time?' Neymar moved away from praising the Barcelona fans and firmly answered, 'Helping Messi to be the best in the world has nothing to do with winning the World Cup. Just like all my teammates, we want to win.'

The polite young Neymar arrived at El Prat airport in Barcelona at 1.02pm, one hour and 45 minutes behind schedule, having boarded a private jet at the Antonio Carlos Jobim airport in Rio de Janeiro straight after playing for Brazil in a friendly against England. The Maracaná Stadium had been refurbished and updated for the World Cup and Neymar had received a nice surprise: the number 10 on his shirt. A symbolic number in football, it was the number Pelé wore for years and years. Felipão – Luiz Felipe Scolari – offered it to him; it was a gesture that showed the faith he has in Neymar. The young forward was to be the team's totem and leader.

Neymar played well in the first half. After ten minutes he had already taken three shots against Joe Hart, the England goalkeeper, but to no avail. In the second half, Neymar went off the boil. The fans continued to shout his name but his tricks failed to come off. The match ended 2–2 and Brazil's new number 10 missed out once again. He would get another chance.

The CBF gave their blessing and Neymar flew off to Catalunya to sign the contract and be introduced to the fans.

The Gulfstream G550 of Julio Iglesias (a devout Real Madrid fan), hired by Barcelona, hosted on board Neymar Pai, Neymar Jr's girlfriend Bruna Marquezine, his childhood friends Gil Cebolla, Gustavo, Gui Pita and Joclecio, who call themselves *parças* (short for *parceiros*: 'partners'). His staff were also there: Neymar's bodyguard Ismael, a huge black guy, and Eduardo Musa who manages Neymar's image.

Twelve hours later, the jet landed at Barcelona airport. Raúl Sanllehí was there to meet the Neymar party. Sanllehí was the man who had gone to Santos to finalise the deal for Neymar's signature. A minibus and two black vans took Neymar and his entourage to the Princesa Sofia Hotel, right next to Camp Nou. Nadine, his mother, and Rafaela, his sister, were waiting for him there. They had been in Barcelona for a week already, looking for a house.

Friends and family took a break. The *tour de force* for Neymar commenced. At 2.00pm, Neymar was smiling for the cameras next to the Barcelona crest, wearing his unmistakable cap on backwards and the white T-shirt of his sponsor, Nike.

Fifteen minutes later, Neymar walked into the Palau Blaugrana where he met his compatriot, Marcelinho Huertas, a player for Barça Regal, the basketball club. Then it was off to the hospital for the first part of his medical: radiography, echography and magnetic resonance.

At 3.29pm, more medical tests: this time at the Ciutat Esportiva de Sant Joan Despí. Neymar received the green light and was certified fit and able to play.

At 4.15 there was finally a break to get something to eat with his relatives and friends.

From Ciutat Esportiva he was taken to Camp Nou, where, at 6.05pm, he signed the contract tying him to Barcelona for five seasons. His salary would be €7 million a year with a further €2 million in performance bonuses (for games played and titles won). The break clause was set at €190 million.

Sandro Rosell, the chairman of FC Barcelona, signed first and then Neymar Jr and Neymar Pai followed. Every page was signed under the watchful eyes of the photographers and cameramen. Then the customary handshake between the chairman and the new star. Photos and more photos, with the vice-chairman and the director of sports, next to the Barcelona shirt.

At 6.20pm, the young Brazilian was in the changing rooms of Camp Nou to receive his kit. His locker would be next to two of his compatriots: Adriano and Dani Alves. The grand finale loomed ever closer.

It was 6.37pm when Neymar Jr walked along the tunnel and up the steps to one of the most famous pitches in the world.

The Camp Nou gates were meant to open to fans at 4.00pm but the 3,000 fans waiting outside made the gate-keeper open the gates fifteen minutes early. Slowly the stands began to fill up; the sunny and humid heat lingered in the air. The stands filled with people, banners and colours: so many young boys and girls from the city and the hinterland. So many Brazilians and South Americans. They had brought banners, flags, shirts, drinks and sandwiches to pass the time. There were tourists and foreigners who wanted to make the most of a special moment and had been to the Barcelona store to see the shirt (numberless) of Neymar Jr, next to that of Leo Messi (number 10).

On the big screen, the words *Benvingut Neymar Jr!* ('Welcome Neymar Jr!')

On the banners: 'Neymar da Silva: let's go and make history', '3,819 miles from New York to see you', 'Florentino [Perez, the Real Madrid chairman], you have no sea, nor Neymar', 'Neymar, we love you', etc. And flags galore: Catalan, Brazilian, as well as those of other South American countries …

But what was this Neymar like, the man whose appearance everyone was anticipating so eagerly? Sergi, sixteen, said, 'He is a star and Barcelona will prove that.' David, seventeen, said, 'He is good but let's see how he gets on here.' Natalia, sixteen, said, 'He is the best in the world.' Ivan, eleven, said, 'With Messi, they will form a partnership that has never been seen before. They will score 100 goals a season.' Carlos, eighteen, chimed in, 'If he gets on with Messi, he will be a success.' Camila, sixteen, said, 'He is an exceptional player and a bit of a hunk.' Lamin, fifteen, commented, 'I play with Santos on the PlayStation because he played for them.'

Everyone had an opinion about the move. And when Pep Callau, the official spokesperson for Barcelona, started to walk round the stadium, few and far between were those who did not speak their mind. Some even burst into song and gave a rendition of the club's anthem. Brazilian music, images on the big screen to pass the time before the big moment. Three hundred and sixty children from FCB Escola, the club's football school, sat down on the pitch next to the light blue walkway which led to the centre of the pitch and the '*arc de triomphe*' that had been installed there. The orange sea of photographers and cameramen swayed from side to side on the lush green pitch. A good sign. The buzz of the crowd started to crescendo.

Neymar was here. He walked out on to the pitch, ball in one hand and waving with the other. The children's flags waved feverishly, the club's anthem boomed around the stadium, Rafaela and Bruna Marquezine took photo after photo from the bench and a tear of joy rolled down their cheeks. The 56,000-strong crowd roared a deafening cheer to welcome the new kid on the block.

Neymar had not beaten the record of 60,000 fans who came to see Ibrahimovic on 27 July 2009, nor the 80,000 fans who went to see Cristiano Ronaldo on 6 July 2009 at the

Santiago Bernabéu, but he doubled the 25,000 who came to see Ronaldinho on 23 July 2003.

What did it feel like for a 21 year old to arrive in another country, another city, and be welcomed by 56,000 fans who came just to see him, to watch him show off a few tricks and hear him utter a few special words?

'It is something quite sensational, marvellous, hard to believe. It was hard to fight back the tears,' is how Neymar explained it later in an interview.

On the pitch, he was a complete professional. He was up to the situation. That said, with his red and blue shirt with no number on it, his new haircut with red highlights but no Mohican, he looked tiny against the backdrop of the immense stadium: a young kid who was rich and famous and who, in front of hundreds of thousands of kids, does what he likes doing: playing football. Under the arch, he pulled a few tricks as the crowd went wild.

Laura Aparicio, Barça TV reporter, was responsible for interviewing him. She asked him how he felt. '*Bona tarda a tothom. Estic molt feliç per ser jugador del Barça i d'haver aconseguit el meu somni.*' ('Good afternoon everyone. I am so very happy to be a Barça player and to have achieved my dream.')

Neymar was well prepared for the occasion and started in Catalan. The fans showed their appreciation. At the end, he signed off in Spanish: '*Muchas gracias y que Dios nos bendiga. Visca el Barça.*' ('Many thanks, God bless you and long live Barcelona.')

The perfect way to end the presentation in front of 56,000 fans. He did a lap of the pitch, booting balls up into the stands; he waved and was overwhelmed with hugs from the kids.

At 6.51pm, fourteen minutes after entering the pitch, he was gone and heading for the changing rooms. The show was over.

A few at a time, the crowd slowly left the stadium, happy in the knowledge that Neymar was now with them: they had their new star.

Neymar's commitments were nowhere near over. In the Auditorium 1899, next to the Camp Nou stadium, the media were waiting patiently for the press conference. Next to Neymar was Andoni Zubizzareta, the sports director for the club and Joseph Maria Bartomeu, the vice-chairman of the club. The latter took the microphone and set the scene with the figures of the transfer: 'Neymar is costing us €57 million, more than we thought we were going to pay when we decided to contract him (€40 million). This was due to other clubs bargaining and pushing the price up.

'In addition, you should note that Neymar has come a year earlier than expected. The amount is split between these four businesses: DIS, TEISA, N&N and Santos. We have managed to get the deal done without intermediaries or agents, as always.'

More than that, Bartomeu was not willing to say. Due to a confidentiality clause in the agreement, he could not explain how the monies were split exactly. It put Neymar in second place, after Ibrahimovic, in the list of most expensive players the club had splashed out on. Bartomeu said that €10 million had already been paid whereas the rest would be paid over three years to the four companies which owned the rights to the player. The questions regarding the monies paid were fast and flowing from the journalists. The answer remained the same. The question would be discussed both in Spain and in Brazil for a long time. Those close to the deal claimed that the amount of the transfer was actually €70–75 million. €32 million was for Santos, without counting the earnings from the two friendly matches (one in the Camp Nou and the other in Brazil) and without counting the €8 million for the option rights to Victor Andrade, Gabriel and Giva, three kids playing for Peixe; €20 million was for N&N, Neymar Pai's company. The rest was to be split between DIS and Teisa.

Zubizzareta revealed the contents of Barcelona's first report about Neymar, which had been prepared by the club's technical team on 31 January 2011 after the Under-20 South American Championship final. He read out a few lines: '[Neymar] is one of the greatest talents in the world right now and if he continues to develop as he has done so far, he can become one of the greatest players in world football.'

Zubizzareta was also responsible for communicating the number on Neymar's shirt. 'Number 11 is Thiago's,' he said. 'We'll see.' (In the event, Thiago was to leave for Bayern Munich, so the number 11 was Neymar's.)

It was the turn of the child prodigy, wearing a Barça crested blue shirt with the collar up. Ney drew strength from his key words:

Heart: 'Madrid is a great club but I followed my heart and decided to come to Barcelona.'

Messi: 'I am one of the most fortunate men in the world to be able to play alongside Messi.'

Dream: 'I would like to thank Barcelona for helping me realise my childhood dream.'

Happiness: 'It is the most important thing. We did not follow the money. I do not believe I am worth €57 million.'

Joy: 'I will play my football. I hope to fit in straight away and to bring joy to the fans.'

The well-prepared answers carried on until 8.37pm when the press conference ended.

Before dinner, with his family and Sandro Rosell, there were a few more interviews to give to local media, Barça TV and TV3. Then the long day was over. Off to the hotel to get some rest.

The next day, the Gulfstream G550 would whisk Neymar off to Brasilia, followed by a helicopter ride to Goiânia, where Brazil were preparing for the Confederations Cup.

Chapter 23

Maracanã

The English writer, Alex Bellos, author of *Futebol: The Brazilian Way of Life*, claimed that the reference points for European history in the 20th century were the two World Wars; for the Brazilians, they were the World Cups.

In June 2013, it just so happened that the dress rehearsal for a World Cup became a 'war'. And for the first time in the country of *futebol*, for the first time in the history of the *jogo bonito* (the 'beautiful game'), football was in the firing line. Not the game, not the teams, not Brazil, but FIFA, the Brazilian government and the grandiose preparations for the 2014 World Cup.

The flame that lit the blue touchpaper was the increase in the public transport fares in São Paulo: a local issue that few would have expected to awaken the 'sleeping giant'. And yet, within a few days, there were demonstrations all over the country, spreading like wildfire due to social media. People were on the march in 80 cities; one million people were on the streets from Manaus to Rio de Janeiro, from São Paulo to Porto Alegre, something which had not happened for twenty years. Mainly peaceful processions were punctuated with sporadic outbursts of violence, ending up with a few getting hurt. The police reacted violently to the protests but there were policemen who, in front of the TV cameras, put down their weapons and joined the protesters in an act of solidarity. The crowds chanted, 'We are not here for the few hundred cents.'

In fact, even when the two largest cities withdrew the fare hikes for the buses, the underground and the trams, the protests did not stop. It was the people rising against the corruption which reigned supreme in the country; people showing their discontent with the schools, the hospitals, out-of-control public spending; people voicing their opinions about the government and the World Cup. It was the protest of a new middle class that Lula da Silva and Dilma Rousseff's governments helped create: a part of society that wanted to be in the first world but, seeing the constructions behind schedule, the failings, the hundreds of unresolved problems in Brazil, wanted to make its voice heard. It was a modern rebellion that had the country's young at its heart.

Before the onset of the protests, Carla Daudes, a 23-year-old Brazilian film director, posted a video online to explain why she was saying 'no' to the 2014 World Cup: 'It will cost $30 billion, more than the last three World Cups put together. Please tell me: do we need more stadiums in a country where illiteracy is at 21 per cent ... in a country listed at number 85 in the human development index, where 13 million people are starving and where many more die while waiting for treatment?'

Juca Kfouri from his office in São Paulo commented: 'The average attendance in the Brazilian stadiums is 15,000 spectators: less than the Soccer League [MLS] in the US, less than the Championship in England and the second division in Germany. Most of our stadiums were built during the dictatorship, when national integration was possible thanks to *futebol*. Well, we are doing the same with democracy. Instead of having a World Cup which is tailored to the needs of Brazil, those in power want to do as was done in South Africa and Germany. They have built and remodelled stadiums which, as we say in Brazil, are "white elephants", just like in

Manaus, in Brasilia and in Cuiabá. These are cities without a football team in the first or second divisions. It is absurd. Why spend all that money on stadiums and not a penny on the hospitals and schools?

'When Brazil was awarded the 2014 World Cup, the dissidents were few but now people are beginning to realise the truth and the Confederations Cup was the straw that broke the camel's back. People are now on the streets to make their opinions known.'

Brazilians had realised that the politicians were taking them for a ride and had used the World Cup to gain entry to the big league of world countries. It was a unique opportunity to show the world what Brazil was: a consolidated democracy, a leader in South America and a player in the big league. The World Cup was to be an incentive for more growth, more wealth, more well-being – it was to change the life of Brazilians, for the better. But it was not hard to see that the benefits of the World Cup would go to FIFA and into the hands of the select few while the average man was being kicked out of his home, out of the *favelas*, to make way for the stadiums, the training pitches, or indeed the sports complexes for the 2016 Olympics.

The deceit had been laid bare. There were rumours of swollen estimates like in the case of Maracana or Mané Garrincha in Brasilia; there was talk of bribes being given here and there, of buildings being promised but never built, of a clampdown on crime which turned out to be the calming of a few *favelas* by moving gangs from one side of the city to the other. It was becoming clear what the World Cup really was. The hundreds of banners and signs carried in the demonstrations around the cities of Brazil and pitched outside the stadiums shouted, 'Is the World Cup a priority for Brazil'; 'I want schools and hospitals not FIFA'; 'FIFA Go

Home'; 'The World Cup does not educate'; 'We do not want the World Cup, we want the metro'; 'No World Cup! Health and Education!'; 'When your child is ill, take him to the stadium?'; 'How many schools are there in Mané Garrincha?'; 'Japan: we exchange our football for their education'; 'Brazil, wake up: is one teacher worth more than one Neymar?'

In but a few days, seeing the protests on the streets of the Brazilian cities, the government did something that no one could have expected. The initial violent police enforcement action was replaced with an attitude of understanding and support for the uprising.

The fare hikes were withdrawn; Dilma announced investment in public transport; the *Supremo Tribunal Federal* (the highest court in Brazil) sentenced a corrupt senator to prison (albeit under house arrest), something which had never been seen before; the royalties from oil were invested in schools and education; it was announced that Congress would work even when Brazil were playing.

FIFA reacted by going underground. It removed its flags from the Copacabana Palace Hotel in Rio, operations HQ, and removed its logo from its official cars. Sepp Blatter, the chairman, who was irritated by the whistles he received at the opening ceremony of the Confederations Cup in Brasilia, stated, 'Football is more important here than the dissatisfaction of the people. The protesters are using football and the presence of the press as a platform to raise the profile of their protest.' He concluded by saying, 'Brazil asked for the World Cup. We did not force Brazil to host it. Brazil knew that to organise a good World Cup, they needed to build stadiums. So if the government has problems with its people, that's its problem, not ours.'

Marco Polo del Nero, vice-chairman of the Brazilian Football Federation and representative for Brazil at FIFA, stated that '199 million people are just focusing on working and there are only a few who are protesting.'

A rumour went round that if the disturbances carried on, FIFA could decide to play the last few matches of the tournament in another country. The flames were quickly doused on this rumour.

The government had a lot on its hands, what with the visit of Pope Francis at the end of July 2013. The atmosphere was tense but Brazil charged headstrong into the winds of angry protest.

Kfouri commented, 'It is curious, but when the country is doing well, the Brazilian team does not and there is no link with the fans. The demonstrations prove that the country is not doing well but Brazil [the team] is on form and the connection with the Brazilian people is renewed, reinforced. The national anthem is sung by the players, the fans and the protesters outside the stadiums with the same passion, the same voice.'

La Canarinha and the protest movement connected – unlike Pelé, who let slip an unfortunate comment ('Let's forget all this mess and think about Brazil') but immediately backtracked and withdrew it. Or unlike Ronaldo, 'O Fenómeno', who said, 'The World Cup is played in stadiums, not in hospitals.' He immediately withdrew the statement, saying that he was misinterpreted. These unfortunate comments aside, the Brazilian team was fully behind the protest. Dani Alves, Fred, Hulk and David Luiz were not afraid to make their opinions known when requested to do so by former players Romario and Rivaldo. Even Neymar got in on the action.

In the first match of the Confederations Cup, against Japan on 15 June, after three minutes, Neymar scored his first goal. Marcelo crossed the ball from the left. Fred controlled the ball with his chest and, with the ball still hanging in the air after the first bounce, Neymar let rip with an awesome strike that hit the back of the net at 98 kilometres per hour after deflecting off the crossbar. The match, in the Mané Garrincha stadium, could not have got off to a better start.

Before the second match on 19 June 2013, the newly signed Barcelona striker posted on his Facebook page: 'Sad for all that is going on in Brazil. I had always hoped that it would not get to the point where people had to occupy the streets to obtain better conditions for transport, health, education and crime control. All of these are the DUTY of a government. My parents have worked hard to offer me and my sister a better quality of life … Today, thanks to the success I am honoured with, my comments could seem like populism but they are not. Let's lift the flag for the protesters all over Brazil. I am BRAZILIAN and I love my country!!! I have family and friends who live in Brazil. For this reason, I want Brazil to be a better, fairer, safer, healthier and more HONEST place!!! The only way I can represent and defend Brazil is by playing football. But as of this match, against Mexico, I will go on the pitch inspired by the movement of the people.'

Against Mexico in Fortaleza, the demonstrations and clashes reached the stadium. Inside, the fans were behind Brazil from the first to the last minute of the game. The signs and banners of protest were there but the fans and the team were on the same side. The national anthem was sung even when the music had stopped. Again it was Neymar who made the difference; in fact it was pretty much a one-man show. After nine minutes, a cross from Dani Alves, deflected by Rodriguez, was met by Neymar's punishing volley. Then in the 90th minute, he caught the Mexican defence off guard and delivered the ball on a plate to Jo, who made it two.

Mexico, Brazil's jinx, who had crucified La Canarinha in the 2012 Olympic final, were out. Neymar was man of the match for the second time.

The last Group A match was against Italy on Saturday 22 June in Salvador de Bahia. Five thousand protested against the spiralling costs of the World Cup. The banners told the story: 'We are in the streets for a better world'; 'We are not fighting the country but corruption'.

The demonstrators were held back by 1,500 policemen. During the match, they managed to get closer and tear gas was dispatched and rubber bullets were fired. As for the football, Brazil went into the match with a mixed track record against Italy. In March, in a friendly in Geneva, it had ended 2–2, and it was Brazil on the back foot that had had to claw back two goals in the second half.

This time Italy did not get a shot on goal in the first 45 minutes. The Brazilians dominated possession but did not achieve much. Brazil finally took the lead in first half stoppage time, the substitute Dante, wearing number 13, scoring the goal. Neymar's free kick was met by a header from Fred; Buffon parried but Dante put it in the back of the net.

The tables were turned in the second half. The *Azzurri* moved upfield and equalised with a beautiful goal from Giaccherini, who received the ball from a flick of the heel of Mario Balotelli. Neymar was not done yet though. When he was awarded a free kick on the edge of the area, the Italians put up a bit of resistance with the referee: they protested that Neymar had dived, that there was no foul, that Neymar was looking for the touch from Maggio.

Neymar got to the task in hand. A perfect shot and the ball left Buffon wrong-footed. A goal in the style of Zico or Didi. This was his third goal in three matches. Balotelli tried to replicate Neymar's goal from further back. He launched a missile but Julio Cesar blocked.

Brazil carried on. Fred scored to make it 3–1. Italy did not give up and pulled it back to 3–2. Maggio tried for the equaliser. But then Fred scored again to put the game beyond reach and the match ended 4–2.

The much anticipated duel between Balotelli and Neymar had ended with the first strike to 'Juninho'. Brazil had won, but it was not plain sailing. The European commentators were not convinced. John Carlin, British author and journalist, summed up in *El País* as follows: 'Those who have the image of Pelé, Rivelino, Tostão, or Zico and Sócrates, or even Romario as Brazilian football will not believe what their eyes have seen in the Confederations Cup, a trial run for next year's World Cup [but let's hope not]. Brazil is reserved, defensive, without joy. There is no football samba. It is pure utilitarianism.'

His view was shared by many. Some talked of *antifutebol*, others hid their disappointment by focusing on the shining light that was Neymar.

In Brazil, they were critical but they were satisfied, as they knew that the Confederations Cup was a trial run for Scolari, the first step to putting together the World Cup team. Besides, they were in the semi-finals against Uruguay. The memories of Maracanazo on 16 July 1950 came flooding back.

Luis Suárez said he was aware of Ghiggia's goal at the front post; Edinson Cavani had only heard about it when he was twenty years old; Diego Forlán was philosophical: 'It is a clear reminder of what we are capable of but it does not help us today.'

Indeed the memories of the past do not help us face the present. It was true that Brazil did not burst on to the pitch with the same impact they had had in the other three matches but they controlled the game nonetheless. Julio Cesar and Neymar were there for Brazil. Cesar saved a penalty taken by Diego Forlán, his former Internazionale teammate. And that was it for Forlán, he did not pick himself up after missing the penalty.

Neymar did not score but he was central to the two Brazilian goals. A long ball from Paulinho right at the end of the first half found Neymar surrounded by Uruguayan defenders. He chested the ball down and had just enough time to boot it at Muslera who was off his line. Muslera parried but Fred was there in a flash and scrambled the ball in.

Five minutes from the end, it was Neymar again. He took a corner kick from the left; Paulinho jumped high and beat Cáceres and Muslera, who hesitated and was caught halfway: 2–1, and Brazil could now focus on who they would meet in the final.

It had not been a pretty match: patchy, dominated in the second half by the *Charrua* (Uruguay) who after Cavani's equaliser almost clinched victory. A football match with little football and a lot of tension and uncertainty, decided in the last few minutes of injury time. Brazil did not have the grace, the poetry, the *jogo bonito* which everyone expected. Brazil were focused on winning the game.

One memorable moment was provided by Neymar's kisses blown to Álvaro González. As the substituted Uruguayan midfielder exited the pitch he passed close to Neymar, who was about to take a corner, and insulted him. Neymar was mute and blew him a kiss. And another. To the pleasure of the crowd.

At Fortaleza, while the police were busy fighting back the protesters, Spain saw off Cesare Prandelli's Italy, beating them on penalties as they had in Euro 2008. After

120 minutes with no goals, the shoot-out finished 7–6 to the world champions.

La Roja (Spain) flew to Rio de Janeiro for the final everyone had been waiting for. Neymar spoke at the pre-match press conference and said, 'Now I can say it. It is the final everyone has been waiting for. Spain are the best in the world at the moment; they are the favourite, but Brazil has great players.'

Neymar said it was a great honour to be playing against his future teammates: 'It will be emotional. I wish them the best of luck – but not for this match.'

The press asked Neymar what the secret to beating Spain was: 'The important thing is not to be afraid. We must be brave enough to do our dribbling, try our tricks. Maracanã will be our twelfth man.'

Who, he was asked, did he fear the most in the Spanish team? 'Iker Casillas. He is in my FIFA team. He is the best goalkeeper in the world and one of the best of all time. I hope I can get one past him.' The press conference was over.

In the 44th minute of the final, Oscar, together with Neymar, went on a blistering counterattack. On the edge of the area, Oscar held the ball up. Neymar backtracked to stay onside and received the ball; he then released an Exocet missile, which slammed into the roof of the net with Casillas recoiling. It was a sensational goal and the number 10 celebrated by diving into the fans.

It was Neymar's fourth goal in the Confederations Cup, and it was a crucial one that put his team 2–0 up, Fred having scrambled a goal in after only one minute and 33 seconds. Neymar was there for that one as well, with a vital flick in the build-up. Fred sealed the game in second-half stoppage time for a final score of 3–0.

The Maracanã went into party mode. Spain, who had not lost an official game since the 2010 World Cup in South Africa (Switzerland 1 Spain 0) were done for. Brazil had put everything into the match and come out fighting: from David Luiz, who blocked a goal attempt from Pedro, to Neymar, who – apart from scoring – drew a foul that got Piqué sent off and forced Vicente del Bosque to replace full-back Arbeloa, who was not up to the challenge. The golden boy attacked and defended.

For his efforts he was named the best player of the tournament by FIFA. He had turned up to the Confederations Cup straight after signing for Barcelona with half the world watching how he would perform. It was not easy being put to the test in this way. But he had passed with flying colours.

In the heart of the Maracanã Stadium on the evening of 30 June 2013, the dream photo could be taken: Neymar biting the champions' medal behind the three trophies he so desired: the Confederations Cup, the Golden Ball for best player and the Bronze Boot for third best goalscorer.

Chapter 24

Barcelona

It was gala evening at the Grand Connaught Rooms in London. Dinner jackets, bow ties, fine dining, speeches and toasts. It was a birthday party. Football was celebrating its 150th anniversary. On this site, in Great Queen Street in the heart of London, the Freemason's Tavern used to stand. It was there that, on 26 October 1883, Sir Ebenezer Cobb Morley, founder and captain of Barnes Football Club, and representatives of eleven other clubs and sporting associations, met 'with the aim of promoting a code of common rules and more generally to adopt articles of association', as it was reported in the *London Daily News*. It was there that, amid several debates, modern football and the first national football federation was born: the Football Association.

The party at the Grand Connaught was hosted by none other than Prince William, chairman of the FA and a keen Aston Villa fan. In his speech, he pointed out that 'football is a great force in the world and can do a great deal of good. There are a lot of people who love it, respect it and enjoy football like nothing else in their life'. At the end, he offered a toast to the guests and to the next 150 years of the FA and football.

A few hours earlier, 1,488 kilometres away, another football party was being celebrated: Barcelona *vs.* Real Madrid. It was *El Clásico* number 225, and the first for Neymar Jr in the Barça shirt.

'It is the match in which every footballer hopes to play, to show their best *futebol*,' explained Neymar to Barça TV. He thought back to other classic matches. The *clásico* he recalled the best was when Ronaldinho, in the Santiago Bernabéu, scored two goals and received a standing ovation from the Madrid fans, on 19 November 2005. Neymar said he had experienced lots of good 'classic' matches in Brazil. The first he played was against Palmeiras, a semi-final, which Santos won; then the final of the Paulistão, which Santos lost to Corinthians; and then against São Paulo. Neymar continued, 'There is the rivalry during the week leading up to the match, just like here. The only thing everyone is talking about is the match; it is the most-talked about topic in the newspapers and by the fans. Even the players who are friends with the players on the other team have a few digs and jibes with their friends on the opposing team. That is the beautiful thing about football.'

He was aware that, for him, the *clásico* on Saturday, 26 October 2013 was extremely important. He was hoping to play well and win.

Almost three months had gone by since Neymar joined Barcelona. After the Confederations Cup, Neymar underwent a tonsillectomy and an operation to correct his nasal septum. Then a short break with friends. Bruna, his girl-friend, had finished *Dancing with the Stars* in Brazil and they joined up with her friends in Europe: Rome and Athens. Monuments and ancient history for her; sun, sea, beaches, relaxation and parties for Neymar. Just what the doctor ordered, before catching the flight back to Ciudad Condal.

He arrived in Barcelona on the morning of 28 July. The next day he would meet his new teammates. A medical would be followed by his first training session in the *Ciutat Esportiva* with Messi & Co. At the end of the session, Neymar tweeted, '*meu sonho virou realidade. Obrigado Senhor!*' ('My dreams have come true. Thank you Lord!')

On 30 July he was already on a plane to Poland for a friendly against Lechia Gdansk. In the PGE Arena, the Polish fans stuck up a banner which was a bit dated (it showed images of Guardiola, Messi, Puyol and Cruyff with the slogan in Catalan *Tots units fem força* ('Together we are stronger'). They wanted to see Messi and Neymar on the pitch. They were disappointed for the sake of a few minutes. Neymar started on the bench and came on in the 78th minute, taking the place of Alexis, but Messi had already been substituted. So Neymar's debut for Barcelona consisted of twelve minutes in a match that ended up a 2–2 draw. Not much, granted, but for Neymar it was enough to put a smile on his face: 'Barcelona is much better than I thought. It is a great feeling. I am very happy to be able to speak to Messi, to be near Xavi and Iniesta.' He said he was working to adapt as quickly as possible to Barça's style of play, '*el más bonito del mondo*' ('the best in the world').

He could not wait to play his first match in Camp Nou.

On 2 August, Neymar got his chance in the 'Trofeo Joan Gamper', a special match. Barcelona were playing Santos, Neymar's old club.

The slogan for the tournament read *Nueva temporada, nuevos sueños* ('New season, new dreams'). All true. Barça had a new coach: Gerardo 'El Tata' Martino, the Argentinian who had played for Newell's Old Boys in Rosario, the city where Leo Messi was born and started playing football. The replacement had been organised quickly after Tito Vilanova had had to resign due to bad health, cancer of the parotid gland. Barça also had a new star: Neymar was making his debut, together with Tata. And Barcelona had just said farewell to Antoni Ramallets, who had died aged 89. The 'Cat of

Maracanã' was one of the historic players of the club, winner of five cups as Barça goalkeeper.

In the heat of an August evening, 81,000 fans filled the Camp Nou stadium and wanted to pay homage to the number 1 who had passed away and to understand what they could expect from the year ahead.

The fans were to go home happy and safe in the knowledge that the future would be a bright one. Barcelona absolutely obliterated Santos 8–0. Leo Messi opened the scoring and in half an hour the game was over. Neymar came on in the second half, after an incident where a pitch invader wanted to hug him: eight security guards were needed to hold the man down. Neymar had the number 11 on his back and received a standing ovation from the crowd.

Neymar played on the left side, where he was marked by Arouca. He was on the pitch with Messi for fifteen minutes. He showed off a few tricks but seemed more interested in passing the ball around rather than going for goal. He avoided going over the top but he nonetheless provided the perfect assist for the sixth goal, scored by Cesc Fàbregas. Towards the end, in the deluge of goals, he got the chance to score but pinged Vladimir's crossbar.

Neymar's post-match comment was, 'It is a strange s ensation. I am happy for the win for my team and my new teammates but sad for my teammates at Santos who I care about.'

The Brazilian papers were hard on Peixe the next day. *Lance* wrote, 'What a disgrace! Without even trying and with Neymar on the pitch in the second half only, Barça humiliates Santos.' The paper coined a phrase for the best duo in the world, the neology 'LioNey': a catchy expression that has slowly gained ground with the press.

After the 'Gamper' came the 'Peace Tour': the Barcelona

team headed off to a clinic in Bloomfield Stadium in Tel Aviv with Israeli and Palestinian children. Thereafter they would begin their Asian tour, which would take them to Thailand and Malaysia.

Santos, on the other hand, headed home with their tails between their legs. It was a crisis and fans held demonstrations before the *clásico* between Santos and Corinthians.

After the team's training session at the CT Rei Pelé and before the press conference (where Edu Dracena, the captain, and Odilio Rodrigues Filho, the vice-chairman, tried to reassure the press), O Rei and Victor Andrade shared their thoughts about Neymar playing at Camp Nou. Victor, who was three years younger than Neymar and came through the youth teams at Santos, had learned a lot from his ex-colleague: 'When I made the first team, he helped me, he gave me good advice on how to behave on the pitch. He told me not to be nervous; he taught me when is the right moment to dribble and when it is better to pass the ball. Do this, do that, hold that position, stay unmarked. I have followed his advice and thank God everything is going well.'

The young kid for Santos explained, 'On the pitch, Neymar was spectacular, quick, agile and improvised all the time. He did what no one expected. He was surely one of the best players I had ever seen and a true teammate. Off the pitch, he was different. He was funny and liked being with his friends and family. I have to say that I had a great time with him.'

Talking about Neymar playing for Barcelona, Victor said, 'It was weird having him as an opponent, especially as three months ago he was playing next to me. It was not a problem as when the referee blows the whistle, you do not think too much about it.'

He continued by saying that they did not talk much about football but more about Neymar feeling homesick: 'It is hard living far away from Brazil.'

What was worrying Ricardo Rosa, physical trainer for Santos, was not Neymar's homesickness but his weight. He saw that the Barcelona staff wanted Neymar to put on three kilos to adapt to European football and he was very concerned: 'It could be a disaster. He could lose his qualities as has happened to other players. Sure, if you look at Neymar, you see he is thin and has no muscles but he is very, very strong. His legs are made for running, for dribbling and for skipping around other players. He is agile, quick and, unlike other strikers, he has incredible stamina. He never gets tired and can repeat moves, one, two, three, four, five times.

'He takes knocks from defenders. Sure, he goes down but he does not get seriously hurt. It would be a shame if they made him put on bulk and muscles.'

Weight was not the only thing causing issues between Spain and Brazil. There was also Neymar's anaemia. The Spanish press spread a rumour that he was on a diet and taking vitamin supplements to deal with a low level of iron in his blood. Luiz Felipe Scolari lost his patience: 'It's as though they [Barcelona] know everything and we are the third world and we do not know anything. After an operation it is normal that he has lost weight but he will gain it back with time. When he eats like a horse at midday, at three in the afternoon and six and nine, he is great. He is on form. If it wasn't like this, he would not play as he is doing for Barcelona.'

Felipão was not wrong, as, during the Asian tour, Neymar was on form.

On 7 August, in the friendly against Thailand in the Rajamangala national stadium in Bangkok, he scored his first goal. In the 11th minute, Messi was on the edge of the area and fed the ball out to the left for Fàbregas, who whipped the ball in. Neymar stuck his foot out and put the ball in the back of the net. The celebration – a quick hug with his teammates – was reserved compared to those he was used to performing in Brazil.

It was different when it came to his first goal that really counted. On 21 August, Barcelona were playing in the first leg of the Spanish Super Cup at the Vicente Calderón. Four days earlier, Neymar had played his first *Liga* match, against Levante. He came on to replace Messi in the 63rd minute (Tata Martino is a fan of mixing things up and rotating players), when the game was already won: 6–0 to Barça.

In the Calderón, David Villa, formerly of Barcelona, now playing for Atlético Madrid, pulled off a fantastic volley: 1–0 to the Red-and-Whites. Messi had to go off at half-time with a muscle problem. It seemed as though Atlético were going to have an easy ride. Alexis and Mascherano were the only Barça players holding the fort. Neymar came on in the 59th minute, replacing Pedro. Seven minutes later, he put Barcelona back on level terms. Xavi passed to Dani Alves on the right; the Brazilian crossed to the back post; Juanfran did not realise Neymar was arriving behind him. The number 11 beat Juanfran to the ball and headed in. Courtois could not get there. It was Neymar's first official goal. He hugged Alves and the others and headed over to the bench to Tata and his teammates. It was a goal that earned Neymar his first trophy with Barcelona. The return leg in Camp Nou finished 0–0 and the cup was Barça's.

Eight matches later came Neymar's first goal in *La Liga*. It was against Real Sociedad on 24 September. It was not a pretty goal: it was the result of mistakes by the other side's defence. Claudio Bravo, the goalkeeper, and Liassine Cadamoro, the central defender, turned an innocent-looking cross from Alexis into a scuffle over the line for the Blaugrana number 11. Neymar confessed after the match: 'The ball crossed the line crying.' He dedicated the goal to his son, David Lucca. Before the match, he had introduced David to the fans, just as Leo Messi had with Thiago, his firstborn.

Two other Brazilian ex-Barça players had got their goalscoring tally off to a start against Real Sociedad: Romario in 1993 and Rivaldo in 1997. A simple coincidence, but Neymar was following in the footsteps of the great Brazilian players who had mesmerised Camp Nou and made history with Barcelona FC. First among these was Evaristo de Macedo: he came from Club de Regatas Flamengo and from 1958 to 1961 he scored 178 goals in 226 matches. Then came Romário Faria da Souza, better known as Romario. He joined from PSV Eindhoven and from 1993 until halfway through the 1994/95 season he played for the Dream Team. Everyone remembers the three goals he scored in a *clásico* against Real Madrid. Then came Giovanni, a star from Santos, then Ronaldo Luís Nazário da Lima, 'O Fenómeno', then Sonny Anderson, then Rivaldo and finally the smiler, Ronaldinho.

Neymar is the latest in a long tradition of great Brazilian players and he was carving out his place and adapting to the Barça style of play.

He had been scoring fewer goals compared to his Santos days but against Real Madrid he made his fifth assist to Messi. He had already played in the Champions League, against Ajax on 18 September. At only 21, he had already played 300 professional games.

On 1 October 2013, against Celtic, Neymar showed his maturity. On the historic pitch where football has been played since 1888, when Brother Walfrid, Andrew Kerins founded the four-leaf clover club in order to drum up funds for charity, Neymar was at the helm, as Messi was not playing. The number 11 was incisive, decisive, brave and defence-breaking. He started with the short game, he dribbled but without overdoing it, he led the attack but helped out in defence as well. Lustig got a yellow card thanks to Neymar and Brown a red after having kicked him in the back. Two fantastic saves from Fraser Forster prevented Neymar from getting his goal in 'Paradise' (as described on one of the Celtic banners in the crowd) but he set up the counterattack that allowed Fàbregas to score.

The match earned him the praise of Tata Martino and his teammates but criticism from Neil Lennon. The Celtic manager accused him of being too theatrical: 'This is a physical game. Neymar does not help anyone by overegging it when he is fouled.'

Here we were again. The story of the player who goes down at the slightest touch. A controversy which got everyone involved, including José Mourinho and Tata Martino. One weighed in against the 'diver'; the other argued that referees did not blow the whistle when Neymar was fouled.

Leaving the controversy to one side, by the eve of *El Clásico*, 'Juninho' was feeling positive. He had played three matches in the Champions League, including one against Milan at San Siro, where he was up against his friend Robinho, two Spanish Super Cup matches and nine in *La Liga*. He had scored a hat-trick in a match against Valladolid. Above all, he had shown that, against all odds, he had been able to adapt to European football very quickly. He had been able to stand in for Messi when the Argentinian was not playing and to support the number 10 when he was not firing on all cylinders. Neymar had made friends in the dressing room and the fans loved him (sooner than expected). His life at Barcelona was going great guns in all respects.

He has showed none of the excesses that other Brazilians have been famous for. He lives in the city in a nice part of Ciudad Condal in a rented house over three floors near to Avenida Pearson. He is far away from Castelldefels where Ronaldinho and Ronaldo lived and where Messi lives. Neymar Pai lives with his son and keeps a close eye on Neymar Jr. Nadine and Neymar's sister Rafaela are in Santos but travel to Barcelona once a month with the 'Toiss', Neymar's best friends. Bruna is in Brazil due to work commitments.

Neymar does not go out much. He goes for a meal or two, mainly to Japanese restaurants like Ikibana, il Nomo and lo Shunka. He often goes with Álvaro Costa, son of Pep, the service manager for Neymar at Barcelona; sometimes with Dani Alves and Adriano, his best friends in the team. It was Dani who helped him find a hairdresser worthy of the task, at Esplugues de Llobregat. When he is not training or playing, Neymar spends a lot of time at home. Brazilian music, videos, takeaways and PlayStation occupy his time: FIFA, Grand Theft Auto and Call of Duty are his favourite videogames. He follows Santos on the TV but is not too interested in following *La Liga* or the Champions League.

The day of *El Clásico* finally arrived. It was 26 October 2013. All the big guns were out: Messi, Cristiano Ronaldo and Gareth Bale, the Welshman who signed for €91 or €101 million, depending on who you speak to, and, of course, Neymar. It was a *clásico* missing certain protagonists: José Mourinho, who had turned the match into a psychological battle as much as anything else, Tito Vilanova, who was poked in the eye, and Pep Guardiola, the footballing philosopher, who was by then plying his trade in Germany.

The list of *El Clásico* debutants on the day was long: Neymar, Bale, Carlo Ancelotti and Zinedine Zidane (the Frenchman had seen many a Real Madrid–Barcelona contest, of course, but never from the bench as assistant manager) and last but not least Tata Martino. *La Liga* had been closely fought at the top of the table and, at this point of the season, Barcelona were just nudging ahead of Real by three points.

Ancelotti goaded, 'Everyone thinks Barça is the favourite and that is fine by us.' Martino's riposte was 'Who is the favourite will be shown during the 90 minutes of the game.'

At eight in the evening, when the guests at football's 150th anniversary were starting dinner in London, the result of the match was already known. Camp Nou was on its feet when Neymar Jr exited the pitch. He had scored and provided an assist. Just like Romario, Eto'o, Villa and Ibrahimovic, Neymar had been a key player in Barcelona's win.

Iniesta on the edge of the area had given the ball to Neymar on the left. The Number 11 had fired the ball hard along the ground and it went straight between the legs of Caravajal, his marker, and Varane who had deflected the ball ever so slightly and put Diego Lopez out of sync. Goal! It was Neymar's first goal in the *clásico* and it put Barça ahead. Neymar continued to impress, providing, on the counterattack, an assist for Alexis, the *Niño Maravilla*, who with a stunning shot signed, sealed and delivered victory to Barcelona.

As is the tradition after a *clásico*, there were the usual squabbles and controversy: the inconsistent officiating by referee Undiano (he failed to give a penalty for a foul by Mascherano on Cristiano Ronaldo); the weak line-up sent out by Ancelotti (the newspapers accused him of gifting the first half to Barcelona). But in the deluge of photographs and news stories, the world press had no doubts that a star was born: Neymar shone, and shone bright. The kid from

Mogi das Cruzes had made the news and filled the column inches. His photo was everywhere in the sporting press.

The best photo was the one on the front page of *La Vanguardia*: Neymar, with his back to the camera, bearing the number 11 to the world and celebrating his goal in front of the stands, arms open like Christ the Redeemer in Rio de Janeiro. The headline that captured the moment perfectly came from *L'Equipe*: 'Neymar the Prince of Camp Nou'.

There is nothing more to say.

Chapter 25

The devil

Diehard Barça fan Jordi Cases is much more than a season-ticket holder on the Camp Nou terraces. The forty-something pro-independence Catalan, who is a pharmacist in a town around half an hour outside Barcelona, has stirred up one of the most significant institutional crises in the club's history. For better or worse, his name will forever be linked with that of Neymar Jr.

Cases symbolises the triumph of David over Goliath – the cry of 'Yes we can!' that the Spanish have screamed at the tops of their voices over the years, whether in football stadiums or at protest marches during the economic crisis. It's a cry reserved for the impossible – or the nearly impossible. He has single-handedly forced the dismissal of Blaugrana president Sandro Rosell and pushed the club to explain itself to shareholders and the courts, in an attempt to reveal how much Barça paid for the Brazilian player.

His detractors think he is a puppet for dissenting voices within the club's own management. There are those – even within Real Madrid – who imply some kind of betrayal, but to date there has been no definitive proof. It is now broadly considered that Cases acted alone – a meddling witness who rose from anonymity to end up splashed across the press and on TV. In the Barça camp he has been referred to as *El Diablo* – 'The Devil'.

On 5 December 2013 he lodges a complaint against

Rosell with the Spanish national court for alleged 'misappropriation of funds' during Neymar's transfer. Cases is convinced the president has not revealed the whole truth to shareholders about the signing and believes that the real amount paid is nearly double the official €57 million sum that was split between the four companies that had rights to the player: DIS, Teisa, Neymar Pai's company N&N Sports, and Santos. Before going to the courts he had sent a certified fax to the club requesting all the details, but hired a lawyer after receiving no response.

The news does not emerge until a few days later, and catches Neymar by surprise during a particularly happy moment. With Messi out injured he has just assumed the captaincy. Even his teammates are amazed by how well he has adapted to Barça's style of play. He still needs to iron out a few kinks, but he has brought a freshness to the squad and the team is in no doubt that it was the right decision to sign him. But during the coming weeks he will face a level of media pressure most players never have to deal with, and certainly not at the tender age of 21. Even his first hat-trick in a Barça shirt – three goals in just fourteen minutes against Celtic in the Champions League on 11 December – will be overshadowed by the controversy surrounding his contract.

Ever since his presentation, there have been many who doubted that he could have been signed for such a 'low' amount. Even Real Madrid president Florentino Pérez claimed he passed up the opportunity to buy the Brazilian player because it would allegedly have cost the Whites €150 million. But Barça continue to deny all the accusations and cite a confidentiality agreement to avoid revealing any further details.

After the Christmas break, events gather pace. On 16 January Barça play a Copa del Rey return-leg match against Getafe. It is only the third time since the start of the season that Neymar and Messi have been on the pitch together. The game ends 2–0 to the Catalans (6–0 on aggregate), but the Brazilian is left with a sprained right ankle and will be out for a month. Just when Leo had returned from two months out, now it's 'Juninho's' turn to take a break. Barcelona are still top of *La Liga*. But just ten days later things go from bad to worse when judge Pablo Ruz accepts the lawsuit against Rosell. It's official: the 'Neymar case' will proceed. According to the judge, Cases' claim contains 'sufficient basis' to investigate all the facts, since it 'could point to a contractual simulation carried out by those who signed the deal, which could indicate a lack of consistency between the original intention and the final agreements and financial obligations in the official signed contracts'. In other words, it is alleged that a parallel contract was signed in order to unofficially finance the transfer, even though that contract was officially for something else.

In addition, Ruz asks FIFA to provide any documentation relating to the signing, and requests that Neymar provide his N&N contract relating to the relinquishing of future financial rights. He also sends an envoy to Brazil to obtain the player's work and transfer contracts, and requests that Barcelona provide the documents relating to the €7.9 million the club paid as an option on three young Santos players and the €9 million paid for two friendlies against Santos.

The following day, 21 January, Sandro Rosell resigns as president of FC Barcelona. 'This board of directors is a team,' he tells the media. 'And this team is spearheading a project that has already borne incredible fruit. I don't want any unjust attacks to negatively impact the club's management or image. That's why I think my tenure must end here.' He defends the club management yet again in a statement:

'In the last few days, unjust and imprudent accusations of misappropriation of funds have resulted in a lawsuit against me in the national court. From day one I have said that all is in order with Neymar Junior's transfer and that it has provoked desperation and jealousy among some of our rivals. Shareholders' right to information must be weighed against protecting the club and the confidential nature of certain matters. Confidentiality is crucial in the footballing world – without it the club could really suffer.'

But judge Ruz's decision is not the only reason he has decided to throw in the towel. Rosell also indicates that his family has 'endured threats and attacks' for some time, and that continuing in his role would 'put them at risk'. It is a sad ending for a president elected with the most votes in Barça history, not to mention a lifelong fan. His father was the club's director general during Agustí Montal's tenure, and he himself went to his first match at Camp Nou at the age of nine. As vice-president to Joan Laporta (2003–10) he succeeded in bringing in Ronaldinho, and in the top role he enjoyed some of his most glorious years, despite constant controversies.

Following Rosell's resignation, vice-president Josep Maria Bartomeu takes the reins. Twenty-four hours later Barcelona admit for the first time that the total sum that changed hands for Neymar was some €86.2 million, excluding his salary. The signing was worth €57.1 million, while the rest corresponds to 'other items'. In particular, the services for which the footballer's father was paid – such as talent-spotting promising young Brazilian players – have been called into question, as it is suspected that such payments were a fraudulent way to purchase the player.

But why have Barça revealed the sum now? Because Neymar Pai has agreed to waive the confidentiality agreement. Nonetheless, the club stands by its earlier position that nothing untoward has occurred. Neither Santos nor DIS are convinced, however, and in light of the new figures now believe they should have received more money.

Meanwhile, the kid from Mogi das Cruzes has been keeping quiet, completely focused on recovering from his injury as quickly as possible. He prefers to stay well out of anything non-sport-related. But by 2 February he has had enough, and posts a picture and an explosive message online defending his father. 'I have kept quiet until now! But I can't bear to hear all these ridiculous things about my transfer any longer … I'm sorry for disobeying you for the first time in my life, dad, but I have to speak out! I want to thank you for the way in which you have overseen my career, for the companies you created to support my work, and the way you have taken care of our family. If I previously played for my favourite team, and now I play for the team of my dreams, I owe it all to you. I know lots of people are talking a lot of rubbish about us, doubting us … I have also realised how many fair-weather friends we have … Dad, when Thiago Silva said he would die on the pitch for me, I thought the same about him … But not only would I die for you, I would give my only son's life for you! So I'm begging you, come back to Spain, I miss you! I'll be back on the pitch in a few days and I need you here with me … Time will show that you have done nothing wrong, that you have just been the best possible dad! I love you!'

On 15 February Neymar is back on the pitch as Barcelona quash Rayo at Camp Nou with a resounding 6–0 win. He scores the sixth, finishing a spectacular move four minutes before the final whistle. The goal deserves a decent celebration, and he goes over to dance in front of the crowd with good friend Dani Alves, breaking out moves inspired by a recent hit song from the Brazilian carnival. But once again he finds himself in the eye of the storm, as some pundits think such a celebration is disrespectful to the opponents after such a humiliating defeat. But Neymar defends himself, attributing it to the Brazilian outlook: 'We enjoy ourselves, whether we're playing, living, whatever we're doing. That's how we are, we just want to make these sorts of moments unforgettable. Daring and joyful are our watchwords,' he writes on Instagram.

But happiness is short-lived. Less than a week later there is more bad news from the courts. The judge has charged Barcelona with suspected tax fraud relating to Neymar's signing. The club is said to owe the Inland Revenue more than €9 million. Barcelona insists on maintaining its innocence, but four days later decides to make a voluntary contribution of €13.5 million to the authorities. Overnight, Neymar's transfer has become worth more than €100 million. Barça tries to paint the payment as a gesture of goodwill 'given the existence of a possible divergent interpretation of the exact amount of tax responsibility arising from the signing' of the Brazilian. However, it is also likely that this payment will reduce any fine by some 60 per cent were the club to be found guilty.

It is to be an *annus horribilis* for Barcelona. On 23 February they lose their *Liga* lead after being crushed 3–1 by Real Sociedad at Anoeta Stadium. Neymar's performance is barely worthy of note – his mind seems somewhere else. The press and the fans are not hiding their disappointment in the NJR–Messi partnership. They have barely been on the same pitch together due to various injuries, and when they have, there has been almost no chemistry. The *Clásico* at the start of the season seems a lifetime ago. In *La Liga* so far, the Brazilian has not received a single assist from the Argentine, and the

Argentine has received just three from Neymar, all back in September. Something is missing from Tata Martino's team. The already highly criticised coach knows that his number 11 is under immense pressure: 'Day to day he doesn't seem too worried, but it's building up inside,' he tells the media. His teammates insist he is doing well, that he's calm and motivated. 'The most important thing is that none of this has affected Ney professionally,' says Xavi Hernández. Iniesta, for his part, acknowledges that it's not good for the team to have to focus on anything other than football, and hopes that 'everything is resolved as quickly as possible'.

On 5 March Neymar Jr takes time out to go to Johannesburg with his national team, and get back to his old self. Lately he seems to have been having more luck in the number 10 shirt than the number 11. He scores three of Brazil's five goals against South Africa, and as if that's not enough, he makes the headlines after a little boy runs onto the pitch and is chased by security guards. Neymar sees him and runs towards him, scoops him up in his arms and carries him over to the rest of the team, who hug and celebrate with him, posing for photos with the little guy. It's Neymar at his most natural – it's this sort of thing that makes him stand out from other players. But before long it's back to reality and Barcelona, and back to disappointment in a clash with Manchester City on 13 March. Barça win 2–1, but the Brazilian hears whistling at his performance. It's not much, but it's the first time he's had that sort of criticism from the Camp Nou crowd.

The following weeks will not be easy for the team. They are barely recognisable from the exquisite, trophy-accumulating Barça of recent seasons. Everything is called into question – even La Masia, the club's world-renowned academy where the next generation of talent is nurtured, is put under the microscope. FIFA accuses the club of infringing article 19 which relates to youth recruitment, and bans it from signing new players for twelve months. Barcelona succeed in delaying the ban through appeal, but the club is still being hounded on all sides.

On the pitch the team suffer two significant blows: they are knocked out of the Champions League in the quarter-finals by Atlético Madrid (2–1 on aggregate), and they lose the final of the Copa del Rey 2–1 to Real Madrid at Mestalla. In the Madrid match Neymar suffers a contusion in his left leg. Meanwhile he has made headlines following the Champions League elimination – not just for scoring Barcelona's only goal of the tie (in the first leg) but for seemingly brandishing his underwear. Critics claim he is guilty of advertising, as every time he lifted his shirt or adjusted his shorts the logo of his longstanding underwear sponsor was clearly visible. The Brazilian insists there is no underlying strategy behind his movements. But it's not the first time the marketing king has been accused of using tricks to promote his products or himself. And it happens again just a few days later, with his 'We are all monkeys' anti-racism campaign. At first it seems like a spontaneous post that goes viral. Someone throws a banana at Dani Alves during a match against Villarreal, and instead of showing his annoyance, the player calmly bites into it. Within minutes, Neymar – who is watching the match on television – has Instagrammed a picture of himself, his son and a banana, with the hashtags #somostodosmacacos #weareallmonkeys. The reaction is huge – even Italian Prime Minister Matteo Renzi gets in on the act. A few hours later the Brazilian media reveal that the whole stunt was dreamt up by the Barça number 11's publicists. It seems nothing is accidental in the world of football entertainment.

Three weeks later, after recovering from his injuries, Neymar is on the teamsheet for the most important match of the year: the final *Liga* clash of the season against Atlético Madrid. Barça have to win if they want to take home the trophy, but the best they can manage is a 1–1 draw. The Brazilian only plays the last half-hour after coming on for Pedro, and for the first time in many years Barça end the season with nothing. It has been a mediocre year for Neymar in sporting terms. He has played in 53 matches, scored four-teen goals and made eight assists. To be fair, all too often Tata has put him on the right rather than the left where he is more comfortable – and the centre of the attack is, of course, Messi's domain. But that's not the only reason. He also misses Brazil, and the controversy surrounding his trans-fer has surely had an effect on him, although he has never let it show in public. He's an elite sportsman, but criticism is criticism, and he has endured plenty in recent months.

One of the toughest blows came towards the end of March from ex-Barça coach Johan Cruyff, who had been a vocal opponent of Rosell's tenure. 'Barcelona have created a problem: they have signed a 21 year old who earns more than everyone else and who has already got it all,' claimed the Dutchman. 'Everyone has to learn at 21 – there is no such thing as a 21-year-old god.'

Chapter 26

Mineirazo

'I could have ended up in a wheelchair.' Neymar is at a press conference six days after the injury that put him out of the World Cup: 'his' World Cup. He has fractured his third vertebra, and it is revealed that if Colombian Juan Camilo Zúñiga had hit him 'two centimetres closer to the middle', he would not have been able to walk.

On more than one occasion the Brazilian has to pause during his account as his eyes well up, and he has to take a deep breath before continuing. He apologises to the journalists, his voice faltering. 'It is difficult to talk about something that happened at such an important juncture in my career,' he says, as he tries to remain calm. He bows his head and wipes away tears in silence.

Neymar is wearing a Brazil shirt signed by all his teammates and a baseball cap with 'NJR' emblazoned on it. His pain is that of a nation who dreamt of bringing home their sixth World Cup, after triumphs in Sweden in 1958, Chile in 1962, Mexico in 1970, the United States in 1994 and Japan and South Korea in 2002. Not winning was not an option for the Brazilians. It's a tale of failure and collective disappointment as difficult to get over as the 1950 'Maracanazo' – a word banned by coach Luiz Felipe Scolari during the entire 2014 tournament.

End of May 2014, Granja Comary

The national team is staying in this oasis of tranquillity on the outskirts of the city of Teresópolis, around 80 kilometres from Rio de Janeiro. Several million pounds have been invested into turning the *Seleção*'s headquarters into a state-of-the-art luxury training centre. The facilities are a veritable compound – the coach doesn't want any prying eyes and he certainly doesn't want the players distracted by the tense atmosphere created by all the anti-World Cup demonstrations going on across the country. The only outsiders who can see any training sessions are accredited journalists and residents in the surrounding wealthy neighbourhood. Scolari even tried to have a wall constructed to prevent the latter seeing in, but he was unsuccessful. He wants the maximum possible privacy for his team because he knows that no other World Cup squad will be subjected to the same level of overwhelming scrutiny.

The coach places as much importance on his players' psychological preparation as on exercise sessions. As well as trainers and masseurs, he has hired Regina Brandão, a psychologist who specialises in sporting stress. They have worked together since the 2002 World Cup and according to the press she's the one who advised Felipão against calling up veterans Kaká and Ronaldinho. Right now, however, her job is even tougher. She has to create a psychological profile of all 23 players as a guide for Scolari. The coach is particularly obsessed with banishing the 'Maracanazo' phantom. After all these years it's still an open wound, and he doesn't even want to hear the word. In fact, he has banned any mention of it inside Granja Comary. But it's trickier trying to enforce the ban on the outside – everyone is talking about it, including the country's former president Lula da Silva.

In every interview Neymar insists he is taking it all in his stride: 'I'm playing in the World Cup, in my country no less. I couldn't be happier.' The kid from Mogi has surprised everyone with his leadership qualities, particularly after an erratic season at Barcelona. Without the pressure to play second fiddle to Messi, and with a strategy that affords him more freedom of movement, he is in his element. He couldn't be in a better frame of mind, and he seems sure that victory is within reach. 'I saw Ronaldo and Romario win it, and that's what I want to do,' he declares shortly before two warm-up friendlies – against Panama on 3 June in Goiânia, and against Serbia in São Paulo three days later. The first is a resounding 4–0 victory. Neymar scores the first in the 27th minute, and plays a part in the final goal as well. The second match is rather more disappointing. Only Fred manages to score and their performance draws boos from the crowd. Brazil's number 10 is unable to create any real opportunities. But his luck will change a week later, in the opening match of the 2014 World Cup.

Thursday 12 June, Corinthians Arena, São Paulo

Brazil are up against Croatia for only the second time in a World Cup. The first was in Germany in 2006, also in the group stages. On that occasion La Canarinha won it thanks to a goal from Cafú. Tonight, the five-time champions are going out on to the pitch all too aware that they have the upper hand. Niko Kovač's team qualified via the play-offs, although they have three excellent players who are used to the big leagues: Real's Luka Modrić, ex-Sevilla player Ivan Rakitić, who as of June 2014 has joined the Barça ranks, and former Bayern player Mario Mandžukić, now at Atlético Madrid. Shortly after kick-off, Julio Cesar's goal is under attack, with a shot from Ivica Olić grazing the post. And in the eleventh min-ute the crowd is stunned into silence after Marcelo puts the

Croatians ahead with an own goal, something no Brazil player has ever done in a World Cup. It's incredible bad luck: the ball catches him on the right leg while on the run, and deflects into the net. The Real defender looks utterly crestfallen.

But Brazil gather themselves and start looking for the equaliser. They fire their first warning shot in the 22nd minute with an effort from Oscar that Pletikosa manages to block. It will be one of the only things the Croatian goalie does right all game. A little while later Neymar receives his first yellow card of the tournament for elbowing Modrić, and in response immediately makes it 1–1 with a left-footed shot from outside the box. He celebrates by pointing to the sky, and Marcelo can breathe a sigh of relief. But after play resumes, Brazil seem to be losing their rhythm. There is something not quite convincing about their performance.

No one could have predicted what happens next. In the 68th minute Yuichi Nishimura awards a penalty for an apparent foul on Fred, something nobody but the Japanese referee seems to have seen. Neymar takes it, left-footed, and puts his team ahead. The goal certainly ups the energy, but the Brazilians are still struggling to get shots on target … right up until injury time, when Oscar seals a 3–1 win. A first victory for the home team, albeit a rather lacklustre one – no strokes of genius, no charisma, and a little too much controversy. Only one player seems to be up to the sort of standard expected of the only team in the world to have played in every World Cup: Neymar Jr. The number 10 is crowned man of the match, and describes his feelings with a single word: 'happy'.

Tuesday 17 June, Castelão stadium, Fortaleza

Everyone's worst fears have been confirmed: this Brazil team is a shadow of its former self. Against Mexico in the second

Group A match they can only manage a 0–0 draw. There is no trace of the team who won the FIFA Confederations Cup just a year earlier, and their place in the last sixteen hangs in the balance. The Mexicans are hungry, and more importantly they have 'Memo' Ochoa, a goalkeeper in the midst of one of the performances of his career. His incredibly quick reflexes enable him to block three dangerous chances: one from Paulinho in the 43rd minute, one from Neymar in the 68th, and a shot by captain Thiago Silva after a cross from the number 10 in the 86th. Apart from that, Brazil muster little else to excite the 60,000 spectators in the packed stadium or the millions watching across the globe. Mexico are dominating with plenty of possession, but they are lacking shots on target. Meanwhile Brazil lack ideas and imagination.

At the final whistle Scolari defends his approach: 'A 0–0 draw is never a good result, but it reflects the type of match we had: a hard-fought one. The *Seleção* is evolving and we have now played twenty matches with this strategy. The team is doing well. People have to understand that we are up against some exceptionally strong squads. Being group leaders doesn't make this draw a good result, because a win would have meant we would already be through. But we have to pay tribute to our excellent opponents.' Meanwhile the kid from Mogi das Cruzes has earned his keep, although he has certainly had better games.

Monday 23 June, Mané Garrincha National Stadium, Brasilia

'This was definitely our best match – not just because of the result, but because of our whole performance. The way we kept up the pressure on our opponents was crucial. We won comfortably and we deserved to. We are on the right path and we will keep improving every day.' Neymar is ecstatic: his team are through to the last sixteen after beating Cameroon 4–1 in the final group match. The young footballer can go home with his head held high, in the knowledge that were it not for his talent and thirst for victory, it could have been an entirely different story. Because, despite the number 10's generous comments, the result is rather deceiving.

Their star player aside, Brazil still have a lot of problems to iron out. The host team have been entirely dependent on the Barcelona forward. In the sixteenth minute Marcelo and Luiz Gustavo went on the counterattack and Neymar got the goal. But once in the lead, Brazil lost their concentration. They should have been aiming for a whitewash; instead they allowed Cameroon to equalise. Allan Nyom went past Dani Alves on the left and crossed to Joël Matip, who made it 1–1 in the 26th minute. Tension started to mount around the stadium. But once again the kid from Mogi went on the attack, and ten minutes later he had put them in front again, becoming the sixth-highest goalscorer in Brazil's history at just 22 years of age. In the second half, goals from Fred and Fernandinho sealed it, and La Canarinha went through as group winners.

Saturday 28 June, Mineirão stadium, Belo Horizonte

First tears of anguish, then joy. The tense last-sixteen match against Chile is the backdrop for some of the most surreal images of this World Cup.

In the eighteenth minute David Luiz nets one for Brazil after a corner. And in the 32nd Eduardo Vargas takes advantage of a mistake by Hulk after a throw-in. He passes to Alexis Sánchez, and Neymar's then-Barça teammate beats Julio Cesar with a shot across goal. One-all. From then on Chile put their best foot forward, while Brazil seem to stall. They are visibly nervous, but they manage to hold on for extra time. During the next half-hour the Chileans look tired, although they come very close to snatching a victory with a shot by Mauricio Pinilla which hits the crossbar.

Down to penalties. And this is where the 33 cameras at the Mineirão capture an alarming scene. Julio Cesar crying. Captain Thiago Silva refusing to take a shot and going to pray in the corner of the pitch. Brazil are paralysed with fear. Even Neymar drops to his knees before getting ready to take his shot. 'I felt like I was running three kilometres rather than three steps,' he would say later, 'but the most difficult part was when I got to the ball and had to shoot.'

Luck is on the Brazilians' side – the shootout ends 3–2 in their favour, and practically the entire team breaks down in tears, as if in a collective catharsis. The number 10, exhausted and suffering from cramp, has his arms around Scolari. Silva is inconsolable. David Luiz buries his face in the pitch. Emotion, tension, anxiety … the pressure has been building on this Brazilian team, and the coach may well need to call on his expert psychologist again. Next up: Colombia.

Friday 4 July, Castelão stadium, Fortaleza

Neymar will certainly remember this as one of the worst days of his life, if not the worst. Everything is going well, his team have already done enough to go through to the semis, when Juan Camilo Zúñiga knees him in the back. Neymar falls face down on the ground, screaming in pain, holding his back. Marcelo runs over to him and the Barça forward tells him he can't feel his legs. The whole team fear the worst. His pain is all too visible as he is rushed off on a stretcher. A few hours later the doctors confirm the fracture to his third vertebra, an incredibly rare injury in football and one that will keep him out for three to six weeks.

Neymar's World Cup is over. The Colombia match, having

been the best the *Seleção* has played all tournament, is to be his last. After all the doubts and errors, the Brazilians have given their best account of themselves while the Colombians have been on the ropes for almost the entire 90 minutes. Even Thiago Silva has managed to make up for refusing to take a penalty against Chile. The captain scored the first after six minutes with a shot at the far post. The second came from David Luiz – an incredible free kick from 30 yards.

By the 68th minute the game seemed decided. But less than ten minutes later Colombia managed to pull one back after Julio Cesar brought down Bacca in the box; James Rodriguez converted the penalty. Two-one at the final whistle, the end of a bittersweet clash for Brazil. In the days that remain before the semi-finals, Scolari has a mission impossible on his hands: convincing his team that they can win without Neymar.

Tuesday 8 July, Mineirão stadium, Belo Horizonte

The headline in newspaper *Folha de São Paulo*, 'Massacred', just about sums up the most diabolical 90 minutes in Brazilian footballing history. No one thought the match against favourites Germany would be easy, and it was clear that La Canarinha would be weak without Neymar. But absolutely no one was expecting a more painful and humiliating 'Maracanazo' than the original.

The German goals came thick and fast after Thomas Müller converted a corner in the eleventh minute. He found himself alone at the far post, and Brazil's defence was already in complete disarray. Before the home crowd could even react, Miroslav Klose scored the second to become the leading goalscorer in World Cup history. Toni Kroos scored the third two minutes later, and the fourth another minute after that, and Sami Khedira made it 5–0 just before the half-hour mark. In less than 30 minutes the Germans had made mince-meat of their opponents, and the five-time champions' fate was sealed.

The second half was not as intense, although no less galling for Brazil. André Schürrle came on to the pitch and scored in the 69th and 79th minutes to make it 7–0 – at which point Neymar switched off the television. He had been watching at home with family and friends, and according to Brazilian web-site UOL Esporte, frustrated with events in Belo Horizonte he now shouted: 'Screw it, I don't want to see any more of this. Let's play poker!' He ended up missing Brazil's only goal, netted by Oscar in the dying seconds of the match.

Saturday 12 July, Mané Garrincha National Stadium, Brasilia

The kid from Mogi is back on the pitch. He is still injured, but he wants to support his teammates after what is now being referred to as the 'Mineirazo'. He receives a stand-ing ovation from the crowd, and after watching some of the team's warm-up exercises he settles down in the dugout.

Brazil is still in a state of shock. For a country with foot-ball in its blood, it is hard to cope with the sort of thrashing they received from Germany. There has been rioting and looting across various cities, including Rio. On the street, in the media and on various social media channels the players and coach are lambasted with criticism and insults. The only one who remains unscathed is Neymar, and he pleads with the nation not to desert the team. 'We have to approach this match as though it's the final, and finish the World Cup smiling, with a victory. It won't take away all the pain, but it's important,' he says at a press conference at Granja Comary the night before the third-place play-off against the Netherlands.

It's a consolation match that serves little purpose and which no one wants to play. Neymar insists there is 'no shame' in being part of a national team that has taken a 7–1 beating, but he doesn't yet know that the *Seleção* still has one final humiliation in store, as the Dutch beat them to third place. Even he finds that too much to bear, covering his face with his shirt on more than one occasion during the match. In the first minute the Netherlands are awarded a penalty for a foul by Thiago Silva on Robben, and Van Persie steps up to the spot to make it 1–0. It's difficult to come back from that kind of start, especially for a team as devastated as Brazil. The game ends 3–0 after goals from Blind in the seventeenth minute and Wijnaldum in the 91st. There are boos from the crowd whenever the Brazilians touch the ball, and in the end the Brazil players are nowhere to be seen when the Dutchmen go up to collect their medals.

At the post-match press conference, Neymar interrupts Scolari to give him a hug. A few days later, the architect of the 2002 Japan and South Korea World Cup win resigns as Brazil coach. It's back to square one, and for the difficult job of rebuilding, the CBF name Carlos Dunga as Brazil's new coach.

Chapter 27

100 per cent Barça

It's just like when he was little: the headband with the words '100 per cent Jesus' emblazoned on it. The first one was made by his mother so that God would protect him, and he wore it for every match. This time he waits until the referee blows the final whistle before putting it on, wearing it to go up to collect Barcelona's 2015 Champions League trophy after beating Juventus 3–1 in Berlin. It is his way of giving thanks for the most important match of his life.

'Today is definitely the best moment in my career. The greatest match. I'm sure this day will go down in history,' he says when he finally comes off the pitch after an hour-long celebration with the team. He has been very emotional throughout all the hysteria with his teammates. At one point he breaks down in tears, sinking to his knees on the pitch, praying with his face practically touching the exact spot from which he scored the final goal of the match. 'I saw that my friends were there. I cried because of the realisation of every-thing that had happened, everything that I had dreamed of since I was a child, all that effort, my family's effort,' he explains. The Brazilian's comments are humble, emotional, although his cheeky nature still shines through. 'What more could anyone ask for? There's nothing more anyone can say about me.'

Champions League, *La Liga*, Copa del Rey. Barcelona have won their second treble in five years. Up until the final weeks no one had been expecting anything like it. And nobody has done more than Neymar Jr, scoring in the finals of both the Champions League and Copa del Rey. In Berlin he has been instrumental in the Blaugrana's victory. He had a hand in the first goal, scored another that was disallowed due to an accidental handball, and ended up netting the definitive third goal in the dying seconds of the match. The shot came after a rapid build-up, surprising Juventus goalie Gianluigi Buffon, who was off his line. Leo Messi got the ball halfway up the pitch and passed to the Brazilian, who took it up the pitch, did a one-two with Pedro and sent the ball into the back of the net with his right foot.

'He has had a spectacular season, with a huge increase in both goals and in performance level, which confirms him as one of the best players around,' says Barça coach Luis Enrique at the press conference after his team's triumph in Germany. In his second season at Barcelona, Neymar has played 51 matches and scored 39 goals, including ten in the Champions League – equal to Leo Messi and Cristiano Ronaldo. The three were joint highest goalscorers in the competition; Neymar was finally neck and neck with the big stars. The investment in the kid from Mogi das Cruzes had paid off and the club could breathe easily.

It was without a doubt a very different season to his first at Barcelona. On 11 August 2014 the Brazilian was back with his teammates after putting behind him one of the most difficult moments of his career: a brutal clash with Colombian Carlos Zúñiga and an injury that spelled the end of his World Cup. He was back in training, ready to face the new season with renewed energy – and single this time after splitting with Bruna Marquezine. It had been a turbulent relationship since day one, but the split seemed permanent this time. What was the cause? There were rumours that she had wanted to tie the knot, but that he supposedly wasn't ready for that commitment. 'No, we are no longer together,' said the actress on the *Fantástico* programme on Brazilian TV channel Globo. 'I care about him a lot, he's someone I'm really fond of.'

Neymar's media exposure was still incredibly intense, with 52 million Facebook followers, more than 23 million on Instagram and nearly 19 million on Twitter. His life and image were still bringing in more than his sporting achievements, something that worried the Barça camp, who wanted him to focus on giving his all on the pitch and improve upon the mediocre results of the previous season, when he had scored nine goals in 26 *Liga* matches, fifteen in 41 in all competitions. They wanted more of a return on their significant economic investment; more goals to help pay back the large sums that all his contractual irregularities had ended up costing the club. His great friend Dani Alves was one of the few who was convinced that the coming season would be the year of Neymar Jr. 'Everyone needs time to settle in,' he said, 'and this will be the year to really see his abilities. He's gaining a much better rapport with Leo, as well as with the staff.'

That was key: his relationship with Messi. It was clear in the second *Liga* match on 31 August that they had strengthened their bond. Neymar started on the bench and didn't come on until the second half. After two serious errors, he redeemed himself with a magical pass to Lionel, who slid the ball between the legs of the opposition goalkeeper, so that Sandro could tap it in, making it 0–1. But there was also a more worrying incident, demonstrating Neymar's 'superstar' tendencies. During his warm-up time on the edge of the pitch, instead of focusing on the match ahead, he was busy signing fans' boots. Was it friendliness, a marketing ploy, or just irresponsible?

But while the Spanish press were busy scrutinising his every movement, the Brazil coach had every confidence in him. In fact, in September, Dunga announced that he would be the *Seleção*'s new captain. 'He is a role model, he's a top-quality player despite his youth,' explained the coach. 'He has experience and he knows how to stay calm under pressure.' A few days later, Dunga's words were confirmed on the pitch at Camp Nou. Neymar started on the bench once again, but later silenced his critics with two goals in five minutes against Athletic Bilbao, the only goals of the match, thanks to assists from Leo. They were his first goals in *La Liga* since 26 March.

The partnership with Messi was working, it was three victories out of three for Barcelona, and they hadn't conceded any goals – they hadn't had such a strong defensive start since 1985.

'I'm very happy about the two goals,' Neymar said at the end of the match, although he admitted that he still was 'not 100 per cent fit, I hope to get back to full strength'. He insisted he felt more settled into life in the Catalan city: 'It was very important to take time to adapt, now I am happier and I hope to do even better.' And he had no problem deferring to Lionel: 'It is a privilege to play with him, he's a star, the best in the world.' He said they were getting know each other 'a lot better' and he believed the relationship would only improve.

But during the following weeks it started to become apparent that the relationship between the Barça coach and the players was somewhat strained. It was put down to the constant changes in line-up. In every match, new coach Enrique was trying different combinations. He wanted every player, without exception, to earn their position. It was a tactic that seemed to increase Neymar's hunger for goals. On Sunday 21 September, at precisely 9.33pm, the Brazilian kicked off the scoring in what would be a 5–0 whitewash over Levante, thanks to a Messi assist once again. But the number 11 didn't finish the match. 'He twisted his ankle and he had been having a bit of pain, so we decided to take him off,' explained Enrique. It was nothing serious, and he was back to full fitness a few days later.

On 27 September he scored his first *Liga* hat-trick against Granada at Camp Nou, where the final score was 6–0 to Barcelona. His first goal was in the 26th minute. Neymar took advantage of an error by the opposition midfielders to make it 1–0. Shortly after the break, he got his second after Leo passed to Munir El Haddadi, whose shot was blocked by the goalie; Neymar came running in for the rebound. The last goal was thanks to a Messi–Neymar move: the Argentinian gave the assist and the Brazilian thanked him with a hug that lifted the number 10 off the ground. The newspapers were starting to talk of 'the happy couple'. Between the two of them they had scored eleven of Barcelona's seventeen goals in the first six matches of *La Liga* – six by Neymar, five by Messi.

'Neymar is a genuine star. I don't judge strikers by their goals, I judge them by how much effort they are willing to put in, how capable they are of adapting, and their desire to work hard, day in, day out. From that point of view Neymar will not let us down,' said the club's sporting director, Andoni Zubizarreta.

But good things don't last forever. On 30 September the Blaugrana lost 3–2 to Paris Saint-Germain in their Group F Champions League match. Neymar scored their second goal but apart from that, like the rest of the team, his impact was minimal. The next day, his father appeared in court to explain the supposed irregularities committed by the club during his son's signing. Allegedly the club's aim was to allow Messi to think he was still the highest-paid player in the dressing room.

For two hours, Neymar Pai tried to convince the judge that he had behaved in accordance with the law, that the companies which received payments as part of the deal really existed and were legal entities, rather than simply a cover to avoid attributing all the money as salary and thereby reducing the amount of tax payable. He also made a surprising admission: that the Neymar family had preferred Barcelona even though Real Madrid was offering them a lot more money – around €150 million. The reason was that at Barça they were offered the chance to raise the player's profile a lot more. The whole process had plagued the player ever since he arrived in the city, and it was to continue causing headaches for him throughout the rest of the season.

But despite everything, Neymar Jr continued smiling and showing the happier side to his life on social media, like the video he uploaded of him singing – albeit rather badly – in the car. Or the one in which he rode alongside 2013 and 2014 world rally champion Sébastien Ogier, occasionally looking nervous, but ending with his usual laughter.

Back on the pitch, October was the month for goals. On Tuesday 14th he had one of his best ever matches for his country, scoring four goals against Japan. At just 22 years old he had already racked up 40 in 44 appearances with La Canarinha. Even he couldn't believe the achievement. 'I have no idea what my limits are, it's giving me goosebumps. It's a wonderful feeling, I'm so incredibly happy to realise this dream. I never imagined in my wildest fantasies that

I would get to play for my country. I feel very happy and I thank God.'

With Neymar in the team Barça also continued to dominate … until 25 October, the date of the first *Clásico* of the year against Real Madrid at the Santiago Bernabéu stadium. It was the debut for the new Barça strike force of Neymar, Messi and Luis Suárez; the Uruguayan was playing for the first time with his new team after completing his ban for biting Italy's Giorgio Chiellini during the 2014 World Cup. But the trio of stars were no match for Real Madrid that day, and the Whites won the first clash of the season 3–1. The consolation goal went to Neymar in the fourth minute. It gave the impression that victory would be easy, but it wasn't to be. Suárez sent him a deep pass, the Brazilian controlled it on the edge of the area, dodged round two defenders and scored. But after that there was nothing to write home about from the Barça side. The following day, the number 11's performance was the saving grace in the match reports.

Between matches, the media were continually interested in his personal life, especially his rumoured relationship with Soraja Sara Vucelic, the bubbly model six years his senior, a former *Big Brother* contestant in Serbia and known as 'the Kardashian of the Balkans'. They apparently met in Ibiza and the player was said to have sent her a private jet so that she could come and visit him in Barcelona. Whether or not the rumours were true, it was an opportunity for *Interviú* magazine to feature a cover picture of Soraja coming out of the sea topless. But the model was not the only one linked with Neymar. He was said to have another lover in Barcelona, a young Catalán lawyer who he supposedly met after flirting with her on Twitter. And the Brazilian model Patricia Jordane also claimed in a

Playboy interview to have had a relationship with the foot-baller. He would neither confirm nor deny the rumours, although his representatives were adamant that 'it's all a lie, he's single'.

November started with a slight hiccup, when Barcelona lost 0–1 to Celta Vigo; suddenly Real Madrid had the advantage. It was Barça's second consecutive defeat in *La Liga*, following on from their disappointment at the Bernabéu. But despite looking a little unconvincing, the team won all their matches throughout the rest of the month – although the match away to Almería was notable for the now unusual sight of Neymar on the bench in the first half. From there he had to watch as his team were boxed in by the home side. But in the second half Luis Enrique changed tack and sent him on to the pitch. Half an hour later he scored the equaliser. After the initial scare, the match – 'our worst match', according to the coach – finished 1–2 to the Blaugrana. In the next game, against Sevilla, the Brazilian scored yet again at Camp Nou, a goal-fest that ended 5–1 and saw Messi become the highest goalscorer in the history of *La Liga*. Just like the previous week, Neymar's contribution came at a critical moment. The visitors had just equalised and it took him just two minutes to turn the scoreline back in Barça's favour, opening it up for their mammoth victory.

On 6 December Barcelona overcame Paris Saint-Germain to win Group F of the Champions League and qualify for the last sixteen. It was the first time that Neymar, Messi and Suárez all scored in the same match, making it 3–1. But the Brazilian wouldn't be back on the pitch until 20 December, first due to ankle niggles, and then because the coach decided to rest him. He came back on in the match against Córdoba, although only as a substitute, listening to the crowd from the bench. Barcelona enjoyed a resounding 5–0 win, but something was still not right about Luis Enrique's approach.

That's how Neymar Jr's year ended. *L'Équipe* named him in its top XI, and described him as a player who 'has repeatedly saved his team from mediocrity'. In an interview with *Globoesporte*, the Brazilian said he was 'very happy' with everything he had achieved: 'I am growing every day, every season. I think it's a great experience. I was very happy at Santos, but I needed a change, I needed bigger challenges, and I hope I can continue to be happy here.' He acknowledged that he felt under pressure after all the gossip about him, but that wasn't what motivated him to improve: 'There is one person who is my greatest influence, and that's my father. His impact on me is much greater than anyone or anything else. I feel calm, I feel free to do my job.'

Neymar went off on holiday, satisfied with a job well done. But on his return a dispute erupted that had been brewing in the dressing room. The Brazilian started January on the bench, along with Messi and Dani Alves. It seemed to be a punishment for coming back later than everyone else from the Christmas holidays, despite having had express permission from the club. But Luis Enrique denied any form of chastisement. 'I made the decision so that those players would be less at risk. They have had fewer training sessions, and a long journey. I felt they shouldn't be put at risk of injury,' he said. With the stars on the bench against Real Sociedad, the match at Anoeta was a complete disaster. Neymar went on in the 58th minute, but the game was already a done deal. The Blaugrana, now behind Real Madrid in *La Liga*, lost following an own goal. And the number 11 wasn't even able to get a single shot on target. It wasn't a huge defeat, but it left a poor impression nonetheless, and the players' morale was shattered. Shortly afterwards the media revealed that after that humiliation, some of them created a WhatsApp group in an attempt to change the attitude of the team. The first message was blunt: 'If we continue like this we won't win anything this year.' After that, things began to improve bit by bit.

Four days later, on 8 January, all Barcelona's top players were back in the starting line-up for the Copa del Rey last-sixteen match against Elche, another 5–0 whitewash against one of the bottom teams in *La Liga*, in which Neymar scored first and last. With several months still to go, the kid from Mogi das Cruzes had overtaken his tally from the previous season. He had scored sixteen goals, as against fifteen in 2013–14. And he wasn't done yet.

In the next game they beat Atlético Madrid 3–1 at home in their eighteenth league match of the season. The match started with a minute's silence for the victims of the *Charlie Hebdo* attack, while all the staff, including the presidents of both teams, held signs that read 'Je suis Charlie'. Neymar got the first goal in the twelfth minute. Messi shook off three defenders in the area and crossed; Suárez couldn't get there, but as if by magic the ball met the Brazilian's boot at the far post and he scored. Shortly afterwards Neymar received a kick from the Uruguayan José Giménez. It was enough of a blow to cause his ankle to bleed, but the referee didn't blow his whistle. Throughout the season so far, Neymar had received 69 fouls over 1,563 minutes – around one every 22 minutes, the most of any Barça player. 'My father always told me that I loved the ball more than I loved actually playing football. When I was little I spent all my time dribbling round the furniture at home,' he said in an interview with *Forbes*, which included him on the list of the 30 most influential sports personalities under 30. 'Football, particularly Brazilian football, tries to be a happy sport. And that leads to people doing tricks with the ball. It's part of our culture. I've learned to defend myself from people who are coming at me.'

But aside from goals, good football and fouls, the match left a lasting image that was more significant than it may have appeared at first: a euphoric Neymar, Messi and 'Lucho' Suárez, running towards the crowd with their arms around each other to celebrate the final goal, scored by the Argentinian. It was a moment that perfectly captured the harmony between the three stars, and how well they had begun to understand each other. 'It's rare that an Argentinian, a Uruguayan and a Brazilian get on so well, but we do,' Neymar admitted. 'We have a great relationship,' added Messi, 'and when there's an understanding off the pitch then it's much easier to play well together on the pitch.' Their love of traditional South American barbecues had been credited with kick-starting their friendship. Teammate Javier Mascherano said they often got together with their families to grill the kinds of meat that were popular back home. Apparently one day Leo also told Neymar not to show him so much admiration, that they were equals and that Neymar scored more goals. And that was that.

The triumph against Atlético seemed to calm the waters in the dressing room. Referring to the much-criticised rotational tactics of Luis Enrique, Neymar insisted that the initial bumpy start had passed and that they were 'all together again'. 'I am very happy,' he declared. 'Now we just have to focus on playing as one team on the pitch. It has been a good game, we did it as a team.'

But his smile was wiped from his face in the very next match – in the 70th minute, to be exact – against Deportivo La Coruña at the Riazor. At that point Barça were winning 0–3 (the match ended 0–4), and the coach decided to bring substitute Pedro on in place of the Brazilian. Neymar didn't hide his anger, avoiding eye contact with the coach all the way to the dugout. He sat down, took off his boots and threw them on the ground in annoyance. He had played in sixteen of nineteen *Liga* matches, but had only stayed on for the full 90 minutes in seven of those. In four he started on the bench and in five he was substituted. He never liked being brought off, and he had made it clear in the worst possible way. 'I don't like coming off, I always want to play, I always want to be on the pitch,' he has said on more than one occasion. And it wouldn't be the last time …

By the end of January, the press and the fans were won over by Neymar's genius. The Brazilian was 'the biggest sensation of Barcelona this season', according to *Marca*. And he knew it. 'I feel important,' he said during a publicity appearance. 'Right now, I am completely comfortable. I love playing, scoring goals, and am gaining in confidence thanks to my teammates' help. This is the best I've felt since I came to Barcelona.' And he proved it yet again on 28 January when he was instrumental in beating Atlético Madrid and helping his team through to the semi-finals of the Copa del Rey (2–3 at the final whistle, 2–4 on aggregate). He shook off the *Atleti* defenders to deafening whistles from the crowd. It was an electric game, which ended with Atlético's Arda Turán throwing a shin guard at the linesman. And the kid from Mogi das Cruzes also got into a confrontation with some of his opponents on his way to the dressing room at half-time, following some gestures he made on the pitch.

'He has a peculiar way of playing when he's winning. No one likes it but he keeps doing it. He always makes lots of gestures when he's winning, and it rubs it in for the opposition,' Atlético captain Gabi later explained. But Brazil coach Dunga defended him: 'If you take away football, samba and a few other things from a Brazilian, it's like he's no longer Brazilian. He has a very different understanding of what football is compared to players of other nationalities.' And his teammate Jordi Alba added, 'Neymar is a really humble, straightforward guy, he likes to play football and he likes to play it a certain way. Everyone who knows him knows that. He has no intention to disrespect anyone. He doesn't foul people, he doesn't insult them.' That afternoon Neymar was the victim of a particularly ugly gesture. Atlético's Juanfran held up seven fingers and then made the signal for elimination – a cruel reference to Germany's 7–1 humiliation of Brazil in the World Cup.

As the season continued both Barça and its star attacking trio looked more and more comfortable. On 4 March the Blaugrana made it through to the final of the Copa del Rey, leaving Villareal in the dust, 6–2 on aggregate. On 8 March, after beating Rayo Vallecano 6–1 – a match that Neymar missed due to a ban – they reclaimed the top spot in *La Liga* from Real Madrid. And a week later they sealed their place in the Champions League quarter-finals after beating Manchester City 3–1 on aggregate. But the Brazilian's life was not all about soccer. He also got the chance to try his hand at American football, accepting the Starclub Challenge to try to beat the NFL record of kicking a goal from 64 yards. He didn't do too badly – 50 yards with an American football and 60 yards with a soccer ball.

In April the Blaugrana racked up one win after another, with just one draw, 2–2 against Sevilla. It was during this draw that the fans saw Neymar's negative side again. He had scored his team's second goal with a superb free-kick, breaking a dry spell of a month and half without scoring. But fifteen minutes before the end of the match, when they were a goal up, the coach decided to substitute him. He came off, but very reluctantly, making irritated gestures with his hands, protesting in front of his other teammates on the bench and throwing his boots on the ground again, leaving them to be retrieved by an assistant. It was like watching the behaviour of a spoilt child. Three days earlier, against Almería at Camp Nou, he had been grumpy about not playing at all. 'I don't fixate on these petty details. I'm only interested in football,' said Luis Enrique, apparently unperturbed. 'This sort of behaviour is becoming fashionable, and it's ridiculous.' He later added, 'I understand that everyone wants to be on the pitch. But the players also have to understand that I'm the coach and I make the decisions.'

At the end of the month they went through to the semi-finals of the Champions League, knocking out Paris Saint-Germain, thanks in large part to Neymar, who scored one in the first leg and one in the return leg, taking them to 5–1 on aggregate. 'I'm very happy with how the season is going and the fact that I was able to help my teammates,' he said. 'We have to keep this up so that we can achieve our main objective – winning the Champions League.' First they had to get past ex-Barça coach Pep Guardiola's Bayern Munich in the semis, which they did, 3–0 at home in the first leg with one from Neymar, and then 2–3 in the away leg with both goals coming from the Brazilian.

And on 17 May they won their first trophy of the season. It was the penultimate round of league fixtures, and Barça triumphed in *La Liga* after beating Atlético thanks to a single goal from Messi. Neymar Jr also had various chances but his shots were deflected. But he was on target in the Copa del Rey final two weeks later. On 30 May at Camp Nou they lined up with Athletic Bilbao to sing the national anthem; and then Barcelona dominated from start to finish. It was a final that would end up having a strangely similar outcome

to the Champions League final against Juventus the following week – 1–3 to the Blaugrana, even including a disallowed
goal for Neymar, on this occasion for a dubious offside rul-
ing. But the kid from Mogi das Cruzes recomposed himself,
just as he would do the following week in Berlin, and ended
up making his mark with a goal. In the Copa del Rey match
it was the second goal, in the 36th minute, following a play
involving Rakitić, Messi and Suárez, setting up Neymar in
front of an open goal.

The Brazilian was also behind the biggest controversy on
the pitch. With the game already sewn up, he tried a flashy
'lambretta' (a reverse flick-over, or 'rainbow kick'), prompting indignation from Athletic Bilbao. The move ended in a
foul, Neymar fell to the ground and his opponents crowded
round him to accuse him of showboating and give him a
dressing-down. They saw the acrobatics as an attempt to
mock their defeat. After the match, once Barcelona had
lifted their 27th Copa del Rey trophy, coach Luis Enrique
also voiced his displeasure: 'In Spain it is looked upon very
badly. If I were an Athletic player I would have reacted the
same, or even worse. In Brazil it is normal, so we have to
understand the context. He didn't do it to humiliate his
opponents. But we will have to control it with time.'

Aside from such moments, Neymar Jr closed out an
incredible season with the best Barça side in history. His
alliance with Messi and Suárez – now dubbed 'MSN' – had
netted 122 goals. He had certainly got over his homesickness.

But his transfer case is not yet over. In the coming months
he will have to testify in Brazil as part of the lawsuit brought
by DIS Group (which owned 40 per cent of the player's
rights), in its attempt to claim more money once it became
known that Barcelona paid more for him than they had
originally revealed. His former club Santos has also filed

a complaint with FIFA against Barcelona, Neymar and his father. And Barcelona president Josep María Bartomeu, his predecessor Sandro Rosell, and Barcelona itself are accused in Spain of tax fraud in relation to the signing, and will stand trial. All these legal proceedings will be ongoing during the Brazilian's third season at Barcelona.

Chapter 28
Confirmation

This was the photo from left to right: Cristiano Ronaldo, Leo Messi, Messi's wife Antonella Roccuzzo, and Ney. Just two and a half years after arriving at Barcelona, there he was sitting with the world's top players, making small talk. He knew it would be mission impossible to win the 2015 Ballon d'Or, but it was only his first time on the shortlist. At the celebratory gala on 11 January 2016 in Zurich, everyone knew that the Brazilian would have his time to shine in the future. And he was all smiles as he accepted the decision in his usual natural way, never missing an opportunity to don a quirky outfit. If in previous years it was Messi who stood out with his garish attire, this time it was Neymar who stole the show, in a dark blue suit with velvet lapels, white shirt, spotted bowtie … and topped off with a dapper hat.

'I never played to be the best in the world or to win the Ballon d'Or,' said the Barça number 11. 'I always played to be the best I could be, to push myself further. Being the best in the world is a result of that hard work. If I am here talking about this today, it's because my work is paying off.'

There had been calls for Barcelona's MSN 'trident' of Messi, Suárez and Neymar to all be nominated. But at the gala in Switzerland Neymar praised not only Leo's genius, but also that of his rival CR7. 'I don't know who is better, Messi or Cristiano, but I admire them both greatly. I have watched them both play since I was young, and it is incredible to be able to be here with them. They each have their own story and their own achievements. They are the greatest players I have ever seen and they have both made history. I see Leo every day and I admire him as a player and as a person. He is very calm and he's a good friend. Cristiano I have followed more on TV. But they have both enjoyed great success for around eight or nine years now, and one day I hope to be like them – in a position to break my own records.'

It was clear from the votes that he was inching closer to achieving that goal, but there was still plenty of work to do: Leo took 41 per cent of the votes, Cristiano 27 and Ney 7. Still, not bad for his first time on the shortlist, and he didn't try to hide his ambition, saying, 'I hope to be back.'

Who would have thought, six months earlier, that he would be experiencing such a joyous moment? It hardly would have seemed possible back in June. At that point he was entirely focused on avoiding another catastrophe with the national team, like the previous year's Mineirazo against Germany in the 2014 World Cup. He needed to regain his confidence, his self-esteem and, more importantly, his goal-scoring abilities. And Carlos Caetano Bledorn Verri was counting on him. Brazil's head coach, better known as Dunga, had pinned all his hopes on a defensive strategy and the magic of a young Blaugrana player in an attempt to get his hands on the 2015 Copa América, or at the very least to restore the Canaries' pride.

On 14 June in La Serena, northern Chile, they were up against Peru. They may have seemed a modest team on the surface, but it was clear that Brazil didn't scare them, although they did manage to clinch it in the dying moments. The commentators were clear that Neymar was a cut above the rest of his teammates, heading their first goal in the fifth minute. It came at a crucial moment, rallying the Brazilians after they had already conceded a goal by Christian Cueva in the first few touches of the game. With Brazil having little more in the way of tactics than passing to the Barça number 11, it all rested on Ney. And he didn't disappoint: he scored, he made nineteen attempts (more than in the entire previous tournament in 2011), he managed six shots on target, he dazzled with a double 'sombrero' – two flicks over the heads of two opponents with consecutive touches – and finally he set up Douglas Costa's winning goal in injury time.

It was an agonising victory, but Neymar made it possible. At the age of 23 he was the youngest player to have scored 44 goals for Brazil, and in the list of historic goalscorers he was up there behind only Pelé, Ronaldo, Zico and Romario. He was a symbol of hope for his country, a warm and charismatic kid, although he occasionally let his emotions get the better of him. Then he showed his worst side – like on 18 June in a clash with Colombia, which ended in a 0–1 defeat for Brazil and was to be his last match of the tournament. He wasn't out injured like in the World Cup, this time he was sidelined due to an unjustified outburst. When the final whistle went, Ney already knew that he wouldn't be able to play in the next match against Venezuela because he had racked up too many yellow cards. Suddenly, without warning, he kicked the ball, hitting Pablo Armero in the back. Was it bad luck, or a deliberate strike? A general brawl ensued between the two sides, and Chilean referee Enrique Osses pulled out his red card.

'They are using the rules against me. That's what happens when you have a mediocre ref,' said Neymar, adding: 'There was a lot of confusion at the final whistle, but there was no need to start sending everyone off. I was pushed.' It was evident from the replay that he was run down by Carlos Bacca – who also ended up with a red card and a torn shirt to boot – but only after Ney head-butted Jeison Murillo. Even

Colombia star James Rodríguez had to intervene. 'Calm down, you can't always win everything,' the Real Madrid player told Ney.

The altercation put an end to a bitter match for the Brazilians, but not to Neymar's anger. He squared up to the referee in the tunnel, hurling insults at him. 'You were trying to make a name for yourself at my expense,' he allegedly said, according to the referee's official match report. He was immediately banned for four matches by the Disciplinary Tribunal of CONMEBOL – the South American Football Federation. 'It was a premeditated act, waiting for the referee in the tunnel and then insulting him,' stated Argentine committee member Alberto Lozada. 'The punishment could have been much worse. He got off lightly.'

Neymar left Chile on 20 June. Even his fellow Brazilians couldn't justify his actions. 'He is behaving in a very aggressive way and that's not acceptable,' said Ronaldo Nazário da Lima. Dunga seemed to be in agreement: 'We need men who can make decisions, even if they get it wrong; we don't need children.' The rest of the squad followed Ney just a week later, after a defeat by Paraguay on penalties in the quarter-finals.

Back in Spain, Ney's season got off to a bad start when he missed both the Spanish and European Super Cups and the start of La Liga after coming down with the mumps. He was back on the pitch at the Nou Camp on 29 August against Malaga, although he finished the match on the bench, watching as a solitary goal from Vermaelen clinched it for the locals. Coach Luis Enrique felt he needed a rest until he was fully recovered. He didn't score in the 2015–16 championship until 13 September, against Atlético Madrid at the Calderón. Their rivals scored first with a shot from Fernando Torres in the 50th minute. But their joy was cut short when Ney equalised just four minutes later. He was one of the ones pushing the hardest for the Blaugrana to take the lead, which they did fifteen minutes before the final whistle, thanks to a goal from Messi.

'I'm very happy with the victory, and of course with the goal,' said a delighted Neymar. 'We equalised quickly at an important moment. It was a pleasure to win this match.' And he had a few words to say about Lionel as well: 'When we have the best of the best on the pitch, we all play better.' But whether by pure coincidence or bad luck, that theory would be put to the test sooner rather than later, as Leo was forced out with an injury against Las Palmas on 26 September. The whole of the Nou Camp fell quiet. All eyes were on Neymar: the strikeforce, the leadership and the fate of the match now rested on his shoulders. Was he up to the task? Could he step into the boots of one of the greatest players in history?

One game later everything seemed in doubt when Seville beat Barcelona 1–2 at home. Neymar's performance was up and down, although he was the best on the team and at least he scored a penalty, ending that particular drought. He hadn't had a great record from the penalty spot since arriving at Barça, missing three out of five. But despite the poor result at the Sánchez Pizjuán, the Brazilian had the air of someone ready to step up, and as the days went by he seemed to settle into his new position of responsibility.

Over the next six weeks, victories came thick and fast for Barcelona in both La Liga and the Champions League under the Brazilian's leadership. 'He's electric, and when he gets into the box at that speed, the defenders either have to foul him or concede a goal,' said the coach after a match against Rayo Vallecano on Saturday 17 October. It ended 5–2 to Barça, with four by Neymar – something he had achieved on four previous occasions: with Santos against both Atlético

Paranaense and União Barberense, and with Brazil's Under 20s against Paraguay and in a friendly against Japan. 'This has been one of my best games since I arrived, it's in my top ten without a doubt. But scoring goals is only possible with the help of the whole team. It wasn't easy,' he told the press, as he clutched the match ball signed by all his teammates. He had celebrated earlier on the pitch, doing the moves to *Watch me* by the rapper Silentó. Even his good friend Dani Alves mimed shining his boots in adulation, while the press started to compare him to Ronaldinho – another great Brazilian to leave his mark at Barça. And Luis Enrique, who had been a team-mate of Ronnie's before coaching Neymar, acknowledged something of a parallel. 'When I played with Ronnie we used to stay to watch him doing tricks with the ball during the warm-up. It's the same with Ney.'

He was undoubtedly on a winning streak. On 25 October against Eibar he scored another three in a convincing 3–1 victory, on 30 October he did away with Getafe in just two plays, one finished by him and the other by Luis Suárez, and on 7 November he netted an unforgettable shot against Villareal in a match that ended 3–0. He received a cross from Suárez, controlled the ball and flicked his trademark 'sombrero' move over Jaume Costa's head. As the ball hit the ground he turned and shot, bringing the Nou Camp crowd to their feet. It was one for the history books. 'I had planned to do that play. I'm delighted,' he admitted after the match. So far he was the top goalscorer of the season. And the scene was set for one of the most crucial dates of the year: the Real Madrid–Barça *Clásico*.

But though he may have been getting results, things were far from perfect. There was gossip about Neymar off the pitch, and it wasn't always positive. His legal woes surrounding his signing were still ongoing. One day it emerged

that possessions worth €42 million had been seized, supposedly because of tax evasion. The following day he posted an
Instagram photo of the new car he had acquired to replace
the Porche Panamera that he had been banned from using.
And while the latter was worth €80,000, the new red Ferrari
458 Spider cost more than three times as much. The kid had
been enjoying something of a charmed existence, narrat-
ing his daily life via social media and already earning more
through endorsements than playing football. The press were
always focused on him, every gesture he made, every new
haircut. It was draining always having to play the starring
role and be in the limelight – particularly when not everything said about him was complimentary. It was his father
who spoke out: they were happy in the Catalan capital, but if
the attacks continued they would consider moving country,
he threatened. 'I don't want to use the word "persecution",
but if we are not able to work in peace then we won't stay
in Spain,' Neymar Pai told the *Què t'hijugues* programme on
Radio Barcelona, striking fear into the heart of the Barça
camp, who must have been wondering if the rumours were
true that he had received offers from Man United or Real
Madrid. 'We have spent the last two and a half years answering the same questions and defending ourselves against the
same accusations. We are coming up to a contract renewal
with Barça, but we'll only pursue it if it's worth it for Neymar,
my business and our family,' he insisted.

Neymar Pai's warning was still ringing in everyone's ears
when his son stepped out onto the pitch at the Santiago
Bernabéu on Saturday 21 November for the first *Clásico* of
the season. Leo Messi had been given the go-ahead from the
medics but he was still starting on the bench. He came on
in the second half: the Messi–Suárez–Neymar 'MSN' trident
was finally reunited. And they didn't disappoint, crushing

their biggest rivals 0–4. Ney scored the second in the 39th minute with an outstanding play. He was finding it difficult to get into the match, but once he netted the goal he transformed into an unstoppable force, pushing the Real defenders to breaking point. Four minutes from the final whistle, fed up with constantly running back for the ball, central midfielder Isco aimed a kick at the Brazilian. Red card. But worse than the foul itself was the behaviour of the Whites fans, who cheered their man as he was leaving the pitch. But others preferred to focus on the match's more positive moments, including pop giants One Direction. While doing some promotional work in Mexico, Neymar had mentioned that he was a huge fan of the British boyband. Band member Niall Horan had even come to Barcelona a few times to watch some matches and had met quite a few of the players. 'Neymar and Messi are the best,' he said. 'It's difficult to find anyone better than them.'

Just three days later, in the Champions League against Roma, Barça pulled off an even more impressive scoreline: 6–1. Although Neymar had a hand in the first goal by Suárez, he didn't score any this time round. In fact, he missed another penalty. But he was back with another double on 28 November against Real Sociedad, in another resounding Barça performance that ended 4–0 with goals from all three of the strikers. 'If they don't all get to score, the party isn't complete for them,' said Luis Enrique. 'We are undoubtedly having a good run, but we have a tough month ahead of us with the FIFA Club World Cup in Japan.'

Ney landed in the Far East with a muscle injury that he had picked up a few days earlier in training. It wasn't serious, and although he missed Barça's first fixture, the semi-final against Chinese club Guangzhou (3–0 to Barça), he was back in time for the final against Argentina's River

Plate on 20 December. It was a particularly special final for the Brazilian, not just because of his fame among South American fans, but because it was his chance to win one after suffering a 4–0 whitewash in the 2011 final with his Brazilian club Santos, at the hands of Guardiola's Barcelona. This time he got to enjoy a 3–0 victory, and although he didn't score he set up Messi's goal to finish off an excellent year for the club, winning five out of six possible titles: La Liga, the Champions League, the Copa del Rey, the European Super Cup and the Club World Cup.

After the Christmas break and the Ballon d'Or gala, 17 January saw one of the most hotly anticipated matches of the season. It was the first time Neymar would come up against the Athletic Bilbao players after their controversial 2015 Copa del Rey final, when one of the Brazilian's cheeky tricks with the ball late in the game was criticised as rubbing salt into the Red and Whites' wounds. No one denied that it would be a tense encounter, but everyone in the Barça camp closed ranks around Ney. 'He should keep enjoying his football. He's not out to humiliate anyone,' said Enrique. 'He hasn't done anything offensive. He's Brazilian, there's nothing disrespectful or dishonourable about his style of play. And he shouldn't have to apologise if he chips the ball over your head.'

At 8.30pm the two teams went out onto the pitch at the Nou Camp, and it was quickly evident that the locals had the edge. The visitors went down to ten men after their goalkeeper Gorka Iraizoz conceded a penalty for a foul on Suárez, and Messi didn't hesitate to convert it, kick-starting a 6–0 hammering that Bilbao would not forget in a hurry. Neymar had plenty to do, scoring the second on the half hour, helping to set up the first of Suárez's three goals, and gifting another to Ivan Rakitić after another stunning play that was pure Neymar. He pushed forward down the left hand side, losing his opponent, moved into the box as if heading for the goal, then suddenly surprised the defenders by dashing away towards the touchline and crossing towards the goal, leaving the Croatian to just tap it into the net. And better yet, he made it look completely effortless.

Three days later the two teams faced each other once again, this time in Bilbao in the first leg of the Copa del Rey quarter-finals. It was another victory for the Blaugrana, albeit a rather more conservative 1–2 this time. 'They got one back at the end which has made things a bit tougher for us, but we played a good game. They're a dangerous team,' said Neymar, who scored the second in the 24th minute. Unfortunately, the abiding image was not of a match well played, but of an unsportsmanlike exchange between Aritz Aduriz and Ney. The Brazilian was down on the ground when the Bilbao striker seemed to step on his shoulder while running past him. Luckily the dispute was resolved pretty quickly. 'I apologised to him as I grazed him slightly. I wasn't my intention to hurt him in any way. This is the sort of incident that should be left out on the pitch. He's a genuinely world class player and I have to congratulate him on his performance,' insisted Aduriz. 'But sometimes I wish he would change his attitude,' he added.

Coach Luis Enrique had his own theory on why the Brazilian always seemed to court controversy. 'Players of his calibre, with his style, who are particularly good in one-on-one situations, are always going to get hassled from all sides. I'm sure it happened to him in Brazil as well.' And Neymar's old coach at Santos, Muricy Ramalho, who knew him better than most, could certainly testify to that. 'They went after him far more when he was in Brazil. The referees there are much more lenient. He looks skinny but he's very strong.

And when someone takes a swing at him he knows how to defend himself. He stands up to his attackers, he's brave. But he doesn't actually intend to provoke anyone, that's just his style of play.'

In the return leg at the Nou Camp a week later, the Blaugrana emerged victorious with a 3–1 win to take them into the Copa del Rey semi-finals. Ney scored the third, despite getting trampled on yet again, this time by Mikel San José in a fruitless attempt to block the goal. He managed to finish the match, although a few days later he tweeted a photo of his bandaged foot as he was about to start an electrotherapy session, with the caption: 'I'm recovering, bit by bit.'

Meanwhile the court case over his controversial signing in June 2013 was looming. On 3 February he was charged with tax fraud and forgery in his home country. He was being represented by his father, just like his team-mate Messi who was also facing allegations of tax fraud. Neymar Pai was shielding his son by dealing with the press on his behalf: 'My son is extremely busy and we don't deserve this,' he said, making no attempt to hide the sense of distress for his son at having to appear before the judge. It was something the player himself had acknowledged just a few days earlier in an interview with the popular Brazilian Sunday TV show *Fantástico*. 'Before stirring up allegations, before trying to imply that we're involved in this or that controversy, they need to show us the evidence,' he said on camera. Meanwhile his father said he wanted to put paid to the harassment that they were receiving, particularly in Brazil.

Despite everything, Ney went on with his life as though it was no big deal. Two days later he celebrated his 24th birthday with a party into the early hours. It was a Friday and there was no training until 5pm the following day, but the press were unforgiving, waiting at the door of the restaurant where they were celebrating, leading to a scuffle with his father. The criticisms were intensifying, and coach Luis Enrique decided to speak out: 'I want to reassure our fans not to worry, they need to relax. Our players are one hundred per cent dedicated to their work and to their team. Like us, our fans know that this is all just part of the media circus. We are not going to get side-tracked by this sort of thing.'

In truth, Neymar had attracted attention as a partygoer ever since he arrived in Barcelona, and it was a matter of concern for a club that had already been through the experience with Ronaldinho, whose lifestyle had often been blamed for the decline of his Barça career. It was yet another point of comparison with his fellow Brazilian, and an issue that would rear its head again at the beginning of March. Ney received an automatic one-match ban after accumulating too many yellow cards, and took the opportunity to return to Brazil for a few days for his sister's twentieth birthday. The same thing had happened exactly a year earlier: he had been suspended and headed back home to celebrate with Rafaella. There was no shortage of journalists quick to point out the coincidence, noting the chain of events that had resulted from a slight handball in the final minutes against Rayo Vallecano a few days earlier, leaving him with a few days clear to hop over to São Paulo.

Unperturbed by the criticism, and with nothing to hide, he wasted no time in posting photos on all the various social networks showing them celebrating her birthday in one of the city's best known clubs with more than 200 family members, friends, popstars, former contestants on Brazil's *Big Brother*, and various other celebrities. There was just enough time for a party, a charity appearance and a new tattoo on his left leg – asking for God's protection – before he headed back to Ciudad Condal in time to score two goals in Barcelona's 6–0 defeat over Getafe.

But although everything seemed to be going smoothly on the pitch, a storm cloud was on the horizon. In mid-March the administrative court of the Federal Revenue in Rio de Janeiro ordered him to pay more than €45 million after being found guilty of tax fraud, Brazil's *Folha de São Paulo* revealed. And on 2 April, Real Madrid beat their rivals 1–2 at the Nou Camp in the second *Clásico* of the season. On the surface it didn't seem like a significant defeat, but it ended the Blaugrana's run of 39 matches without loss, and more importantly, it left the La Liga title hanging in the balance. To make things worse, the following week the website Football Leaks published all the previously undisclosed details of Neymar's contract with the Catalan club. He was said to receive €5 million gross per season, although the figure was deceptive because it didn't take into account the ever increasing bonus that had earned the player more than €45 million in the five years since his signing.

At the end of April, despite the coach's insistence that his players were used to performing under pressure, Barcelona were losing ground in the Spanish championship, and were knocked out of the quarter-finals of the Champions League by Atlético Madrid. The club's run of bad form mirrored Ney's, whose performance had dropped somewhat since January. Even the fans had begun to whistle at him. But they were still in the lead, despite the Whites and Atlético being hot on their heels and praying for a mistake. In the end the mistake never came, as Barça held on without losing another point, winning their second consecutive Liga under Luis Enrique on 14 May away to Granada (0–3). Luis Suárez scored all three goals, but the whole team rallied to secure the victory, including Neymar.

The Blaugrana's euphoria could be felt across the Los Cármenes stadium. Meanwhile hundreds of Granada fans invaded the pitch, and one decided to take out his frustration on the Brazilian. 'I don't know where he came from, but I got punched in the mouth,' Ney said later. 'Thank goodness it was nothing serious. It was just a knock, it's all fine.' A few hours later he posted a clip online of him singing '*Campeones campeones, ole ole ole*' with his father.

Back in Barcelona that evening, the club put on a party in one of the best hotels in town, although Ney was noticeably absent, preferring to celebrate with his own close circle, including fellow Brazilian Dani Alves. The following day he joined his teammates for the victory parade, sharing the trophy win with the fans. He looked ecstatic, beaming all the way, making jokes, enjoying the moment … and even devouring a hamburger after asking some of the fans to bring him one.

There was reason to celebrate once again a week later, on 22 May, when Barça were crowned Copa del Rey champions at the Vicente Calderón against Seville. Neymar scored in the 122nd minute to make it a definitive 2–0, finishing 2015–16 with 30 goals and eighteen assists in 43 matches. Another season for the record books.

The Copa América Centenario kicked off on 3 June 2016 in the United States. But the club decided that Ney would play no part. 'FC Barcelona would like to thank the Brazilian Football Confederation and its president, Marco Polo del Nero, who have accepted the proposal put forward by the club that Neymar should only have to compete in the Olympic Games in Brazil in 2016, which are taking place from 3 to 21 August. That means Neymar Junior is exempt from the Copa América,' Barça explained in a statement.

Without the pressure of the tournament in the States,

Ney was free to focus on the Olympics in his home country, and his efforts paid off. On 20 August, the Canaries and their star player got their revenge by beating Germany in the final. The Brazilians went ahead in the 27th minute with a Neymar goal from a set piece. The odds were in Brazil's favour for the next half an hour, until the Germans equalised, threatening yet another Greek tragedy. The scoreline remained the same during extra time, and it all came down to penalties. Germany's Nils Petersen missed the fifth and Neymar headed straight over to the penalty spot. He knew it was all resting on him – if he scored, the gold would be his. He didn't disappoint. The entire Maracanã crowd leapt to its feet, and Ney was unable to contain his emotion. He had made it as an Olympic champion, and thanks to him, the Canaries could put one of the saddest periods of their history firmly behind them.

Chapter 29
99 per cent faith

8 March 2017. A few minutes after 10.30pm, Neymar fired a long, hopeful ball into the box at Camp Nou. The Paris Saint-Germain defence headed clear, sending it straight back to Neymar's feet. He was far from the goal, almost 45 yards. He cut round one opponent with his right, drifted infield and lofted the ball over a seven-man defensive wall to the edge of the six-yard box. An unmarked Sergi Roberto strained to reach it with his toe, sending it into the back of the net.

It was pandemonium. The whole team rushed over to pile in on Roberto, Luis Enrique ran along the touchline to embrace assistant Juan Carlos Unzué, and Camp Nou erupted in a single roar.

FC Barcelona had just made history. No one had ever managed to pull off what the Blaugrana had achieved that night. It was an unprecedented Champions League turnaround, coming back from 4–0 down in the first leg to win the return 6–1 (6–5 on aggregate) to reach the quarter-finals.

How could something like that have happened? Let's go back to 15 February to make sense of it. 'Although there's only 1 per cent chance, I have 99 per cent faith,' Neymar posted on social media that day, less than 24 hours after the resounding defeat at the Parc des Princes in Paris. It was a positive message, in contrast to the comments he made on television just after the match: 'It's difficult, practically impossible. But we can't give up.' He had just suffered through one of the worst nights in his team's memory, in which every aspect of their game was ravaged by a far superior Paris Saint-Germain. Two goals from Di María, one by Draxler, and one from Cavani were the punishment endured by an ineffectual Barça, whose only saving grace was goalie Ter Stegen – and Ney. 'Neymar was the only one pushing them to turn it around, but he was all alone,' wrote Juan Irigoyen in *El País*. 'Neither Suárez nor Messi, and certainly not the midfielders, were helping the Brazilian.'

The three weeks between the two matches felt like an eternity, although at least the Blaugrana managed to stay alive in La Liga with four consecutive victories. Meanwhile, attention was diverted away from the pitch on 1 March as Luis Enrique announced he was stepping down as coach, prompting immediate speculation about who would take over. And as if that wasn't enough, the press were insisting that Messi still hadn't renewed his contract, which was due to expire in 2018. Neymar could rest easy as far as contracts were concerned. He had signed to extend his in October, tying him to the club until 30 June 2021. The figures were dizzying: a salary of nearly €25 million a year – second only to the Argentine – and a buyout clause that would increase every year, reaching €250 million in 2020. 'I'm very happy to renew my contract, now that I have settled in here,' he told Barça TV on the day of the signing. 'I wanted the best for my family and for myself, and that's what we have here. Barça will always be special and close to my heart.'

So on the eve of the return leg against Paris Saint-Germain at Camp Nou, Ney remained totally focused on the match. Focused, and confident – as his final Instagram message of the night insisted: '99 per cent faith'.

Right from the start it was a dream match for Barça fans,

after Luis Suárez headed the opener in the third minute. And an own goal from Kurzawa put the Blaugrana halfway back on track, making it 2–0 just before half time. After the break Neymar took control of the match. In the 50th minute he was brought down by Meunier inside the box after an exchange with Iniesta down the left wing. The ball bounced away over the touchline, play stopped, and the entire stadium was asking the same question: was it a penalty? Even referee Deniz Aytekin had to consult with one of his assistants. But it didn't take long before he gave the penalty. Messi converted it, and the miracle inched ever closer: 3–0.

Edinson Cavani tried to breathe some life into the visitors' game in the 62nd minute, making it 3–1, but Hurricane Blaugrana enveloped Unai Emery's team in the final magical fifteen minutes. Ney was giving it his all, he seemed to be omnipresent. After an incredible effort, he scored a stunning goal from a direct free kick in the 88th minute, and went on to convert a penalty in the 90th after a foul on Suárez. That was normally Messi's job, but everyone knew whose match this was. It was 5–1, it was down to the wire.

With stoppage time almost over, Neymar was on hand again to assist Sergi Roberto in the 95th minute, unleashing mass hysteria. 'My first thought was to shoot, but I saw two players, Messi and Piqué, on the move. I hadn't seen Sergi Roberto. I crossed for Messi and Piqué,' he commented a couple of weeks later during an interview on *Canal Esporte Interativo*. Regardless, the result remains: that 1 per cent chance of going through converted into a hundred before the disbelieving eyes of the entire footballing world.

'In orchestrating Barcelona rally, Neymar proves ready for the baton,' read the *New York Times* headline that night. 'Neymar stands apart to make the impossible possible for Barcelona,' said the *Guardian*. 'Neymar crowned king,' claimed *El País*, as the Brazilian continued to be lauded and praised by rivals and former players alike. '[Neymar] put in one of the best performances I've ever seen,' said Steven Gerrard on BT Sport. 'He's the heir to the throne of Ronaldo and Messi,' agreed Rio Ferdinand.

March was clearly his month: on the 28th he scored another goal for the record books, this time on the other side of the Atlantic. It was the 64th minute in the Brazil–Paraguay World Cup qualifier at the Arena Corinthians in São Paulo, and Marcelo passed to Neymar in his own half, down the left hand side. He paused for a moment, made as if to head towards the centre of the pitch, and suddenly surprised everyone with a dodge towards the outside, fooling his opponent and making a run for it along the touchline. A second Paraguayan player came to challenge him, but Neymar was too quick, launching the ball in front of him and then sprinting to catch it up, leaving his marker far behind. And though his teammates were ready on the attack, Ney kept going right to the edge of the area, ball glued to his feet. After a 65 yard run, he was in front of goal with three defenders closing in. Would he cross? Or pass the ball back for his teammates? No – a firm tap with the inside of his foot, a light deflection off defender Cristian Riveros' knee, and moments later the ball spun into the net without the goalkeeper getting a hand to it.

Goal for Neymar – goal for Brazil. It was his 52nd in 77 appearances for the Canaries, and all by the tender age of 25. The only other player to match this achievement was O Rei Pelé. By the end of a rough match in which the number 10 had been fouled four times in the first few minutes, Brazil had done enough to qualify for the next World Cup. Ney needed a World Cup win – or rather two wins – to put him anywhere near on a par with Pelé, who led Brazil to victory in 1958 and 1962. In his first outing Ney had had to make do with fourth place. This victory against Paraguay paved the way for to the 2018 Russia World Cup, which represents another chance to get one step closer to the legendary former number 10.

Back in Barcelona on 2 April, Ney scored his team's fourth goal in a match against Granada at the Los Cármenes stadium (1–4). It was in stoppage time, and it didn't make any difference to the final result, but it was an important one for the Brazilian, as it was his 100th goal in an official match with the Blaugrana, in 178 matches. Messi took 188 matches to get to that total. They had however both fallen a long way short of the record 100 goals in 103 matches set by the legendary László Kubala.

Ney's performances against PSG and with the national team, and the fact that he had already notched up eleven goals and ten assists in the year so far, were already generating headlines such as the one in *As*: '2017: catapulting Neymar towards the Ballon d'Or.' And then former Brazil star Romário declared on Fox Sports' *Boa Noite*: 'We're entering the Neymar era, he has played some incredible matches with Barça and Brazil. He needs to win a World Cup and then he'll be in with a chance.'

But soon after his Pelé-worthy run of success, the Brazilian hit a particularly rough patch. He didn't score for another month until 6 May when he got one against Villarreal. Unfortunately by that point his team were already out of one of the three competitions they had had their eye on since the start of the season – the Champions League.

Luis Enrique's men had gone into the first leg of the quarter-finals against Juventus with mixed feelings. A defeat in La Liga by Malaga had broken the winning spirit they displayed against PSG. But the memory of such an epic match still kept the fans buzzing with anticipation. Despite this, they made the same mistakes in Turin as they had in Paris, losing the first leg 3–0. This time critics attributed it to Mathieu, who was overpowered by the Juve strikers, and a lack of good shots from the MSN trio. Barcelona only managed four shots on target, Neymar barely set foot in the box, nor did Messi or Luis Suárez.

The team attempted to repeat their historic comeback and, given the PSG result, no one dared breathe a word about elimination before the start of the return leg. But one crucial detail counted against Barça: Gianluigi Buffon's men had only conceded two goals during the eight matches of the competition so far, so the Blaugrana would need to score at least three to avoid being knocked out. In the end, Juve's solid defence dominated from start to finish at Camp Nou. Neymar kept former teammate Dani Alves on his toes on the left wing, but his crosses weren't converted by the rest of the MSN strikeforce. After 90 minutes of anguish, the scoreline hadn't budged: 0–0. Juve were through to the semi-finals and Barcelona had to watch their dreams of winning their sixth Champions League just 25 years after their first evaporate into thin air. At the final whistle Ney could be seen crying on the shoulder of Alves, who hours later would post a photo of their embrace online with the caption: 'I love you, brother.'

With no time for a break, another trial by fire was looming just four days later – *El Clásico* at the Santiago Bernabéu; the coin toss for La Liga in front of 80,000 Madrid fans. Real, who had been as erratic as Barcelona throughout the season, were three points ahead with a game in hand. With only five matches remaining, a victory for *Los Blancos* would more or less quash the Blaugrana's hopes. A draw would favour them as well, while a Barça victory would leave things wide open.

Once again, the duel didn't disappoint, with Barcelona winning 2–3 thanks to a heart-stopping finish and a stellar performance from Messi. He scored Barça's equaliser to make it 1–1, and popped up again in the 92nd minute with the winner. Neymar was not on the pitch, following a ban for mocking the referee at the Malaga match three weeks earlier. It wasn't the first time in the season that his conduct made front page news. In a match against Leganés on 17 September, he showed off some fancy footwork with the scoreline already firmly in his team's favour, drawing criticism from commentator Michael Laudrup. 'At 0–4 you can't be showboating and provoking your opponents,' said the Dane, a former star of both Barça and Real. The discussion over whether Neymar provoked his rivals and exaggerated fouls continued throughout the season, and was sparked whenever he went down in the box. In fact, he ended La Liga with the most fouls of any player, 126, and the most yellow cards of anyone at Barça, with eight.

Not all the media attention surrounding the Brazilian related to his performance on the pitch. In 2017 he also made his on-screen debut with a cameo in *xXx: Return of Xander Cage*, the third in the *xXx* franchise starring Vin Diesel. And although Ney appeared on screen for less than a minute, his scene – sitting in an oriental restaurant with Samuel L. Jackson – became one of the talking points of the film. During publicity for the movie, director D.J. Caruso even said: 'For me, Neymar is triple X – he's one of the greatest footballers of all time, he's got the looks, and he has a rebellious attitude that fits perfectly with the *xXx* persona.'

Back on the pitch following the match at the Bernabéu, the team decimated Osasuna 7–1, and now that Neymar had returned they remained unbeaten until the deciding game, on 21 May. The match against Eibar was to be a rollercoaster of emotions for the Blaugrana. Real Madrid had managed to score in the first few minutes of their fixture against Malaga, while Barça had let themselves go. It was 0–2 by the 60th minute, with two surprise goals marking an unprecedented achievement for the Basque team at Camp Nou. The Blaugrana fans were silent, disappointed, and there were long faces among the players. As if trying to recreate the PSG match, Neymar rose to the occasion, with Messi's help this time, pushing for the comeback. The Argentine set off on a run, crossed diagonally into the middle, on the edge of the area, perfectly positioned for the number 11 to take a shot unmarked, which beat the goalkeeper. The ball glanced off the post first time round, but Eibar defender David Juncà fumbled his clearance into the net and Barça got their first goal of the game. It was the 62nd minute. Ney pointed both hands to the sky, perhaps giving thanks for some divine assistance, and ran back to midfield with barely a celebration.

In the 66th minute another run from Messi set up a chance for the Brazilian, but his shot went just a few centimetres wide of the right post. It was Suárez who got the equaliser with a header in the 72nd minute, and then Messi who scored from the penalty spot in the 76th after a swift red card for Ander Capa for a foul on Neymar in the box. The Argentine went on to net another in injury time, making it a definitive 4–2. But the comeback was in vain, as the news from the Costa del Sol confirmed that Real, who only needed a draw, had won their match. La Liga 2016–17 was over, and *Los Blancos* were victorious.

The Copa del Rey was Ney's last ditch attempt for a title with Barcelona that season. The previous August, when the season began, the Blaugrana had lifted the Spanish Supercup after beating Sevilla in a double-header. But Ney had been absent due to the Olympics, and he wasn't on the team sheet for either of the matches.

Against Deportivo Alavés on 27 May in the Copa del Rey, Luis Enrique's men were the favourites, although it didn't show. Their rivals, despite having no national or international titles to their name, were a solid, experienced team who had finished in the top ten in La Liga under the guidance of Mauricio Pellegrino. Plus, they had already surprised Barça back in September with a 2–1 win at Camp Nou.

Barcelona had to make do without Luis Suárez, who had been banned following two yellow cards in the semi-final against Atlético Madrid, but their strikeforce didn't seem to be too badly affected. They were on the attack from kick-off, and in the fifth minute Jordi Alba's header was just wide of the post. In the eleventh minute there was more bad news for the Blaugrana as a dazed Mascherano had to leave the pitch after a collision. Alavés began to dominate, with Ibai Gómez hitting the post in their best chance so far. But Neymar and Messi stepped in with an impressive response in the 30th minute. The Argentine received the ball in his opponents' half, directly in front of Pacheco's goal, and made a run towards the edge of the area. He passed to Neymar who returned it after just two touches, positioning the ball perfectly for Leo to tap home with the inside of his foot. Neymar celebrated yet another assist, the most in any season for him with a total of 21.

Theo Hernández kept the match alive with a stunning free kick two minutes later. It was 1–1 and Alavés were hopeful. In the 44th minute, Leo pushed through the rival midfielders and passed to the Sergi Roberto on the right, who fed a perfect pass to an unmarked Neymar, just yards out: 2–1. Another unexpected record for the Brazilian, who was now the first player in more than 50 years to score in three consecutive Copa del Rey finals. The previous record holder had been none other than Ferenc Puskás who had held the record since 1962. Of course, the Hungarian star lost two of those finals, something that hasn't happened to the Brazilian. He was now able to add a third win to his previous two, sealed with Paco Alcácer's goal in first half stoppage time. The scoreline remained at 3–1 throughout the second half, giving Barcelona their 29th Copa del Rey trophy – more than any other team. The victory meant the first title to play for in 2017–18 would be the Spanish Supercup – a double-header against Real Madrid to start the season with a bang.

With a lack of titles, the 2016–17 season was notable for Neymar for other weird and wonderful reasons. According to the CIES Football Observatory, the Brazilian was now the most expensive player in the world. In a study published on 12 June and based on its own unique algorithm, it claimed that he would currently sell for €210.7 million, putting him some way ahead of second and third places (Dele Alli and Harry Kane, respectively), and miles ahead of Messi, who was fourth with a value of €151.7 million, and Cristiano Ronaldo, who was eleventh on €112.4 million.

And Ney topped another unusual list: best dribbler in the major European leagues. His more than 160 runs in La Liga put him top, joined by Chelsea's Eden Hazard. And finally, ESPN's World Fame 100 ranked him as the sixth most famous athlete in the world, after his two biggest rivals (Ronaldo was top, Messi third), as well as LeBron James, Roger Federer and Phil Mickelson. He had dropped down from fourth place the previous year, but his stats were still incredible: 68.2 million Instagram followers, 58.6 million Facebook fans and 27.3 million Twitter followers. Numbers which will surely only increase with the 2018 World Cup on the horizon.

Chapter 30
O Rei in Paris

Pelé arrived in Paris in June 1960. Two years earlier, he had
astounded the entire world and brought France to tears. At
the World Cup held in Sweden, he had become the youngest
ever world champion aged just seventeen and finished the
tournament as the second top scorer behind Just Fontaine.
Against Fontaine's France on 24 June 1958, the king-in-
waiting had taken charge, finding the back of Claude Abbes'
goal on three occasions in the semi-final. Final score: 5–2
to Brazil.

Two years later, Racing Paris invited Pelé's club side
Santos to the prestigious Tournoi de Paris. Guests of honour, the Brazilians were joined by CSKA Sofia and Stade
de Reims. Pelé, accompanied by the four other members
of the Vila Belmiro quintet (Pepe, Coutinho, Dorval and
Mengálvio), took things into his own hands. At the Parc des
Princes on 8 June, he got past five Reims defenders before
beating Dominique Colonna with a diagonal shot. Against
the Bulgarians in the final he opened the scoring, finishing
off a delicious one-two with Coutinho. Santos won the tournament, then moved onto the next stage of their European
tour.

He returned to Paris three years in a row. Pelé was fond
of the French capital because, he admitted, it was the French
press who elevated him to the rank of king, *O Rei*, after the
World Cup in Sweden, but also because he thought the city

was beautiful; it was one of his favourites. So much so that in 1966 he returned with his wife Rosemeri dos Reis Cholbi, a few weeks after their wedding. But it was not until the spring of 1971 that Edson Arantes do Nascimento would return with the Santos Globetrotters, a year after leading Brazil to their third World Cup win, beating Italy in the final in Mexico.

Pelé's visit had been talked about since the start of 1971 and a swarm of photographers and cameramen were waiting for him when he stepped off the plane at Orly airport on 30 March. O Rei travelled down the Champs Élysées in a convertible, brandishing the Jules Rimet Trophy. An enthusiastic crowd cheered the champion along the route. The Hôtel de Ville was his last stop in Paris, where Brazil's number 10 was awarded the Vermeil medal. He then went to the Stade Yves-du-Manoir in Colombes, where Santos faced a team of players from Olympique de Marseille and Saint-Étienne. It was Pelé's triumphant return to Colombes eight years after France v Brazil had ended 2–3 on 28 April 1963. This time it was a friendly match organised for charity by *Télé 7 Jours*, which was about to celebrate its tenth anniversary. Thirty thousand spectators, stars of French show business, a live television broadcast and Brigitte Bardot, dressed in the colours of the French flag, got the evening started. All the ingredients for an unforgettable evening had been brought together. It was a shame that the spectacle on the pitch left a lot to be desired: it ended in a lacklustre 0–0 draw. But there had to be a winner so preparations were made for a penalty shootout. Pelé wanted to take all five shots but he was not allowed to and the French team eventually won 3–1.

The story did not end there for O Rei, who once again found himself on the front page of *L'Équipe* less than three months later. 'Pelé to Paris for 9 million [French francs]? It's possible!' By now it was 22 June 1971 and the French sports daily had dropped a bombshell. The news was picked up by the Brazilian press, who were stunned and incredulous. It was impossible to think that Pelé would leave his club and country. But the story was true and the negotiations between Paris Saint-Germain and Santos were taking place. Guy Crescent, the then president of PSG, confirmed it. Supported by a group of investors and with the agreement of the French Football Federation, Crescent had founded a club capable of competing with the very best teams in France by merging Paris FC and Stade Saint-Germain to create Paris Saint-Germain, and it did not stop there. Now that his team, a mixture of amateurs and experienced professionals such as Jean Djorkaeff (captain of the national team and father of Youri), had succeeded in climbing to the first division, Crescent wanted to cause a stir: it was time for fireworks. And who better than Pelé to get the world talking about PSG?

On 5 July 1971, Guy Crescent flew to Brazil to try to convince Pelé, who declined the first Parisian offer on television. Faced with serious financial difficulties, Santos were not in a position to refuse the offer from France, the equivalent of $1 million; everything depended on Pelé, who was visibly courting the attention. The club president returned to France with an agreement, but negotiations eventually collapsed. Pelé changed his mind, apparently for family reasons, or, as he would explain at the end of the year when visiting Paris with his wife, he chose to honour his contract with Santos. What was the truth? As is often the case, it was hard to get to the bottom of the story, to find out whether the reason Pelé would never wear a Paris shirt was down to a series of publicity engagements that had to be respected, fear on the part of Santos' directors as to how their fans would react, or even pressure exerted by the Brazilian government.

Paris Saint-Germain fans had to wait five long years before

they could admire O Rei at the Parc des Princes. On 14 April 1976, Pelé wore the white number 10 shirt of the New York Cosmos. For $6 million over three years, a contract more worthy of an actor than a footballer, O Rei moved to the Big Apple. The deal would require the mediation of Henry Kissinger, the US Secretary of State, without whom the Brazilian government would never have let their national treasure leave. It also required Pelé, who had actually retired by this point, to return to the pitch to resolve his mounting financial problems. But there he was, O Rei at the Parc des Princes. PSG won the game 3–1. Five years it had taken PSG fans to see Pelé, now aged 36, though the circumstances were slightly different to those first envisioned.

In the summer of 2017, the wait for O Rei 2.0 was much shorter and this time the man in question was wearing the right shirt. PSG's fans would soon be able to admire a smiling Neymar Junior in his new red and blue shirt, shaking hands, kicking a ball about and greeting the assembled crowd at the Parc des Princes. This moment would arrive barely three weeks after *AS* and *Sport*, the Madrid and Barcelona dailies, had reported an initial contact between the Brazilian star and PSG. Apparently, Neymar's father was to meet with the president of PSG, Nasser Al-Khelaifi, over the coming days. And that was not all: 'Neymar is unhappy at Barcelona,' claimed *Sport*. 'A member of his inner circle is insisting that the time to leave Barcelona has come. His friends and family are asking him to come out from Messi's shadow to try to grow away from the Camp Nou and seek some glory of his own.' Whether journalistic speculation or transfer market rumour, PSG fans had heard the same tales a year earlier, before they burst like bubbles. But it quickly became clear that this time would be different.

At 3.09pm on 18 July, the Brazilian website *Esporte*

Interativo wrote: 'Neymar has accepted PSG's offer.' Five words above a mocked up image of Neymar wearing a Paris shirt. According to the Brazilians, Barcelona's number 11 had signed a five-year contract for €30 million per season, plus bonuses. And what's more, the club from the French capital was prepared to pay his release clause of €222 million. The official announcement would take place within a few weeks. An immediate denial came from Spain: 'We are 200 per cent certain that Neymar won't leave,' stated Jordi Mestre, the vice president of the Blaugrana. PSG also denied it whilst Neymar remained tight-lipped as he enjoyed a day off in Formentera with his father and friends.

On 19 July, Barcelona departed for their pre-season tour of the United States. Neymar was in attendance. In an interview with *Goal.com*, the Brazilian claimed that he was 'happy' at Barça: 'At the moment, we have to work on making next season even more successful, both individually and as a team.' On 20 July, Josep Bartomeu, President of Barcelona, assured *Associated Press*: 'Neymar is not on the market.' That same day, on the pages of *L'Équipe*, Unai Emery confided: 'Neymar? The club and its supporters would be delighted if he came. PSG need to count on a player who is one of the five or seven best players in the world, in addition to those they already have. It's a difficult objective. He may come … but then again he may not.'

Neymar continued to say very little, though he remained active on social media. On Friday 21 July he posted a photo on Instagram showing him at training, stretched out pensively on the grass, with his left hand resting under his chin. There was no caption.

On Saturday 22 July, he impressed fans at New York's MetLife Stadium against Juventus in the International Champions Cup. In the first match of the Ernesto Valverde

(Luis Enrique's successor) era, the number 11 played 45 minutes, scoring twice to give Barcelona the win. The second was a gem. He slalomed across the area to dodge Lichtsteiner, Benatia, Barzagli, Khedira and Asamoah in quick succession, then, with his right foot, fired the ball past Buffon. He celebrated the goal by raising his fist in the air, nothing more. No message to the fans, in either direction. It was to the disappointment of the commentators and journalists, who were hoping for a sign. It was Gerard Piqué who got everyone excited, posting a clear message that had only one possible interpretation. At 10.55pm on 23 July, the Catalan defender posted a photo of himself with Neymar on Twitter with the words: '*Se queda*' (He's staying). It was a cold shower for Parisian aficionados, but brought joy to Barcelonans and plenty of doubt to those who had spoken of the existence of an agreement.

Nevertheless, the rumours persisted. It was suggested that the heavyweights of the Blaugrana dressing room (Leo Messi and Luis Suárez) had put pressure on the Brazilian and succeeded in convincing him; the young man had never wanted to leave and it was all coming from his father, who wanted to pocket a few million more. Doubt had been cast and it seemed the transfer of the century would not take place. Those two words from Piqué caused a real earthquake on social media and amongst the press.

A few days later, the landscape changed again. Gerard Piqué attended a press conference at the FedEx Field in Washington DC alongside Javier Mascherano. He was urged to explain his tweet: 'It was just a personal opinion. Only Neymar can announce whether he's staying or not. When I posted the picture I wanted to express how much I want him to stay. It's not official, it's not up to me to give information about it. But I hope he stays.'

In other words, he was not sure at all. It was simply what he wanted. But Piqué did not stop there and went into more detail about the reasons that might prompt Neymar to leave:

It's understandable that he's looking for a new start. He's 25 and he has a unique talent. He has options on the table. It may be all about the money but I don't think it is. It may be about his ambitions in the sport, but there's no doubt that there's nowhere better for that than Barcelona. It may be for personal reasons, because he wants to play a more important role, be the leader of a team, because the best player in the world, Leo, is here. And I can understand that. Ney came here when he was twenty and Barça have had to fight to keep him, even if his transfer could bring the club a lot of money, there isn't another player like him on the market. I want to tell him: 'Don't go to Paris, don't play in a league where, with all due respect, you won't have such a high profile; your season will come down to the Champions League and if you don't win it you won't be entitled to the recognition you deserve.' As teammates and friends, we're trying to get him to think about it, as when it comes down to it Neymar is young, he's only 25, and he has the right to have doubts.

On Thursday 27 July, the headline on the front page of *L'Équipe* read: 'Paris in talks with Barcelona.' PSG were said to have already come to an agreement with the player and were trying to lower the release clause fee of €222 million, but it seemed the Catalan club had no intention of negotiating. Meanwhile, Neymar gave Barça a second win on its American tour. In the 31st minute, he made sure of the result against José Mourinho's Manchester United. The

Brazilian superstar shone but the tension was palpable. On 28 July, Neymar almost came to blows in training with Nélson Semedo, Barça's new Portuguese recruit, and left the pitch after throwing his training bib to the ground.

In Tangier, on 29 July, PSG won the Champions Trophy with a 2–1 win over Monaco. Dani Alves, who had recently arrived in the French capital, scored with a stunning free kick, a response to Sidibé's opening goal. After the victory celebration, he took the time to have his say on the Neymar affair: 'The easiest solution for Neymar is to stay in Barcelona. But fortune favours the brave.' He was not the only Brazilian to share his opinion. In Tegucigalpa, where he was playing in a charity match, Ronaldinho, a former PSG and Barça player, said that Neymar 'needs to listen to his heart and be happy, to do what his heart tells him'. And in Miami, when speaking to *ESPN* on the pitch, Bartomeu began to concede ground: 'We want to keep Neymar but there's a release clause in his contract. If he wants to leave he has to pay.'

The final match of Barça's American tour took place on Saturday 29 July. A Florida version of El Clásico that saw plenty of action: five goals, a ton of chances and a real spectacle to delight the 65,000 spectators in the Hard Rock Stadium. Barça won 3–2 thanks to goals from Messi, Rakitić and Piqué. Neymar played 75 minutes, showed some fantastic movement and provided two assists, which earned him this comment from Luis Suárez: 'Most of the players want him to stay. As far as I'm concerned, he's one of the three best players in the world at the moment. He's a pleasure to play with and it would be a real shame if he left.'

From the United States to China. Neymar then flew to Shanghai at the request of a sponsor. Everyone was waiting for a statement about his future but nothing came, even though the saga seemed to be nearing an end. *Sport* ran with the following: 'He is leaving. His departure has now been rubber-stamped internally. The Blaugrana club is waiting for the player to tell them his final decision in the coming hours before making a swift start on looking for his replacement.'

Tuesday 1 August became the day of the aeroplane mystery. Neymar triggered an alert by posting a photo of himself in Dubai on Instagram. The visit led to endless speculation. There were those who said Brazil would be his next destination, others who thought it would be Qatar, others still who were imagining him en route to signing his contract in Paris, when finally, Neymar landed at El Prat airport in Barcelona. Wearing a basketball cap and headphones, still not a word passed his lips.

At 9am on 2 August, Neymar arrived at Barcelona's training complex, Ciutat Esportiva Joan Gamper, in a blue Audi RS7. He did not change into his training gear, instead he headed directly to the office of Ernesto Valverde to tell him he was leaving Barcelona. The manager gave him permission to skip training. He had to decide his future. Neymar then visited Raül Sanllehí, Barcelona's director of football, and Òscar Grau, CEO. It was a short meeting as half an hour later, the Brazilian left the training centre, never to return, but not without saying goodbye to his teammates one by one in the dressing room. Some had known the end of the story since the beginning of the season, almost all were fearing the worst by the time of Leo Messi and Antonella Roccuzzo's wedding on 30 June in Rosario. Many were sad, convinced that the club had not managed to persuade Neymar to stay in Barcelona.

The saga of the summer was coming to an end. Now came the time for comments, headlines and a range of opinions about the transfer of Neymar Junior that shook the world, both inside and outside sport. '€222 million for Neymar, the most expensive transfer in history,' proclaimed the front page of *El País*. 'The transfer that has changed the history of football,' replied *Marca*. 'Goodbye Neymar, hello Coutinho, Dembélé,' predicted *Mundo Deportivo* on its front page. *L'Équipe* simply stated: 'He's coming.' The Portuguese daily *A Bola* contented itself with a single word, 'Madness'. There was something for everyone. The colossal fee for the transfer was the main focus. €222 million compared with the €105 million spent in the summer of 2016 by Manchester United to lure Paul Pogba away from Juventus, with the €101 million spent by Real Madrid to wrestle Gareth Bale from Tottenham's grip and the €95 million paid by the Spanish club for Cristiano Ronaldo. €42 million more than PSG would pay Monaco for Kylian Mbappé. A crazy amount. *El Mundo* described it as a 'transfer of power that threatens to destabilise the football market', and as financial fair play going up in smoke. *La Repubblica* asked: 'Why is Qatar spending €600 million [between the release clause and salary] for Neymar's goals? It is no longer just about football but about breaking the isolation inflicted on Qatar and improving its image.'

Setting political issues to one side, Spanish newspapers such as *El País* emphasised the legal troubles Neymar was leaving behind him, remembering that 'Sandro Rosell, his primary supporter, was in prison for tax evasion,' and that 'Ney's transfer [from Santos to Barcelona] was dissected by the Spanish and Brazilian courts due to inconsistency in the figures.' A glance at the front page of *Sport* was all it took to understand the perspective of the Blaugrana club's devoted fans: 'Gone for good!' read the caption beneath the photo of Neymar leaving the Ciutat Esportiva for the last time. While the headline in *AS* raged: 'Pay up and get out.' They were furious and felt betrayed by a player with whom they had identified, their beloved superstar, the anointed successor to Messi. Many likened him to Luís Figo, the Portuguese player who left Barça for Real Madrid, the pinnacle of treachery, in 2000.

Thursday 3 August was the day of reckoning, time for commentators and reporters to look back and analyse Neymar's four seasons in a Blaugrana shirt. The figures: 105 goals in 186 matches played and ten titles. His departure was a disaster for the magic trio. Messi, Suárez and Neymar had scored a total of 363 goals in three seasons. Would it ever be beaten?

Thursday 3 August was also the day when Neymar's lawyers tried without success to pay his release fee to the Liga. That afternoon, they visited the offices of FC Barcelona to hand over the €222 million. That evening, Neymar signed the contract binding him to PSG. On Twitter, the new PSG number 10 was congratulated by Pelé in a short message accompanied by a black and white photo of O Rei holding the Jules Rimet Trophy with the Eiffel Tower in the background. The famous image of 30 March 1971. Even Emmanuel Macron, President of France and an OM fan, welcomed the arrival of Neymar: 'Yes, it's good news,' he said, of something he considered to be a sign of the appeal of his country.

4 August 2017, Paris, around noon

Elegant in his blue suit and white shirt, a smiling and obliging Neymar entered a press room where the 378 assembled journalists were waiting. He was accompanied by his parents, sister, agent and friends. For 47 minutes, he answered questions asked in French, Spanish, Catalan, Portuguese and English.

Why did you sign for PSG?
'Because of the club's ambition. The ambition of Paris Saint-Germain is a lot like mine. I wanted a bigger challenge. My heart told me it was time to come to Paris. I'm here to do the best I can to help our team win titles.'

Did you leave Barcelona because of Messi?
'No, it's the opposite. One of the reasons I went to Barça was to play with Messi. He's an idol, the best in the world. There was no pressure at all, only during the first week. I was nervous. I was training with my idols. But after that first week I was one of them. Playing with the best is much easier. It's what every player wants to do. I want to thank Messi; I learned a lot from him in four years.'

Leo wrote on Instagram: 'It was an enormous pleasure to share all these years with you, my friend. I wish you lots of luck in this new stage of your life. See you soon.' But today, Neymar was happy to be in Paris: 'My heart told me it was time to sign.'

What do you say to those who think you signed for PSG for the money?
'They know nothing about my life. I've never been motivated by money, that's never been my priority. I think about my happiness and that of my family.'

Do you feel the burden of being the most expensive player of all time?
'No. It's not a burden. I weigh 69kg and I'll stay at 69kg!'

'It's expensive today, but in two years' time, it won't be,' said Nasser Al-Khelaifi, the chairman of PSG. 'We will earn much more than we're spending. It's a joint project.'

Afterwards came the customary photo alongside the

chairman and his number 10 shirt, which had already sold out (10,000 sold on the first day), then another on the pitch at the Parc des Princes to the delight of the army of photographers. It was chaos outside the stadium. Everyone wanted to catch a glimpse of O Rei 2.0, who sneaked out surrounded by a dozen bodyguards dressed like the agents in *Men in Black*.

5 August, 3.30pm

The DJ Martin Solveig had been brought in to get the Parc des Princes jumping. Wearing a yellow number 27 shirt, the new number of the Argentine Javier Pastore, he took to the decks, shouting into the microphone: 'Parc des Princes, if you love Brazil make some noise! You'll need to make more than that later when Neymar arrives!' The fans responded and when Neymar came out onto the stage the stands went into meltdown: there were 48,500 fans. Supporters from the Ultras Paris group chanted 'Neymar! Neymar!' to the rhythm of 'Brasil! Brasil!' from 'Aquarela do Brasil' and the ground came alive. '*Merci!* I'm very happy. I've come here for a great challenge. I'm counting on all of you. I came here to win trophies. Paris is magical!' Ney shouted from the podium set up in the middle of the pitch. Alongside him, the chairman Nasser Al-Khelaifi applauded his entrance. 'Where are we?' asked Neymar, and 48,500 people responded in unison: 'Paris!' It was a great way to win over the fans. The new number 10 then walked towards a corner, shaking hands as he went, greeting fans with a shaka sign before throwing his shirt into the crowd. That was the end of the entertainment; it was time for the game to begin. PSG were playing Amiens in their opening league game of the season, without their €222-million player, who was still missing a document needed to officially seal his contract. He watched the game from the stands, surrounded by members of his family, friends, agents and intermediaries. That night there was another spectacle in his honour, the Eiffel Tower lit up in red and blue with the slogan: 'Welcome, Neymar Junior!' PSG had put on quite a show.

13 August, 11.50pm
Barcelona were overwhelmed by Real Madrid in the first leg of the Spanish Super Cup: 3–1 to *Los Blancos* thanks to magnificent goals from CR7 and Asensio. Deulofeu took Neymar's place but failed to shine.

10.45pm One goal and one assist. The most expensive player on planet Earth did not disappoint on his debut in a Paris shirt. At the Stade de Roudourou, the Brazilian met all expectations against Guingamp. He received plenty of praise. He went through his entire repertoire, including nut-megging Lucas Deaux, dribbling, bursts of pace, displays of great imagination and inch-perfect passing. In the 62nd minute, he provided Edinson Cavani with an assist to make the score 2–0. He picked up the ball in the middle of the pitch and spun on his ankle to find the perfect trajectory to meet the running Uruguayan, who wrong footed Karl-Johan Johnsson. Finally, the new number 10 scored his first goal late in the game, with Cavani returning the favour in the 82nd minute. He crossed from the byline, finding Neymar in the area and the Brazilian made it 3–0. 'People thought I would die when I left Barça … but I'm more alive than ever!' said Neymar on his way out of the dressing room. 'I'm very happy. We have a great team and we can achieve things this club has never achieved before. But we have to move forward step by step.' He was right. This was just the beginning.

Chapter 31

Annus horribilis

'I can say that this is the saddest moment of my career, it's very painful because we knew we could get there, we knew we had the ability to go much further, to make history … but it didn't happen. It's difficult to find the strength to go back to football.' With these words, Neymar summed up Brazil's defeat by Belgium in the quarter-finals of the 2018 FIFA World Cup in Russia – a sad moment for the whole of Brazil, and the end of a disastrous World Cup for the number 10.

Ney didn't distinguish himself by his goals or performance, but rather by his dives and constant disagreements with the referees. He spent a total of fourteen minutes on the ground after diving, sparking several memes in his honour, such as Mexican club Tijuana Xoloitzcuintles players diving on the pitch while shouting 'Neymar', as well as compilations of every single clip of him diving. It had been an 'annus horribilis' – not just in terms of his performance at the World Cup, but a horrible year during the season in Paris as well. Let's look back …

Neymar arrived at Paris Saint-Germain in the summer of 2017 as a king, the new king of Paris and French football, club president Nasser Al-Khelaifi's star signing worth €222 million and practically worthy of a castle in his honour. In September, just a few weeks after his debut in France's Ligue 1 against Guingamp, he settled into Bougival. It was one of the most stylish neighbourhoods in the city of love, an exclusive suburb just a few miles from his new team's training ground. His new home was a 10,000-square-foot mansion with an indoor pool and 50,000 square feet of grounds, previously home to famed French actor Gérard Depardieu as well as Ney's own idol and fellow Brazilian Ronaldinho. It certainly reflected that of the star of a club hoping to make it up there with the other great European teams.

The Ney effect at the Parc des Princes was immediate, marking a change in playing style for the club. The former Blaugrana number 11 organised, passed and scored – but his impact caused problems with his teammates. One particular skirmish happened with striker Edinson Cavani on 17 September against Olympique Lyonnais. In the 57th minute the referee called a foul in favour of PSG, and 'El Matador' Cavani recovered the ball to take the free kick. But Dani Alves had other ideas and, after talking to the Uruguayan, Neymar stepped up to take the free kick, which was blocked by the rival goalkeeper. Fifteen minutes before the final whistle, the same thing happened again. A foul on Mbappé landed a penalty for PSG. Neyamr went to get the ball, but this time Cavani wouldn't hand it over and insisted on taking the penalty, which was nudged wide in an incredible save by Lopes. Meanwhile the media relished the clash between the two stars. At the press conference, coach Unai Emery promised to deal with the matter internally, explaining: 'I usually let the players decide amongst themselves on the pitch who should take free kicks and penalties, but if that doesn't work, I will have to ensure they both get to take them so that it doesn't become a problem for the team.'

A few months later, Ney acknowledged the friction between him and Cavani, 'but we resolved it just three days later,' he said. 'We sat down and we talked. We are two great players, two men, we sorted it out without discussing it with anyone else.'

Once any controversies had blown over, the integration of Ney with his teammates began to bear the fruits that Al-Khelaifi had hoped for. In the resounding 8–0 defeat over Dijon on 17 January 2018, Neymar played as if he was in the school playground, weaving around half the opponents, assisting and scoring four goals against the poor Dijon goalie. PSG's strike force was perfectly coordinated, any differences between the teammates seemed to be in the past, and Neymar's place was solidified. On 27 January PSG were victorious once again, 4–0 against Montpellier. The match was a testament to the improvement in Ney's relationship with El Matador, as noted by *L'Équipe* with its headline: 'Cavani and Neymar share the limelight at PSG.' During the match Cavani was crowned the club's highest goalscorer with 157, overtaking the previous record set by Zlatan Ibrahimović. And it was a good game for Neymar as well, as he scored a double, taking him to seventeen goals in sixteen matches. The first goal came from the penalty spot, while the second came out of a play between Di María and Cavani, who gave him the assist.

Ligue 1 seemed like child's play for the Parisians, and it was easy enough for the kid from Mogi das Cruzes. The real test for PSG and Al-Khelaifi would be the Champions League. The group phase had been nothing short of triumphant for the club. Twelve goals against Celtic and only one conceded across both legs. Nine goals and a clean sheet against Belgian team Anderlecht. The only slip-up had happened on 5 December in the return leg against Bayern Munich. In the first leg at home the Parisians had won 3–0 with Neymar giving an assist to Dani Alves for the first goal and then scoring the third. But the return leg was a disaster:

3–1 to Bayern with no real excuse. In the end PSG went through top of the group thanks to a better goal difference than the German team.

On 14 February 2018 they faced Real Madrid in the final sixteen. The last time they met, in 2016, the Parisians beat the Spanish team 3–1 in the International Champions Club. But the Champions League was another level entirely, not to mention a fresh chance to see two of the greatest players in the world – Cristiano Ronaldo and Neymar Jr – go head-to-head. PSG's hopes were resting on the Brazilian and his experience. They were bolstered by their excellent form since their win over Dijon. But Neymar Jr and Mbappé just couldn't match their opponents. Ney had 86 touches and tried his best to create danger, but Nacho and Varane stopped him getting his way. Apart from two shots, neither of which were particularly threatening, there was almost nothing of note. The plays between the strikers didn't work the way they did in Ligue 1. Ney only managed seven passes to Mbappé in the entire match, and none to El Matador. As observed by *L'Équipe*, PSG seemed to have a complex about playing against Spanish clubs. The kings of Paris and their new player were no match for the Champions of Europe. Adrien Rabiot's goal in the 33rd minute had given hope to the French team, but it wasn't enough. Cristiano equalised after the break, then scored again six minutes before the end, before Marcelo finished the job in the 86th to make it 3–1. It would take considerable effort for Emery's men to avoid elimination now.

A week later on 25 February, PSG faced Olympique Marseille in *Le Classique* French derby, coming out unscathed with a 3–0 victory. Neymar was on good form, but was injured in the 77th minute after a tackle by Bouna Sarr. He fell to the ground, his face contorted in pain, before being stretchered off in tears.

'It's a sprained ankle, but we're doing more tests,' said Unai Emery at the post-match press conference. 'He's being careful, but we have to be optimistic. If I had to say right now whether he'll be able to play against Real Madrid, I would say yes.' But the following day brought a bleak prognosis. 'External sprain of the right ankle, as well as an associated crack of the fifth metatarsal,' according to the medical report posted on the Monday evening on PSG's official website. The club didn't specify how long he would be out, but this type of injury usually required two or three weeks at least. With this complication, Ney's presence on the pitch in the return leg against Real seemed practically impossible. 'Neymar almost certainly ruled out,' read the headline in *Marca*.

A month later, Neymar flew to Belo Horizonte in Brazil for an operation. Brazilian national team doctor Rodrigo Lasmar confirmed that he had suffered a fracture and would be off the pitch until the end of the French championship. He hoped he would be able to play in the World Cup.

Meanwhile, PSG were knocked out of the Champions League after a 1–2 defeat in the return leg against Real. Emery's men were no match for Zinedine Zidane's, and the incredible atmosphere created by the PSG Ultras to spur on their team were not enough to secure a victory. And Real Madrid held their ground despite the inferno of flares, smoke and banners that filled the Parc des Princes. Cristiano opened the scoring with a header. Then Cavani equalised in the 71st minute, but the goal did nothing to animate the home side. Then ten minutes before the final whistle, a shot by Casemiro was deflected by Marquinhos into his own goal. Game, set, match.

It was a huge disappointment for the Paris contingent – particularly for Al-Khelaifi, who had to endure his team being knocked out in the final sixteen despite the millions

spent on Neymar and Mbappé. Everyone was eagerly await-
ing Neymar's return. At the beginning of May, two months
after the operation on his right foot, the number 10's private jet touched down in the French capital. The Brazilian
couldn't train with his teammates but he was with them in
the stands for the final of the Coupe de France, against
the modest Les Herbiers who played in the fourth league,
known as the Championnat National 2. PSG won the cup
2–0 without any problem, their third title of the season. On
31 March they had beaten Monaco 3–0 to win the French
League Cup. And on 15 April, the 33rd matchday of Ligue 1,
they had trounced Monaco again, 7–1 this time, claiming
their Ligue 1 title at the expense of last season's winners.

Despite not having played since 25 February, Neymar won
plenty of trophies too. On 13 May he was named player of the
season by UNFP (France's National Union of Professional
Footballers), beating teammates Mbappé and Cavani, who
won the previous season. His nineteen goals and thirteen
assists in twenty matches had been worthwhile. Ney went up
to lift his trophy, but his mind was already on the World Cup.

On 3 June, Brazil and Croatia met for a pre-tournament
friendly at Anfield. In the 50th minute, three months after
he was injured against Olympique Marseille, Neymar made
his return to the pitch. In the 68th minute he received the
ball from Philippe Coutinho in the box and went past two
Croatian defenders to unleash a powerful shot with his right
foot, which flew over Danijel Subašić's head. The kid from
Mogi was back. And he knew who to thank, running into
the arms of La Canarinha doctor Rodrigo Lesmar, who had
been following him since February. The match ended 2–0,
and Brazil were confirmed as the favourites for the trophy.

But Russia would be a disappointment. On 17 June they
debuted against Switzerland, in a match that ended a feeble

1–1 as the Brazilians couldn't overpower the tough Swiss defence. Neymar had shone a week earlier, but was now nowhere to be seen. Against Costa Rica on 22 June it was evident they were struggling, as they started the match looking clumsy and lacking in creativity. In the second half they began to dominate the play and intimidate their opponents, but goalkeeper Keylor Navas was working miracles, and it was only in the first minute of injury time that Coutinho managed to take control of the situation, as he had done against Switzerland. After a cross from Marcelo, a header by Firmino and a touch by Gabriel Jesus, the Barça number 14 scored to make it 1–0. With the match sewn up, Neymar took advantage of a pass from Douglas Costa to score in an open goal in the 96th minute. It was the Brazilian's first World Cup goal and he fell to his knees at the final whistle, breaking down in floods of tears.

Against Serbia, Brazil were full of surprises. Tite's squad came out focused and didn't leave their opponents any room for manoeuvre, knowing that a win by Serbia would knock them out of the tournament. In the end Brazil won it 2–0 to go through to the final sixteen, finishing top of Group E. But Neymar was still not making much impact. His saving grace was a corner that Thiago Silva converted with a thunderous shot to seal the win. The €222 million-player had been eclipsed by Coutinho, who had proven himself effective and indispensable in every single match so far.

On 2 July they were up against Mexico in Samara and finally it was time for Neymar to shine. The Mexicans were certainly worthy opponents, but they were no match for Neymar on his best day. Within the first few minutes he was in the box taking on goalie Memo Ochoa. By the second half it was abundantly clear which was the better team. In the 51st minute Neymar initiated a play a few yards outside the box, dodged his way around three Mexican players and passed to Willian. The Chelsea player moved into the box and sent the ball back to Ney on a perfect diagonal to enable him to tap it into the net. The entire stadium leapt to their feet as Neymar celebrated, silencing the press and everyone who had criticised him for his diving. But it wasn't over yet. Four minutes before the final whistle he broke free of his marksman on the left wing and received the ball from Fernandinho, going on a solo run until he was face to face with Ochoa. The goalie deflected the Brazilian's shot with his foot but couldn't prevent Firmino scoring from the rebound. It was 2–0 and they were through to the quarter-finals against Belgium.

The Brazilians were the favourites, but things didn't go as they had hoped. In the seventh minute a shot by Thiago Silva hit the post. What a missed opportunity. Five minutes later Belgium took a corner, Kompany went for the header but it hit the near post, flying back and deflecting off Fernandinho's shoulder into his own goal. It was the beginning of the end for the Brazilian national team. In the 30th minute an incredible play by Romelu Lukaku found Kevin de Bruyne, who dribbled to the edge of the area and unleashed a powerful shot across goal that slammed in right at the bottom of Alisson's goal post to make it 0–2. Bolstered by the arrival of Firmino, Douglas Costa and Renato Augusto in the second half, Brazil managed to compose themselves, but any chances were repeatedly denied by goalie Thibaut Courtois. Finally in the 76th minute Augusto broke through with a header. In the 93rd minute Neymar had a chance to prove himself the nation's saviour, but Courtois wasn't having it. From a corner, the ball sailed through the air of the Kazan Arena to the number 10, who took the shot. It was heading for the corner of the net, but the Belgian goalie flung out his left arm, blocking it to keep the scoreline at 1–2, and crushing Brazil's dream of winning their sixth World Cup.

Neymar was not the number 10 they had hoped for, nor the leader that his country and the footballing world had been waiting for. It was deeply disappointing, an incredibly sad moment for Ney: 'I didn't even want to look at a football after the World Cup. I didn't want to see a ball because I just wanted to switch off a bit. I experienced feelings of mourning, of sadness, of wanting to be alone. I didn't want to see anyone, but that sadness can't last forever, because I've got my son, my family and my friends. They don't want to see me sad and I have many more reasons to be happy than to be sad.'

While Ney was in mourning, having his downtime, the European press speculated about his future. There was even talk of him leaving PSG for Real Madrid. 'I'm tired of hearing about it,' he said on 20 July at a charity event for the Neymar Jr Institute in São Paulo, his first public appearance since the World Cup. 'The press have created this story and fuelled these rumours. They need to stop this speculation.' And he reiterated that his future lies in Paris. 'I'm staying, I have a contract with Paris Saint-Germain,' he told Fox Sport. 'I went there to be challenged, to experience new things and in search of new goals. Nothing has changed in my mind. And everyone knows how much affection I have for the club president, the country and the fans.' Let's hope the next season will be more successful than the last.

Acknowledgements

I would like to thank Juca Kfouri, Martín Fernández, Paulo Coelho, Gian Oddi, Álex Sabino, José Miguel Wisnik, Newton Glória Lobato Filho, Pintado, Moacir Teixeira, Atilio Suarti, Maria Antonia Julião Faracco, Betinho, Fino, Edu Marangon, Manuel, Elton Luiz, Alcides Macrí, Lima, Lino Martins, Vágner Mancini, Dorival Júnior, Muricy Ramalho, Victor Andrade, Ricardo Rosa, Armênio Neto, Pepe, Zito, Tostão, Robinho, Léo Baptistão, Walter Casagrande, Luiz Felipe Scolari, Vicente del Bosque, Leda Catunda, Francisco Bosco, Allan Sieber, Hilário Franco Júnior, Cosme Salles, Didí, Alexandre Esnarriaga, Helena Passarelli, Alexandre Barreira, Thiago Campos, Darwin Valente, Manuel Giménez, Dolores de Haro, Duncan Heath, Robert Sharman, Charlie Wright, Laure Merle d'Aubigné and Roberto Domínguez.

Dedicated to Olmo, Lorenzo, Elvira, Alda and Tullio.